Herzog on Herzog

Paul Cronin was a researcher and translator on Faber and Faber's
Cassavetes on Cassavetes and is the editor of two forthcoming
volumes in the University of Mississippi's 'Conversations with
Filmmakers' series (Errol Morris and Roman Polanski). Currently
he is writing a book about cameraman Haskell Wexler for the
American Society of Cinematographers, and has edited a collection of writings and lectures by director Alexander Mackendrick
entitled *On Film-making*. His film *'Look Out Haskell, It's Real!'
The Making of Medium Cool* has been screened on television and
at festivals worldwide, and he is co-founder of the production
company Sticking Place Films (www.thestickingplace.com).

Herzog on Herzog

edited by Paul Cronin

ff

faber and faber

Faber and Faber, Inc.
An affiliate of Farrar, Straus and Giroux
18 West 18th Street, New York 10011

Library of Congress Cataloging-in-Publication Data
Herzog, Werner, 1942–
    Herzog on Herzog / edited by Paul Cronin.
        p.   cm.
    Interview of Werner Herzog by Paul Cronin.
    Includes bibliographical references (p.   ) and index.
    Filmography
    ISBN-13: 978-0-571-20708-4
    ISBN-10: 0-571-20708-1
    1. Herzog, Werner, 1942– —Interviews.   2. Motion picture
producers and directors—Germany—Interviews.   I. Title.

PN1998.3.H477 A3 2002
791.4302'33'092—dc20

                                                2003427567

www.fsgbooks.com

Contents

Introduction

'Those with "something to fall back on" invariably fall back on it. They intended to all along. That is why they provided themselves with it. But those with no alternative see the world differently.'

David Mamet

'*Ich möchte als Reiter fliegen, in einer blutigen Schlacht.*'
['I want to fly like a rider midst the bloody tussle of war.']

The Enigma of Kaspar Hauser

Most of what you've heard about Werner Herzog is untrue. More than any other director, living or dead, the number of false rumours and downright lies disseminated about the man and his films is truly astonishing. In researching Herzog's life and work, a process that involved trawling through endless sources, it soon became clear how frequently some would contradict others. And while recently spending time with the man, I confess to having deviously longed to trip him up, find holes in his arguments, uncover a mass of contradictory statements. But to no avail, and I now conclude that either he's a master liar, or more probably, he's been telling me the truth.

Fortunately there are some basic facts that are indisputable. He was born in Munich, Germany, in 1942, and as a child lived in Sachrang, a remote mountain village near the Austrian border. He started travelling on foot at the age of fourteen and made his first phone call when he was seventeen. To finance his early films he worked the night shift as a welder in a steel factory while at school, resulting in *Herakles*, made in 1961. He directed five features starring Klaus Kinski, and François Truffaut once called him the most important film director alive. But *nota bene*: he didn't direct Kinski from behind the camera with a rifle. He didn't put anyone's life at risk when making *Fitzcarraldo*. He is not insane, nor is he eccentric. His work is not in the tradition of the German romanticists. And he is not a megalomaniac. Rather, he's an extremely pleasant, generous and modest man who happens to be blessed with extraordinary vision and intuitive intelligence. A fierce sense of humour too that can leave you reeling, and as such written interviews with the man can be seriously inadequate. For example, how to transcribe the following with the playfully sardonic tone with which it was told? 'I remember having a public discussion with the diminutive Agnès Varda, who seemed to take offence at my postulation that a film-maker, rather than having this or that quality, should be able to clear his or her own height. She didn't like that very much.'

Yet Herzog's body of work of forty-five films (eleven features, the rest 'documentaries') is no joke, one of the most important in post-war European cinema and perhaps the key to what is known as the New German Cinema. *Signs of Life* (1968) is a wonderfully assured first feature which introduced to us the classic Herzog anti-hero: maniacal, isolated and dangerous. In 1970 the Left accused him of fascism when, he explains, 'instead of promoting the inevitable world revolution I ridiculed it' in *Even Dwarfs Started Small*, the bizarre tale of rebellious dwarfs taking over the asylum. His 1971 film *Land of Silence and Darkness* tells the story of the deaf and blind Fini Straubinger and remains one of the finest 'documentaries' ever made, while his international breakthrough came in 1972 with *Aguirre, the Wrath of God*, Herzog's first collaboration with actor Klaus Kinski, who plays a crazed Conquistador leading his men downriver on a raft to their doom in search of El Dorado.

In 1974 Herzog cast Bruno S., a forty-year-old shell of a man who had spent most of his life institutionalized, as the sixteen-year-old Kaspar Hauser in *The Enigma of Kaspar Hauser* and hypnotized his entire cast during the shooting of *Heart of Glass* two years later. He rushed to a volcanic Caribbean island about to explode to film *La Soufrière*, paid homage to F. W. Murnau in his version of *Nosferatu* (1979) and in 1982 dragged a boat over a mountain in the middle of the Amazon jungle for *Fitzcarraldo*. More recently Herzog has developed an extraordinary body of 'documentary' work by showing us the burning oil-wells of Kuwait in *Lessons of*

Darkness, telling the story of Carlo Gesualdo (Prince of Venosa, sixteenth-century musical genius and multiple murderer) in *Death for Five Voices*, and exploring the life of Vietnam POW survivor Dieter Dengler in *Little Dieter Needs to Fly*. Over the past twenty years he has also directed over a dozen operas across Europe and the Americas, has published several volumes of prose, and has appeared in several films as an actor.

As a film director his place in cinema history is assured. And when it comes to the man himself, I could find nothing more incisive than this comment from Herzog's own mother: 'When he was in school, Werner never learned anything. He never read the books he was supposed to read, he never studied, he never knew what he was supposed to know, it seemed. But in reality, Werner always knew everything. His senses were remarkable. If he heard the slightest sound, ten years later he would remember it precisely, he would talk about it, and maybe use it some way. But he is absolutely unable to explain anything. He knows, he sees, he understands, but he cannot explain. That is not his nature. Everything goes into him. If it comes out, it comes out transformed.'

Herzog is a figure sorely underappreciated in his native Germany and has been somewhat ignored in English-language film scholarship. As such, this is a book that has been screaming to be written for years, the primary obstacle having been Herzog himself. Two years ago, when I first contacted him about the possibility of this book, I received a handwritten fax. It read: 'I do not do self-scrutiny. I do look into the mirror in order to shave without cutting myself, but I do not know the color of my eyes. I do not want to assist in a book on me.' So *Herzog on Herzog* could never have been edited by an academic or aesthetician, for this is a film director who does not respond well to deep ideological and critical investigations into his work. 'When you question someone about his child, you don't wonder about the way it was born,' he wrote to me last year. 'So why do this with a film?'

The conversations in this book take a chronological approach as each film – from *Herakles* in 1962 to *Invincible* in 2001 – is discussed in turn. The text also provides a forum for Herzog's well-honed takes on the things, ideas and people that have preoccupied him for so many years. An overtly analytical approach has been forgone in favour of what is a very practically orientated text and one which I hope gives new meaning to that oft-cited Nietzsche quote, 'All writing is useless that is not a stimulus to activity.' I am also conscious of the fact that there are very few people out there who have seen every single Herzog film, and as such have attempted to edit our conversations so that even if the reader hasn't seen the film under discussion, there will still be something immediate and tangible to appreciate: a story or anecdote maybe, which in turn might lead to a theme or – to use Herzog's own language – something more 'ecstatic' even than that.

Most of our time together was spent in January and February 2001 in London where Herzog was doing post-production on *Invincible*. In January 2002 we sat down once again in Munich, and then a month later in Los Angeles. The resulting text presented here has been cut down from a much longer manuscript, as the more 'confessional' elements, and those not directly related to the films themselves, were excised. Herzog has always been careful to make a distinction between what is 'private' and what is 'personal', and anything that was not directly related to the films was sliced away. What's more, over the course of our lengthy talks we would often repeatedly touch on the same subjects from different angles, and so Herzog's answers have been compiled into single responses which has sometimes resulted in lengthy responses to very short questions. 'You should let the readers know this,' Herzog told me. 'I sound so talkative in the book, but I'm really not that garrulous.'

Several months ago, as I was in the thick of editing the transcripts, I spoke to Herzog on the phone. 'When will the book be ready?' he asked. 'You must do the five-day version. It doesn't need structure, it needs *life*! Leave the gaps in it, leave it porous. Shake the structure out and just write the book.' Well, I (kind of) did this, but still feel the text has structure – and much life – to it. And though it is impossible to capture a man's life in 300 pages, though there remain so many things left unsaid (or at least unpublished) about Herzog's life and work, though the man is, for me, only slightly more discernible now than he was when I first met him, I do feel *Herzog on Herzog* fairly successfully captures the ideas, insights and sensibilities of this important film director.

Through my research for this book I found excuses to travel to some of my favourite cities and visit some extraordinary libraries and archives. Thanks are due to library staff at the following institutions who provided invaluable assistance: the British Film Institute, London; the Cinémathèque Québécoise, Montreal; the Norsk Filminstitut, Oslo; the Danske Filminstitut, Copenhagen; the Hochschule für Fernsehen und Film, Munich; the Film Museum, Berlin; the Cinémathèque Royale, Brussels; the Cinémathèque Municipale, Luxembourg; the Cinémathèque Suisse, Lausanne; and the Filmmuseum, Amsterdam. Thanks also to staff at the German Historical Institute, London; the Imperial War Museum Library, London; the Bibliothèque du Film, Paris; the Center for Motion Picture Study at the Academy of Motion Picture Arts and Sciences, Los Angeles; the New York Library of the Performing Arts; and the Film Study Center of the Museum of Modern Art, New York. Special thanks to Lucki Stipetić, Monika Kostinek and Irma Strehle at Werner Herzog Filmproduktion, Munich.

My own time with Herzog has been nothing if not challenging (this is the best of all possible adjectives), and brings Chekhov (via Mamet) to mind:

ASTROV: This or that, that we're living, you know, is our *life*. (*Pause.*)
IVAN PETROVICH: It is?
ASTROV : Quite.

On a personal note I owe much to those who have been supportive of this project, whether they know it or not: Ian Bahrami, Joe Bini, Ray Carney, Susan Daly, Walter Donohue, Jay Douglas, Roger Ebert, Lizzie Francke, Snorre Fredlund, Jeremy Freeson, Herb Golder, Marie-Antoinette Guillochon, Remi Guillochon, Lena Herzog, Martje Herzog, Rudolph Herzog, David Horrocks, Richard Kelly, Harmony Korine, Peter-Pavel Kraljic, Tatjana Kraljic, Joshua Kronen, Howie Movshovitz, Julius Ratjen, S. F. Said, P. Adams Sitney, Gavin Syevens, Amos Vogel, Kate Ward, Haskell Wexler and Peter Whitehead.

Special thanks to Werner for his time and vision. This book is for Abby, David and Jonathan, without whom my work over the years would have been impossible.

Paul Cronin
London
March 2002

Facing the stark alternative to see a book on me compiled from dusty interviews with all the wild distortions and lies, or collaborating – I choose the much worse option: to collaborate.

Werner Herzog
Los Angeles
February 2002

1
The Shower Curtain

Before we start, are there any philosophical insights you'd like to give your readers so they might sleep easier at nights?

Well, let me say just this, something for human beings everywhere, whether they be filmmakers or otherwise. I can answer your question only by quoting hotel mogul Conrad Hilton, who was once asked what he would like to pass on to posterity. 'Whenever you take a shower, always make sure the curtain is inside the tub,' he said. So I sit here and recommend to people the same. Never *ever* forget the shower curtain.

When did you first realize that filmmaking was something you were going to spend your life doing?

From the moment I could think independently I knew I was going to make films. I never had a choice about becoming a director. This became clear to me within a few dramatic weeks at the age of fourteen when I began to travel on foot and converted to the Catholic faith. After a long series of failures it was only a small step into filmmaking, even though to this day I have problems seeing it as a real profession.

You're known as a filmmaker who likes to explore far-flung corners of the world. When did you start to travel?

Even before I had officially left school I lived in Manchester for a few months, a place I was drawn to because of a girlfriend. I bought a run-down house in the slums of the city together with four people from Bengal and three people from Nigeria. It was one of those nineteenth-century terrace houses built for the working class; the back yard was full of debris and garbage, and the house was full of mice. That is where I learned English. Then, at the age of nineteen, immediately after my final school exams in 1961, I left Munich for Greece and drove a truck as part of a convoy to Athens. From there I went to the island of Crete where I made some money and then took a boat to Alexandria in Egypt with the intention of travelling to the Belgian Congo. By that time the Congo had won its independence and almost immediately the deepest anarchy and the darkest violence had set in. I am fascinated by the idea that our civilization is like a thin layer of ice upon a deep ocean of chaos and darkness, and that in this country everything overwhelmingly dangerous had come into the open. Only later did I learn that of those who had made it to the most dangerous Eastern Congolese provinces at the time, almost all had perished.

So where did you go from Alexandria?

I travelled basically along the Nile to the Sudan, and today I thank God on my knees that on the way to Juba, not too far from Eastern Congo, I became very sick. I knew that to survive I had to get back as quickly as possible, and luckily I made it back up to Aswan. At that time the dam was still under construction. The Russians had built the concrete foundations and there were lots of German engineers working on the electrical intestines of the dam. One of them found me after I had taken shelter in a tool shed. I had a very high fever and did not even know how long I had been there. I have only very blurred recollections of it all. Rats bit me on my elbow and in my armpit, and apparently they wanted to use the wool from my sweater for a nest because when I stretched out I discovered a huge hole. I remember being woken by one rat who ran up and bit me on the cheek, and then saw it scurry away into a corner. The wound didn't heal for many weeks and I still have the scar.

I finally made it back to Germany where I eventually made my first couple of films. Once in a while I did show up at Munich university, where I was supposed to be studying history and literature, but I certainly cannot claim to have been a very serious student. I hated literature at school but kind of enjoyed listening to one woman professor at the university who was very intelligent and demanding. I know she gave me certain insights that I am very glad to have now.

How did your parents react to your plans to become a filmmaker?

We should not speak of parents in the plural, since my father never played a part in my life. But in August 1961 my mother, Elizabeth, sent me two letters – on consecutive days – which I received when I was on Crete. In them she wrote that my father, Dietrich, was anxious to dissuade me from becoming a film director, as before leaving Munich apparently I had made some pronouncement that I was going to do just that upon my return. I had already written several screenplays and had submitted various proposals to producers and TV stations from the age of about fourteen or fifteen. But my father was quite convinced that my idealism would be crushed within a few years because he thought I would never achieve what I wanted to. He thought I did not have the energy or perseverance and sense for business to survive in the intrigue and hard milieu of the film business.

What was your mother's attitude?

My mother took a more sensible approach. She was not dissuasive like my father, rather she tried to give me a realistic idea of what I was getting myself into and what might be a wise move. She explained to me what was going on economically in West Germany at the time and in the letters she asked me to think about my future very carefully. 'It's too bad that we never talked about it in detail,' she wrote. But my mother was always very supportive. I would run away from school and disappear for weeks at a time and she would not know where I was; sensing that I would be away for a time, she would immediately write a letter to school saying I had pneumonia. She realized that I was one of those who should not be kept in school indefinitely. On several occasions I would walk and hitch-hike to northern Germany, staying in abandoned houses or villas if no one was around, and got very good at getting into these places without leaving a trace.

In these letters my mother tried to convince me to return to Germany so I could start an apprenticeship she had set up for me in a photographer's lab. I had to get back by September so as not to miss another year. For her the rush was on. She had spoken to an employment expert who told her that filmmaking was a difficult profession to break into and that because I had only high-school exams I should start in a photo lab. After that I could move up to a movie lab, which he said would be the basis to start as an assistant director in a film company. But I had something else in mind and could not be persuaded.

You were born in 1942 in Munich, the largest city in Bavaria. What was it like growing up in the immediate post-war era?

A couple of days after I was born, the house next door to us in Munich was destroyed by a bomb and our place was damaged. We were lucky to get out alive – my cradle was sprayed with flying glass – so my mother moved me and my brothers out of the city to Sachrang, a small mountain village on the German–Austrian border. The Kaisergebirge mountains in the Austria Tyrol and around Sachrang were one of the last pockets of resistance in Germany at the end of the war, one of the final places the occupying American soldiers moved into. At that time the SS[1] and the Werewolves[2] were on the run and passed through the village, hiding their weapons and uniforms under the farmers' hay before finding refuge in the mountains. As a child I was very aware of the border between Germany and Austria as a result of my mother often taking me and my elder brother across to Wildbichl in Austria. She used the two of us to help smuggle various things back to Germany, the things that could not be found on our side of the border. In the post-war period smuggling was quite an accepted thing to do; even the police were involved in it.

My childhood was totally separate from the outside world. As a child I knew nothing of cinema, and even telephones did not exist for me. A car was an absolute sensation. Sachrang was such an isolated place at that time – though it is only about an hour and a half's drive from Munich – that I did not know what a banana was until I was twelve and I did not make my first telephone call until I was seventeen. Our house had no water-flushed toilet, in fact no running water at all. We had no mattresses; my mother would stuff dried ferns into a linen bag and in winter it

4

was so cold I would wake up in the morning to find a layer of ice on my blanket from frozen breath. But it was wonderful to grow up like that. We had to invent our own toys, we were full of imagination, and the guns and arms we found – remnants of the SS soldiers – just became part of what we owned. As a boy I was part of the local gang and invented some kind of flat sailing arrow which you would throw with a whip-like action, which made it sail more than 600 feet. A wonderful invention. Very difficult to aim, but it would sail on and on and on. We invented an entire world around us. Part of me has never really adjusted to the things I find around me even today. I am still not very good on the phone. I jump whenever it rings.

It might sound bizarre to people today, but things like our discovery of the arms cache made for a wonderful childhood. Everyone thinks that growing up in the ruins of the cities was a terrible experience, and for the parents who lost absolutely everything I have no doubt that it was. But for the children it truly was the most marvellous of times. Kids in the cities took over whole bombed-out blocks and would declare the remnants of buildings their own to play in where great adventures were acted out. You really do not have to commiserate with these kids. Everyone I know who spent their early childhood in the ruins of post-war Germany raves about that time. It was anarchy in the best sense of the word. There were no ruling fathers around and no rules to follow. We had to invent everything from scratch.[3]

What are your earliest memories?

I have two very distinct early memories. One is of the bombing of Rosenheim one night. My mother ripped me and my brother out of bed and carried both of us, wrapped in a blanket, one boy in each arm, up the slope behind our house. In the distance we could see the entire sky of orange and red. She said to us, 'Boys, I took you out of bed. You must see this. The city of Rosenheim is burning.' For us Rosenheim was the big city at the very end of the world. There was a valley and twelve kilometres away at the end of the valley was Aschau, where there was a hospital and a train station, and beyond that was Rosenheim. That was somehow the limit of my universe. Of course as a child I never went as far as Rosenheim. Apparently what happened was that bombers had flown into Italy, could not drop their bombs because of bad visibility, and flying back over the Alps dropped them on the first place they could clearly see so they did not return loaded.[4]

The second very vivid memory is of seeing Our Lord himself. It was on Santa Claus Day, the 6 December, when Santa Claus appears with a book listing all your misdeeds of the year, accompanied by a demon-like figure, Krampus. The front door to the house opened and suddenly a man stood there. I must have been about three and fled under the couch and peed my pants. He was wearing brown overalls, no socks and had oily hands. He looked at me so kindly and was so gentle. Right away I knew it was the Lord himself! I later found out he was a guy from the electricity company who happened to be passing.

One thing that my mother once told me was that I fell quite ill when I was five or six. We could not call an ambulance because even if we did manage to get hold of one, we were too deeply snowed in. So my mother wrapped me in blankets, tied me on a sled and pulled me all night to Aschau where I was admitted to hospital. She visited me eight days later, coming on foot through deep snow. I do not remember this, but she was so amazed that I was absolutely without complaint. Apparently I had pulled a single piece of thread from the blanket on the bed and for eight days had played with it. I was not bored: this thread was full of stories and fantasies for me.

Bavaria was in the American zone of occupation. Do you remember the US soldiers?

Sure. I remember the jeeps driving in and thinking that this was all the Americans in the whole world, though it was only about sixty-five of them. The GIs all drove with one leg dangling out on the bumper and they all had chewing gum. And for the first time I saw a black man. I was totally mesmerised because I had only heard about black people from fairytales. He was a big wonderful man with a tremendous voice. I can still hear it today. I would speak with him for hours, and one time my mother asked me how I managed to communicate with him. She said that I replied, 'We talk in

American.' Once he gave me some chewing gum which I kept for a whole year, continuously chewing it. Of course, we were constantly hungry and looking for food, and this is one reason why I felt such a connection to Dieter Dengler many years later. In *Little Dieter Needs to Fly* he talks about peeling the wallpaper from the walls of bombed-out houses. His mother would cook it because there were nutrients in the glue. This is something we never needed to do; things were not quite that bad for us. One time I stumbled across some workers who had shot a crow and cooked it in a pot next to the road. For the first time in my life I saw an eye of fat floating on the surface of the water. Never before had I seen fat like that, it really was quite a sensation. With one of the sub-machine guns we had found in the forests around town I tried to shoot a crow too but never succeeded. I was thrown to the ground by the recoil, and my mother – who knew how to shoot a gun – was, contrary to my expectations, not angry and did not punish me. Instead she took the gun and said, 'Let me show you how to use this.' She taught me how to secure it and unload it, and even took me into the forest and shot a single round into a thick beechwood log. The bullet went straight through and I remember splinters of wood flying out of the other side. She said to me, 'This is what you should expect from a gun, so you must never point even a wooden or plastic gun at anybody.' I was so stunned by the violence of it that I was immediately cured of my preoccupation with these kinds of things, and since that day I have not even pointed my finger at anybody.

What were you like as a child?

I was very much a loner. I learned how to concentrate by necessity because in Munich the whole family lived together in just one room. There were four of us in this tiny place, each doing their own thing. I would lie on my back on the floor with a book and read for hours no matter how much talking and activity was going on. Often I would read all day long, and when I finished, I would look up to discover that everyone else had left hours ago.

It was my older brother Tilbert who really took charge once we moved to Munich. He did not like school and was thrown out after a couple of years, and he immediately started in business, very quickly rising like a comet through the ranks. By the age of sixteen he was the main breadwinner in the family, and only because of him was I able to continue in school, even though I would work myself when I could. I owe a great deal to him. My younger brother Lucki is someone with whom I have worked very closely over the years. We have different fathers, but for me he is a full brother. He had great musical talent as a youngster but quickly realized he would not be good enough to compete with the slew of other pianists out there and went into business, he too rising like a comet. I think this scared him because he soon took off to Asia for a while, visiting India, Burma, Nepal and Indonesia. I wrote him a letter asking for help making *Aguirre*, and he crossed the Pacific and made it to Peru to give us much needed assistance. Finally he started to work with me full-time and has run my film-production company since then.

Is Herzog your real name?

My father's name was Herzog, but in my parents' divorce my legal name became Stipetić, which was my mother's maiden name. Herzog means 'duke' in German and I thought there should be someone like Count Basie or Duke Ellington making films. Whatever protects me from the overwhelming evil of the universe.

What were the first films you saw?

There was a travelling projectionist for remote provincial schools who would bring a selection of 16-mm films with him, and when I was eleven I saw my first two films. Even though I was quite stunned that this kind of thing was possible, I was not very taken with the first film, which was about Eskimos building an igloo. It had a very ponderous commentary and was very boring, and I could tell that the Eskimos were not doing a very good job. The second film about pygmies building a liana bridge across a jungle river in Cameroon was a bit better. The pygmies worked very well and I was very impressed that they could build such a well-functioning bridge without any real tools. You saw one of the pygmies swinging across the river on a liana just like Tarzan and they were hanging from the suspension bridge like spiders. It was a sensational experience for me and I still like the pygmies for having done it that way.

Later we watched *Zorro*, *Tarzan* and *Dr Fu Manchu*, things like that. Most of them were cheap American B-movies, though one of the *Fu Manchu* films was a moment of revelation for me. In this film a guy is shot and falls sixty feet from a rock, does a somersault in mid-air and then a little kick with his leg. Ten minutes later the exact same shot appeared in another gun battle, and I recognized it because of this little kick. They had recycled it and thought they could get away with it. I spoke to my friends about this and asked them how it was possible the same shot had been used twice. Before this moment I thought it was some kind of reality I had been watching on screen, that the film was something like a documentary. All of a sudden I could see how the film was being narrated and edited, how tension and suspense were created, and from that day on cinema was something different for me.

You've often spoken of your admiration of F. W. Murnau's films. When did you first see the German Expressionist Weimar films of the 1920s?

I never saw any of those films as a child. In fact, I did not see the Expressionist films until after I heard Lotte Eisner[5] talk in Berlin many years later.

Did you ever get a chance to see any of the avant-garde work that was being done at the time?

I do recall that when I was about twenty-one a young man named P. Adams Sitney[6] came to Germany and brought with him a good many reels of film, things like Stan Brakhage[7] and Kenneth Anger.[8] I was very impressed that there were so many other films out there very different to what I was used to seeing in the cinema. It did not even matter to me that I could tell these were not the kinds of images that I myself wanted to work with. Seeing that there were very bold people out there doing things that were so unexpectedly different intrigued me so much that I wrote about them and visionary filmmaking, and then asked a film magazine to publish the article, which they did in 1964.[9]

I showed you a list that a British critic compiled of the 100 best films ever made and was quite surprised how many of them you hadn't even heard of, let alone seen.

I am not really what you would call cinematically literate, not compared to many film directors. I average maybe one film a month and that is usually at a film festival where I will see them all at once. I might recall a film I saw years ago and still ache with pain about how beautiful it is. When I see a great film it stuns me, it is a mystery for me. What constitutes poetry, depth, vision and illumination in cinema I cannot name. It is the bad films that have really taught me about cinema. The negative definition: for God's sake don't do it like that. The sins are easy to name.

This also applies to my own films. My most immediate and radical lesson came from what was my first blunder, *Herakles*. It was a good thing to have made this little film first – rather than jump into something much more meaningful to me – because from that moment on I had a much better idea as to how I should go about my business. Learning from your mistakes is the only real way to learn.

Can you talk more about the intense religious period you went through?

Like I said earlier, I had a dramatic religious phase at the age of fourteen and converted to Catholicism. Even though I am not a member of the Catholic church any longer, to this day there seems to be something of a distant religious echo in some of my work. Also at the age of fourteen I started to travel on foot for the first time. I wanted to go to Albania, that mysterious country which was completely closed off to the rest of the world at that time, but they would not let me in. So I walked as far as the Adriatic, keeping close to the Albanian–Yugoslavian frontier all the time, maybe fifty metres at most. I never dared enter Albania though. It was my first real escape from home life.

You set up your own production company at a very early age. In fact every single film you've made – including the early shorts – has been produced through Werner Herzog Filmproduktion. What motivated you to take such an active role in producing?

I must have been around seventeen when I got a call from some producers who liked a proposal I had submitted to them. Previously I had avoided actually meeting with any of these kinds of people because I was so young and felt I would not be taken seriously. What caused the reactions I usually got from film producers was probably the fact that my puberty was late and I looked like a tiny school child until I was sixteen or seventeen. Instead I would write letters or speak to them on the phone, some of the first phone calls I ever made. But finally, after the telephone conversations, these producers seemed to be willing to accept me as a first-time director.

When I finally walked into their office I saw two men sitting behind this huge oak desk. I vividly remember the moment second by second. I stood there, totally humiliated as they looked beyond me, waiting, as if the father had come into town with his child. The first one shouted something so abusive that I wiped it from my memory while the other slapped his thigh and laughed, shouting, 'Aha! The kindergarten is trying to make films nowadays!' The whole encounter lasted fifteen seconds, after which I simply turned around and left the office knowing full well that I would have to be my own producer. The meeting was the culmination of many setbacks and humiliations and proved to be a pivotal point for me. I knew there and then that until the end of my days I would always be confronted by this kind of attitude if I went to others to produce my films.

One of my mother's best friends was married to a wealthy industrialist who had a huge mansion, and she took me to see this man so he could explain to me how to set up a production company. He started with this ridiculous loud voice and just shouted at me for nearly an hour: 'This is completely foolish! You idiot! You have never been in business! You don't know what you are doing!' Two days later I founded Werner Herzog Filmproduktion.

But you're hardly a typical Hollywood mogul, are you?

My company was really only an emergency measure simply because no one else would finance my films, and to this day I have only ever produced my own films. Right up to around the time of *Nosferatu*, I worked out of my small apartment in Munich with a telephone and a typewriter. There was no clear division between private life and work. Instead of a living room we had an editing room, and I would sleep there too. I had no secretary, no one to help me with taxes, book-keeping, contracts, screenplay writing, organization. I did absolutely everything myself; it was an article of faith, a matter of simple human decency to do the dirty work as long as I could. Three things – a phone, typewriter and car – are all you need to produce films. Inevitably, as my work reached larger international audiences and there were more and more retrospectives planned and too many people to stay in touch with, it just became too difficult to operate the office on my own.

I remember that when Twentieth Century Fox were first interested in co-producing *Nosferatu* they wanted me to travel to Hollywood. I did not want to go so I invited them to Munich instead. I met them at the airport and squeezed all four executives into my Volkswagen bus with no heater on a freezing winter morning and drove into the Bavarian countryside. Later, they were astonished that I had budgeted only $2 for the screenplay as I needed only 200 sheets of blank paper and a pencil.

Where did you get the money to finance your early films?

During my final years at high school I earned my own money by working the night shift as a welder in a steel factory, as a parking-lot attendant, things like that. Maybe the most important piece of advice I can give to those of you heading into the world of film is that as long as you are able-bodied, as long as you can make money yourself, do not go looking for office jobs to pay the rent. I would also be very wary of excruciatingly useless bottom-rung secretarial jobs in film-production companies. Go out to where the real world is, go work as a bouncer in a sex-club, a warden in a lunatic asylum or in a slaughterhouse. Walk on foot, learn languages, learn a craft or trade that has nothing to do with cinema. Filmmaking must have experience of life at its foundation. I know that so much of what is in my films is not just invention, it is very much life itself, my own life. You can tell when you read Conrad or Hemingway how much real life is in those books. Those are the guys who would have made great films, though I thank God they were writers.

For my first film *Herakles* I needed a good amount of cash, relatively speaking, because I wanted to start shooting in 35 mm and not 16 mm. For me filmmaking was only 35 mm; everything else seemed amateurish. 35 mm had the capacity to demonstrate, more than anything else, whether or not I had anything to offer, and when I started out I thought to myself, 'If I fail, I will fail so hard that I will never recover.' I found myself part of a group of young filmmakers. There were about eight of us and most of them were slightly older than me. Out of the eight planned films, four never went into production, and another three were shot but never finished because of sound problems. The failure of the others was very significant: it dawned on me that organization and commitment were the only things that started and finished films, not money. When it came to *Fitzcarraldo*, it was not money that pulled that boat over the mountain, it was faith.

You've said that Herakles *is more an exercise in editing than anything else, that you were experimenting with a medium that you were a complete novice in.*

Looking back at *Herakles* today, I find the film rather stupid and pointless, though at the time it was an important test for me. It taught me about editing together very diverse material that would not normally sit comfortably as a whole. For the film I took stock footage of an accident at Le Mans where something like eighty people died after fragments of a car flew into the spectators' stand, and inter-cut it with footage of bodybuilders, including Mr Germany 1962. For me it was fascinating to edit material together that had such separate and individual lives. The film was some kind of an apprenticeship for me. I just felt it would be better to make a film than go to film school.

What are your views on film schools? I gather you'd prefer people just went out and made films than spending years at school.

I personally do not believe in the kind of film schools you find all over the world today. I never worked as another filmmaker's assistant and I never had any formal training. My early films come from my very deepest commitment to what I was doing, what I felt I had no choice but to do, and as such they are totally unconnected to what was going on at the film schools – and cinemas – of the time. It is my strong autodidactic streak and my faith in my own work that have kept me going for more than forty years.

A pianist is made in childhood, a filmmaker at any age. I say this only because physically, in order to play the piano well, the body needs to be conditioned from a very early age. Real musicians have an innate feel for all music and all instruments, something that can be instilled only at an early age. Of course, it is possible to learn to play the piano as an adult, but the intuitive qualities needed will not be there. As a young filmmaker I read in an encyclopedia the fifteen or so pages on filmmaking. Everything I needed to get myself started came from this book. It has always seemed to me that almost everything you are forced to learn at school you forget in a couple of years. But the things you set out to learn yourself in order to quench a thirst, these are things you never forget. It was a vital early lesson for me, realizing that the knowledge gleaned from a book would suffice for my first week on the set, which is all the time needed to learn everything you need to know as a filmmaker. To this day the technical knowledge I have is relatively rudimentary. If there are things that seem too complicated, I experiment; if I am still not able to master it, I hire a technician.

You've talked in the past about how collaborative film is, and how many different and varied skills it requires.

Filmmaking is a more vulnerable journey than most other creative ventures. When you are a sculptor you have only one obstacle – a lump of rock – on which you chisel away. But filmmaking involves organization and money and technology, things like that. You might get the best shot of your life but if the lab mixes the developing solution wrongly then your shot is gone for ever. You can build a ship, cast 5,000 extras and plan a scene with your leading actors, and in the morning one of them has a stomach ache and cannot go on set. These things happen, everything is interwoven and interlinked, and if one element does not function properly then the whole venture is prone to collapse. Filmmakers should be taught about how things will go wrong, about how to deal with these problems, how to handle a crew that is getting out of hand, how to handle a producing partner who will not pay up or a distributor who won't advertise properly, things like this. People who keep moaning about these kinds of problems are not really suited to this line of business.

And, vitally, aspiring filmmakers have to be taught that sometimes the only way of overcoming problems involves real physicality. Many great filmmakers have been astonishingly physical, athletic people. A much higher percentage than writers or musicians. Actually, for some time now I have given some thought to opening a film school. But if I did start one up you would only be allowed to fill out an application form after you had travelled alone on foot, let's say from Madrid to Kiev, a distance of about 5,000 kilometres. While walking, write. Write about your experiences and give me your notebooks. I would be able to tell who had really walked the distance and who had not. While you are walking you would learn much more about filmmaking than if you were in a classroom. During your voyage you will learn more about what your future holds than in five years at film school. Your experiences would be the very opposite of academic knowledge, for academia is the death of cinema. It is the very opposite of passion.

Tell me about your ideal film school.

This is something we can talk about later when we discuss *Film Lesson*, the programmes I made for Austrian television, but let me say here that there are some very basic skills that any filmmaker must have. First of all, learn languages. One also needs to be able to type and to drive a car. It is like the knights of old who had to be able to ride, wield a sword and play the lute. At my utopian film academy I would have students do athletic things with real physical contact, like boxing, something that would teach them to be unafraid. I would have a loft with a lot of space where in one corner there would be a boxing ring. Students would train every evening from 8 to 10 with a boxing instructor: sparring, somersaults (backwards and forwards), juggling, magic card tricks.

Whether or not you would be a filmmaker by the end I do not know, but at least you would come out as an athlete. My film school would allow young people who want to make films to experience a certain climate of excitement of the mind. This is what ultimately creates films and nothing else. It is not technicians that film schools should be producing, but people with a real agitation of mind. People with spirit, with a burning flame within them.

In a way Herakles *seems to be about the strongman, a figure that seems to resonate throughout your life and work.*

I have always felt a close affinity to strongmen and my most recent film *Invincible* has one as its main character. For me, 'strongman' is a word that reverberates beyond mere physical abilities. It encompasses intellectual strength, independence of mind, confidence, self-reliance and maybe even a kind of innocence. All these things are clearly an important part of Zishe Breitbart's inner strength in *Invincible*. I am also very careful to make a distinction between strongmen and bodybuilders. I detest the cult of bodybuilding, something I feel is a gross deviation. My fascination with strongmen probably stems from my childhood heroes when I lived in Sachrang.

One of them was an old farmhand called Sturm Sepp ['Stormin' Joe']. I think he must have been about eighty years old and was over six feet tall, though you could not tell because he was always bent over. He was a strange, almost biblical, figure with a big full beard and a long pipe in his mouth. He was always silent; we never got him to say so much as a word about himself, or indeed to utter anything, even though we would always try to annoy him when he was out mowing in the field. As kids we all thought Sturm Sepp had at one time been incredibly strong, in fact so strong that once when his mule collapsed as it was pulling tree trunks down the mountain, Sepp himself had loaded several enormous trunks on his shoulder and carried them down singlehanded. And ever since, as a consequence of this feat of strength, he had been bent over at the waist. The legend also circulated among us that during the First World War he had single-handedly taken a whole squad of French soldiers prisoner, twenty-four men in all. The story went that he had been so quick, running round and round the hills so rapidly and popping up again and again in different places, that the French, who were encamped in a small hollow down in the valley, must have thought they were surrounded by a massive detachment of Germans. I can still picture the scene in my mind.

My other childhood hero was Siegel Hans. He was a young lumberjack, a really brave, daring young chap who had incredible rippling Mr Universe muscles and who was the first villager to get a motorbike. We truly revered and admired him. Once, when the milk lorry broke through the wooden bridge, they fetched him to help and he climbed down into the stream, took off his shirt, revealing his bulging muscles for all to see, and tried to heave the lorry back up again with his bare hands. It could not be done, of course, because it weighed seven to eight tonnes. But the very fact that he climbed down into the stream and even attempted it was enough to inspire in us an awe that I cannot really comprehend today.

The local farmer called Beni was also a very strong guy and for a couple of years Siegel Hans would always be challenging him to a fight. But Beni never wanted to and the two of them would just sit opposite each other in the pub with beer mugs in their hands just staring at each other, just like in that scene in *Heart of Glass*. Finally, one day a fight erupted and the whole village cheered them on. 'We gotta know who is the strongest in the village!' everyone shouted. Soon it was very obvious that Siegel Hans was the strongest man in the village. Siegel Hans happened to be involved in the biggest smuggling operation of the time too. A whole load of coffee had been brought across the border with the collusion of customs officers. Unfortunately they were busted, but when the cops came for Siegel Hans at night he leapt out of a window of his house and fled with his trumpet straight up the nearest mountain, the Geigelstein. Once he had reached the summit he started to blow on his trumpet, and the customs men and police set off in pursuit. But when they eventually arrived at the peak, suddenly they heard Siegel Hans blowing his trumpet from the mountain-top opposite. And so it went on, to and fro, I think for about twelve days in all. The whole village revered him for this, went into positively religious ecstasies over him, and we kids – I for one, at least – gained a model for life. I think in the end he gave himself up. At the time I remember thinking to myself that in order to evade the police for so long, he had actually run around the entire German border, thus evading the police down in the valley. Just like when you shoot a bullet from a very powerful rifle it ultimately will hit you in your own back because it travels around the world and orbits the planet.

You were only nineteen when you made Herakles?

I started very young. Soon after finishing *Herakles* I won the Carl Meyer award[10] for my screenplay, *Signs of Life*. It sounds ridiculous how I behaved at the time, but I was so convinced of myself and my abilities. The jury held its session in Munich, and when a jury member rang at my door after midnight and told me that I had won the award – worth 10,000 Deutschmarks – I looked at him and said, 'You do not have to wake me past midnight to tell me that. I knew it anyway!' The award was a real step forward, even though the film would not be made for a few years. At the time I definitely felt that the award gave me real momentum and would carry me for maybe a decade.

My next film, also shot in 35 mm, was *The Unprecedented Defence of the Fortress Deutschkreuz* which was financed by the money I got from the screenplay award. The four actors got something, but the basic expenses were for the raw stock and the lab fees. It is a short film about a group of young men protecting an abandoned castle from imaginary attackers. It is the same kind of theme that I worked with in *Signs of Life* a few years later. People think they are being besieged, yet there is actually no enemy and they are left in the lurch.

There was a film you made in between Herakles *and* The Unprecedented Defence of the Fortress Deutschkreuz, *wasn't there?*

You are speaking about *Game in the Sand*, which was certainly more of a proper film than *Herakles*, but actually only three or four people have ever seen it as I was careful to take it out of circulation almost immediately after finishing it. It is the one film that I will never publicize in my lifetime. I might even destroy the negative before I die. It is about four children and a rooster, but it is hard to speak about it because during the shooting I had the feeling that things were moving out of control.

You do have a reputation as a risk-taker, someone who goes to extremes. Some people are convinced that you'd even risk the lives of people in order to make your films.

Physicists, experimenting on materials, discover things about a particular metal alloy when they subject it to extreme heat, extreme pressure or extreme radiation and the like. I think that, put under extreme pressure, people give you many more insights into their innermost being and tell us about who we really are. But I would not be sitting here talking to you if I ever risked the life of anyone in order to make a film. I have never gone out seeking inhospitable terrain to film in and I have never taken idiotic risks, nor would I ever do so. I do not deny that – like every film-maker – sometimes I do have to take mild risks, but only in a very calculated and professional way. I would always make sure that what we were doing put us firmly on the safe side, and what's more, generally it was me who always tested the waters. Perhaps mountaineers are motivated to seek out the most difficult routes, but that does not apply to me. As a filmmaker such an attitude would be wholly unprofessional and irresponsible. Being my own producer means, financially speaking, it is in my interests to work as efficiently as possible, and the idea that I am always looking for special difficulties during shooting could not be further from the truth. It has never been my preference to make things more difficult than they already are. The reason *Fitzcarraldo* took so long to make had nothing to do with the risks I had taken or the safety of the actors. The problems were natural disasters and, in fact, once we started shooting with Kinski, we actually managed to wrap principal photography ahead of schedule.

Some years ago when I was directing an opera, I wanted to have a stuntman crashing down from the rigging twenty-two metres above the stage, as if a mountain climber had fallen from a rock face. The problem was that he had to hit a very narrow space: an opening in the floor with a large cushion underneath. It was proving to be very difficult to hit this spot from such a height.

We could not afford a stuntman, and as nobody wanted to take responsibility of testing this fall, I had myself hoisted up. From an altitude of about thirty-five feet I jumped down and got severe whiplash in my neck. I realized that it was just ridiculous to try from fifty feet, and immediately scrapped the whole idea of the jump.

Why did it take so long to get Signs of Life *into production?*

Even after shooting the three early shorts and winning the prize for the screenplay of *Signs of Life,* I sensed that at the age of twenty-two no one would help me finance the film, so I decided to accept a scholarship to study in the United States. It pretty much gave me free choice about where to go. I did not want to go somewhere overly fancy and so I chose Pittsburgh, a place where there were real working people and steel mills. But by the time I arrived in the early 1960s the city was already heavily in decline. The steel mills were shutting down and life for many people was falling apart. Only three days after I arrived I returned my scholarship and as such ended up with no money, no host family and no passage back home.

I did not know there was such a difference in quality between American universities, and felt that the one I had chosen was a bad place for me to be. So I ended up penniless and was pushed around from place to place for weeks until finally I was picked up on a country road by the Franklin family. The mother had six children between seventeen and twenty-seven, her husband had died and there was a ninety-three-year-old grandmother. I owe them so much, this wonderful, crazy family who put me up in an attic where I lived for six months. Of course I needed to earn some money, so I started to work on a project that was part of a series of films for NASA. That I made films for NASA always appears on those five-line biographies, and even if it is somehow true, it is completely irrelevant. I did have access to certain restricted areas and was able to talk to many of the scientists, but just before I was about to start work on the film they ran a security check and discovered I had no permit to stay in the country unless I was a student. I had violated my visa status and very soon afterwards was summoned to the immigration office in Pittsburgh.

It was evident I was about to be expelled from the country and shipped back to Germany, so I took a rusty old Volkswagen and went to New York during a very bitter winter. I lived in the car for some time, even though its floor was rusted right through and I had a cast on my leg at the time because I had broken it quite badly after jumping out of a window. It was winter and there were snow storms, and because I could not move my toes properly they nearly froze. I needed to wrap wads of newspaper around the foot in the cast to make sure I did not lose the immobilized toes through frostbite. And at night, when it gets cold, say at 3 or 4 a.m., the homeless of New York – who live almost like Neanderthal men – come and gather together on some empty, utterly desolate street and stand over fires they have kindled in the metal rubbish bins without speaking a word. Eventually I just cut the whole cast off with a pair of poultry shears and fled across the border into Mexico.

And that's where you learned Spanish?

And where I also developed this real fascination and love I have for Latin America. Of course, while I was there I had to make a living and discovered that there was a weak spot on the border between the twin cities of Reynosa in Mexico and McAllen in Texas. There was a lot of daily commuting between these towns, Mexicans working in McAllen during the day and returning at night. Tens of thousands each morning who all had special stickers on their windshields that would allow them to pass virtually free through the border. I stole one of those stickers and bought some television sets for people who wanted them down in Mexico where they were very expensive. One time a rich ranchero asked me to buy him a silver colt pistol which he was not able to find in Mexico, so I bought one and took it down there for him. I made fairly good money on all these things. From this came the legend that I was a gun runner.

Then I spent a couple of weekends as a rodeo rider in *charreíadas*. The way it worked was that they would have three cowboys or *charros* in the ring who would catch the bulls, usually very fast animals. They would use lassos to bring the bull to the ground and then tie a rope around its chest. You have to squat on the animal and grab the rope while he is on the ground. They release him and immediately he explodes in rage. I have seen bulls jumping clear over a six-foot stone wall. Every single week I was injured and one time had to fix up my bad ankle one time with two rulers I got from some schoolkids. I could not even ride a horse, something that soon became patently clear to the spectators, so I appeared under the name El Alamein, which after Stalingrad was the biggest defeat of the German forces in the Second World War. They all just loved to cheer the idiot on!

One time I was in the ring with a bull who got on his feet and just stood there staring at me. I screamed, '*Burro!* You donkey!' I can still hear the cheers of the young women in the crowd. Of course, it was pretty angry at me and tried to pin me to the stone wall. I caught my leg between the animal and the wall, and sustained an injury that was so bad I quit the job there and then. Today it all sounds quite funny and I do see it with a certain humour, but my time down there was quite banal and partially miserable too. It was '*pura vida*' as the Mexicans say, 'pure life'. But I thank God on my knees that after America I did not go straight back to Germany.

Where did you go after leaving Mexico?

I travelled around Europe for another few months and only then returned to Germany, where I started pre-production on *Signs of Life* almost immediately. Still nobody took me seriously, even after the Carl Mayer Award and my short films which had been shown at the Oberhausen Short Film Festival and places like that. At that time Munich was very much the cultural centre of Germany, so I made contact with other filmmakers. This is when I first met Volker Schlöndorff[11] who was about to make his first film, *Young Törless*. He wanted to see who was doing the same kind of thing and whether we could help each other. He has been helpful ever since, the most loyal of all the friends I have among filmmakers, even though his films are so different to mine. Rainer Werner Fassbinder[12] was also around. One evening he rang at my door – it must have been around 1968 – and asked me to produce his films. At that point he had made two interesting shorts which he showed to me. I said to him, 'Listen, Rainer, do it like me, for God's sake. You must produce your own stuff, be independent.' And he did. He looked like a real peasant and I immediately sensed he had something very forceful about him which I liked very much.

Many of your films have been made outside of Germany. Yet even a film like Fitzcarraldo, *filmed in the Amazon in Peru, was called 'Bavaria in the Jungle'. You haven't lived in Germany for many years, but do you feel you've retained your German sensibilities? And what does it mean to be Bavarian?*

It does not matter where the films were physically filmed. Geographically, I have travelled widely, but I do feel that all my films are not only very German, they are explicitly Bavarian. There is a different culture down in Bavaria. It is an area that, historically, has never considered itself part of Germany. My first language was Bavarian and it was a real culture shock for me when for about a year I went to school in Swabia where the kids spoke a different language. I was teased and mocked by the kids who would imitate my thick accent; at the age of eleven I had to learn *Hochdeutsch* which was a painful experience for me. Irish writers write in English, but they are Irish. I might write in German, but I am very much a Bavarian. Being Bavarian means as much as it means to be Scottish in the United Kingdom. Like Scots, Bavarians are very hard-drinking, hard-fighting, very warm hearted, very imaginative. The most imaginative Bavarian of all was King Ludwig II.[13] He was totally mad and built all those castles that are so full of this quintessentially Bavarian dreaminess and exuberance. I always felt that he would have been the only one who could have done a film like *Fitzcarraldo*, apart from me. You see this kind of baroque imagination in Fassbinder's films, the kind of unstoppable and ferocious creativity he had. Like his work, my films are not thin-blooded ideological constructs that we saw a lot of in German cinema in the 1970s. Too many German films of that era were thin gargling water instead of real thick stout.

You haven't lived in Bavaria for quite some time. Is there anything you miss about the place?

In an interview a few years ago Edgar Reitz asked me what my favourite season is. I said the fall, even though quite often I am in places where there are no seasons. I have lived in California for some years now and I miss the changing seasons more than anything else. I may just be a very simply woven animal who needs different seasons. Dammit, now you've got me thinking about warm Bavarian pretzels coming right out of the oven with some good butter and a thick beer. You just cannot live without things like that. This is what being Bavarian is really all about.

Tell me about your screenplays which are formatted very differently from the average screenplay.

For many years I have thought of my screenplays – the early ones of which are written in prose with very little dialogue – as representing something like a new form of literature. I do not really care much about the very physical form of my writing, but have always felt that if I had to write this stuff down then at least I could attempt something new with the form. It is connected to the fact that I have tried to give my screenplays a life independent from the films they help give birth to and not make them mere cookbooks with recipes that need to be followed during a film's production. This is why my screenplays have always been published without photos incorporated into the text, because I did not want to have any reference made to the films themselves. For me the screenplays have always been pieces of literature that stand alone.

Did you get any help from the system of film subsidy in Germany at the time? Many young German filmmakers were able to make their first films relatively easily thanks to the government's wide-ranging policies on film production.

For a time West Germany had probably the most subsidized film industry in Europe, if not the world. But it was never that easy to make films in Germany. Back when we were all starting out in the 1960s, Alexander Kluge[14] was probably the single most important figure when it came to securing the financial assistance we needed for film production; I have always felt that he was very much the spiritual and ideological force behind German film in the late

24

1960s.[15] Apparently he was the one who single-handedly wrote the Oberhausen Manifesto,[16] even though a couple of dozen other filmmakers signed it. Kluge also pushed through the film-subsidy legislation which led to television stations across Germany agreeing to co-produce the work of young filmmakers. It also meant that films could not be screened on television for at least two years after being theatrically released.

There was an organization called *Kuratorium junger deutscher Film*,[17] devised by filmmakers themselves, which gave a first start to many young German filmmakers. You had to submit your scripts to them and wait and see if your film would be one of the few they decided to give money to. It was not a lot of money – about 300,000 DM for each film – and you had to have the rest of the funding in place before they accepted your application. But even though I already had some money to make *Signs of Life* and I felt myself to be an ideal candidate, I was denied *Kuratorium* money for two years. I had made three short films, each of them had in some way caught the attention of the media and the film festivals, and of course the screenplay for the film had even won the award a couple of years earlier.

Why do you think you were denied the money?

I think, quite simply, it was because at the time there was nobody who had, at the age of twenty-two, produced and directed his own full-length feature film. When *Signs of Life* was finally released, it was a total flop with audiences and nobody wanted to distribute the film, even though it won the National Film Award[18] [*Bundesfilmpreis*] in Germany, which thankfully meant money for my next film. It also won the Silver Bear at the Berlin Film Festival, so the press was up on the film and people knew about it. A newspaper in Wiesbaden, near Frankfurt, wrote a full-page article about the film, and because of this a cinema invited me to come to a screening. I got to the place and only nine people were there. That kind of shock is still in my bones. I have always had to struggle – film after film – to get audiences' attention in Germany. Let me say that this might not be such a bad thing, for I never felt the subsidy system was the healthiest way to run the film industry in West Germany.

You talk of happiness not being something you are in search of, that you just don't function in those terms. But clearly your work is tremendously important to you.

I have never been one of those who cares about happiness. Happiness is a strange notion. I am just not made for it. It has never been a goal of mine; I do not think in those terms. It seems to be a goal in life for many people, but I have no goals in life. I suspect I am after something else.

Can you articulate what that is?

To give my existence some sort of a meaning. It is a very simplified answer, I know, but whether I am happy or not does not count that much. I have always enjoyed my work. Maybe enjoying is not the right word: I have always loved it. It means a lot to me that I have the privilege of working in this profession, even though I have struggled to make my films the way I really wanted to, and get them as close to the vision I have been seeking. Of course, I am very aware that there are so many people out there who have good ideas and who are aspiring filmmakers, and who never find a foothold within the system. Inevitably they fail, and that is sad. But like I said, at the age of fourteen, once I realized that for me filmmaking was a duty, then I really had no choice but to push on with my projects.

One aspect of who I am that might be important is the communication defect I have had since a young child. I am someone who takes everything very literally. I simply do not understand irony, a defect I have had ever since I was able to think independently. Let me explain by telling a story. A few weeks ago I received a phone call at my apartment from a painter who lives just down the street from me. He tells me he wants to sell me his paintings, and because I live in the same neighbourhood, he says he wants to give me a good deal on his work. He starts to argue with me, saying I can have this painting for only ten dollars or even less. I try to get him off the phone, saying, 'Sir, I am sorry but I do not have paintings in my apartment. I have only maps on my walls. Sometimes photos, but I would never have a painted picture on my wall, no matter who made it.' And he kept on and on until all of a sudden he starts to laugh. I think: I know this laughter. And he did not change his voice one bit when the painter announced that it was my friend, Harmony Korine.[19]

In fact, something much worse happened years ago when I got a call from the Ministry of the Interior right after it was announced that I was to receive the National Film Award for *Signs of Life*. This was fantastic news because it meant 300,000 DM for my next production and, of course, a trophy and a handshake at the Ministry of the Interior. It was the minister's personal assistant who called me. 'Are you Werner Herzog? The minister would like to have a conversation.' I am connected to the minister, who starts stuttering and says, 'Ah well, Mr Herzog. We have publicized the news that you have won the *Bundesfilmpreis* but, ahem, I have to personally take the matter in hand and humbly apologize. I regret to say that in reality it was not you who won the award, rather someone else.' I remained stunned yet composed and replied, 'Sir, how could this have happened? You as Minister of the Interior are responsible for many things, including internal security and the safety of our borders. In what kind of a state is your house? This letter I have has not only your signature, it has two more signatures. I accept this, but how could it have happened?' It went on like this for ten minutes when suddenly the minister starts to scream with laughter so hard that I recognize the voice of my friend Florian Fricke. 'Florian, it's you, you bastard.' When he called as the personal assistant he did not change his voice, but I took them as two different people. That is how bad my communication defect is. I am just a complete fool. There are things in language that are common to almost everyone, but that are utterly lost on me.

And compared to other filmmakers – particularly the French, who are able sit around their cafés waxing eloquent about their work – I am like a Bavarian bullfrog just squatting there, brooding. I have never been capable of discussing art with people. I just cannot cope with irony. The French love to play with their words and to master French is to be a master of irony. Technically, I am able to speak the language – I know the words and verbs – but will do so only when I am really forced to. Only twice in my life has this happened: one time when I was under arrest in Africa, surrounded by really raucous and drunken soldiers who pointed a rifle at my head, another at my heart and a third at my balls. I tried to explain who I was and the commander screamed at me:

'*On parle que le français ici!*' The second occasion was when we were making *La Soufrière* on Guadeloupe, which is French-speaking, although 95 per cent of the population is purely African. The man we found asleep under the tree who had refused to be evacuated from the island when it was just about to explode spoke Creole French. I woke him up and we spoke in French on camera. So under extreme force I will speak the language, only when there is a real necessity. Otherwise I avoid it.

But though you might not understand irony, you do have a sense of humour, don't you?

Of course I do. There is a big difference between irony and humour. I can understand humour and laugh at jokes even if I am not very good at telling them myself. But when it comes to irony, clearly I do have a serious and obvious defect.

An endearing defect though.

Not if you saw me sitting in a Parisian café.

NOTES
1 The *Schutzstaffel* started out as Hitler's personal bodyguard in 1925 and continued to grow until the end of the war in 1945, absorbing such organizations as the *Waffen SS* (the SS army formed in 1939) and the *Totenkopfverbände* (the Death's Head concentration camp guards).
2 Underground SS-led guerrilla groups formed in 1945 as last-gasp resistance against Allied forces in Germany.
3 There were several films shot amongst the city ruins of Germany, part of an inevitably short-lived wave of filmmaking in the immediate post-war era called the *Trümmerfilme*, 'rubble films'. See Robert R. Shandley's *Rubble Films: German Cinema in the Shadow of the Third Reich* (Temple University Press, 2001).
4 Rosenheim (birthplace of Hermann Göring) burned on the night of 18 April 1945, less than two weeks before Hitler killed himself in Berlin. Herzog was about two and half years old. That evening 148 American B-17s dropped 431.2 tonnes of bombs on the marshalling yards of the town in an attempt to destroy enemy transport systems. Rosenheim was in fact the intended target of this mission.
5 See Chapter 5.
6 P. Adams Sitney (b. 1944, USA) is a film historian currently at Princeton University, author of *The Visionary Film: The American*

Avant-Garde 1943–1978 (Oxford University Press, 1979). From Christmas 1963 to August 1964 Sitney was curator of the International Exposition of the American Independent Film, which travelled to several cities including Munich (January 1964), Amsterdam, Stockholm, Paris, London and Vienna. The trip was organized by New York-based Lithuanian filmmaker and curator Jonas Mekas, who established and still runs America's leading avant-garde cinema, Anthology Film Archives in New York.

7 Stan Brakhage (b. 1933, USA) is one of America's most important avant-garde filmmakers and writers, and has taught for many years at the University of Denver, Colorado. His best-known work is *Dog Star Man* (1961–4). See also his book *Film at Wit's End: Eight Avant-garde Filmmakers* (Documentext, 1989).

8 Kenneth Anger (b. 1927, USA) is the director of the infamous landmark work in gay cinema, *Scorpio Rising* (1964), and the author of the equally infamous book *Hollywood Babylon* (French edition published 1959, English edition 1975). See Bill Landis's biography *Anger* (Harper Collins, 1995).

9 'Rebellen in Amerika', *Filmstudio*, May 1964.

10 Named after the Austrian-born scriptwriter of films such as *The Cabinet of Dr Caligari* (Wiene, 1920), *The Last Laugh* (Murnau, 1924) and *Sunrise* (Murnau, 1927).

11 Volker Schlöndorff (b. 1939, Germany) directed one of the first internationally acclaimed works of New German Cinema, *Young Törless* (1966), and went on to make *The Lost Honor of Katharina Blum* (1975) and *The Tin Drum* (1980), which won the Oscar for Best Foreign Film.

12 Rainer Werner Fassbinder (1945–82, Germany) was one of the leading lights of the New German Wave. In a period of only sixteen years he wrote and directed over thirty feature films, including *The Bitter Tears of Petra von Kant* (1972) and *Fear Eats the Soul* (1974), plus numerous plays and the television mini-series *Berlin-Alexanderplatz* (1980). See Ronald Hayman's *Fassbinder* (Simon and Schuster, 1984) and *The Anarchy of the Imagination: Interviews, Essays and Notes of Rainer Werner Fassbinder* (Johns Hopkins University Press, 1992), edited by Michael Töteberg and Leo A. Lensing.

13 King Ludwig II, who ruled Bavaria from 1864 to 1886, was known as the 'fairy-tale king'. Only eighteen when he assumed power, Ludwig preferred to live in his own fantasy world and in 1868 started building a series of beautiful castles at the foothills of the Bavarian Alps (today very popular tourist attractions). After the German Empire conquered Bavaria, he was eventually declared insane, in part because he was spending so much money on these seemingly useless buildings, and died soon afterwards in mysterious circumstances.

14 Alexander Kluge (b. 1932, Germany), long considered the 'father' of New German Cinema, was a law student and writer before working as Fritz Lang's assistant. He co-wrote the Oberhausen Manifesto (see footnote 16) and established the Institut für Filmgestaltung in Ulm in the wake of the German filmmakers' demands expressed in the manifesto. His legal background meant he was at the forefront of filmmakers' demands for a series of new state and federal government film-production subsidies, as well as new channels of production and distribution with state television stations. His films include *Brutality in Stone* (1960) and *Yesterday Girl* (1966). In 1962, along with Edgar Reitz, he established the first film school in West Germany, the Institut für Filmgestaltung. The Deutsche Film und Fernsehenakademie in Berlin (who rejected Fassbinder's application to study there) followed in 1966.

15 This is the New German Cinema, or New German Wave, the name given to a very disparate group of filmmakers from West Germany. The era of New German Cinema can probably be most easily demarcated by the working life of director Rainer Werner Fassbinder (1966 to 1982).

16 The Oberhausen Manifesto, signed by two dozen German filmmakers on 28 February 1962 at the Oberhausen Short Film Festival, proclaimed, 'The old film is dead. We believe in the new one,' and that this 'new film' needed 'new freedoms. Freedom from the conventions of the established industry. Freedom from the outside influence of commercial partners. Freedom from the control of special interest groups. We have concrete intellectual, formal, and economic conceptions about the production of the new German film. We are as a collective prepared to take economic risks.' The manifesto was an attempt by young German filmmakers to combat the post-war domination of their country's film markets by the United States, something that meant indigenous film production was being steadily decimated. In the wake of Oberhausen came a whole slew of federal projects to support film production, distribution, study and archiving in West Germany. See *West German Filmmakers on Film: Visions and Voices*, edited by Eric Rentschler (Holmes and Meier, 1988), p. 2, for the complete Oberhausen Manifesto, and Chapter One of Thomas Elsaesser's *New German Cinema* (Rutgers University Press, 1989) for a summary of the manifesto's impact on film in West Germany.

17 The *Kuratorium* was 'explicitly charged with putting the proposals of the Oberhausen Manifesto into practice' (Elsaesser, 1989, p. 22) by advancing 'German film-making and stimulate a renewal of the German film in a manner exclusively and directly beneficial to the community'. It was non-profit-making and was funded by the Ministry of the Interior. Submitted scripts were read by young film

critics – not bureaucrats – and between 1965 and 1968 the *Kuratorium* assisted in the financing of twenty films.

18 Awarded annually by the Federal Ministry of the Interior.

19 Harmony Korine (b. 1974, USA). Writer (*Kids*) and director (*Gummo, julien donkey-boy*).

2

Blasphemy and Mirages

Around the time of your first feature, Signs of Life, *what became known as the New German Cinema was born. By 1969 Fassbinder had made his first few films, including* Love Is Colder than Death, *Schlöndorff had made* Young Törless *and Wenders[1] had produced his first shorts. Did you feel that you were part of an important new movement?*

The so-called New German Cinema really did not have much significance for me because I started making films before even the Oberhausen Manifesto was written. I did not take part in the manifesto and did not even know they were writing it. Though I did show films at the film festival at Oberhausen, I was never part of that group. Basically, it was a coincidence that I belonged to the first generation of post-war Germans, many of whom attempted to articulate themselves in new ways cinematically, not difficult when we think of German cinema in the 1950s.[2] Remember, by 1968 I had already produced several films and from the very earliest days spent time outside of Germany, so I could never realistically be seen as a spokesman for New German Cinema. Throughout the key decade of New German Cinema – the 1970s – I was making films all over the world. What's more, I feel I have made some of my most important works in the 1980s and 90s and into this new millennium, and though many of my recent films are not as well known, many are better than my early works. For me the lifespan and history of the New German Film has no relevance to what I am doing these days.

I certainly never saw the New German Cinema as a coherent

movement, artistically or ideologically, even though what was happening in Germany was certainly an interesting development in European cinema. But there were other movements of equal importance, like *Cine Nôvo* in Brazil with directors like Ruy Guerra[3] and Glauber Rocha.[4] But what *was* very clear to my generation was that by the early 1960s we German filmmakers desperately needed to grow up and take our destiny into our own hands, and this is exactly what we did. It is this which united German filmmakers in the late 1960s, not the films themselves, and certainly not the themes of our work.

There were actually a couple of waves of filmmakers. The first was the Oberhausen Manifesto people, though most disappeared completely. I think Kluge and Reitz are probably the best known out of the two dozen filmmakers who signed it. The people in this first wave were generally older than people like Fassbinder, Wenders and myself. Then there was the second wave, and I was part of the early second wave. Actually Fassbinder and Wenders really came a little bit later; they are almost the third wave. Of course, there were others who came after us with some very fine films, but they never really seemed to persevere or else they started to work exclusively in television where there was always more money.

Did it take a while for the rest of the world to catch on to what was happening in German cinema?

You might even say that by the time most people realized there was good work being done in Germany, the New German Wave was subsiding. But for a short time a handful of German filmmakers certainly found it much easier to screen their films internationally, though by no means everyone.

It is not easy to say when German writers and painters – and especially filmmakers – will be able to take their place fully and freely in international culture. Many years ago when I was in America I pulled up to a gas station in the deep south, I think it was Mississippi. My car had number plates from Pennsylvania and the guy at the pump called me a Yankee and flatly refused to sell me any gas. A century after the end of the Civil War and for some in the south the hatred still remains. I know that many people feel the same way about Germany today and the slow pace of collective consciousness is maybe one reason why recent German filmmakers have had such a hard time exhibiting their films outside of their country. After the war there were two jobs of reconstruction: the cities had to be rebuilt physically, but just as important was the necessity of rebuilding Germany's legitimacy as a civilized nation again. This is *still* a struggle. Half a century on and Germany is still not completely there. Even though I have not lived in Germany for some years, it is very clear that today it is not a country known for its cinema. I feel there is a profound lack of vision, courage and innovation in German cinema today. Many young filmmakers emerge from film school, make one film, maybe a second and then disappear. They try too hard to emulate Hollywood. It is almost as if I have to make films for several generations at once.

You could hardly proclaim German cinema to be in the dark ages. There doesn't seem to be that much happening in a country like Italy either these days.

That is probably true, and of course Germany has never been known as a nation of cinema-goers. It is a graveyard over there. In this respect the French and Italians were always much more advanced. And what I found problematic was that even during the peak years in the 1970s it never really occurred to most German filmmakers that they should be trying to reach international audiences. German films in the 1960s and 1970s – to say nothing of what was being produced in the 1950s – were so impossibly provincial that it was difficult to export them internationally. No one outside of the country would have ever wanted to see most of what was being produced, and this is one reason why I have always looked further than our national borders. It is also one reason why I was not so bothered about how my films were received in Germany. Or rather, it is why I was *very* hopeful that they would be well received overseas. It was very gratifying to see that *Aguirre, the Wrath of God* and *The Enigma of Kaspar Hauser* could be screened to audiences at repertory cinemas in London or to native Indians in Peru and be understood and appreciated.

In the 1970s you were out of the country filming probably more than most other German directors. Did you have any extensive contact with other West German filmmakers at the time? What about the distribution company Filmverlag der Autoren?

I was never directly involved with Filmverlag.[5] I was invited to be a part of the organization, but I said no. The concept was certainly good: filmmakers who had no access to distribution companies would create their own distribution company. Outside of Germany distributors were extremely choosy and only a tiny fraction of what was being produced was ever seen internationally. Sure, you could see some Fassbinder and Wenders, maybe some Kluge, but never anything of Achternbusch[6] or Schroeter.[7] But I did not like the concoction of personalities at Filmverlag, plus there was something disparate about it that did not feel quite right to me. Maybe if it had been just Fassbinder and me and a couple of others then I would have trusted it, but there were some people involved who had an agenda and who seemed very disunited in their work. Later on they did take over some of my early films and distributed them.

But I suspect I was probably something of an outsider when it came to dealings with other German directors. When I would meet Fassbinder, some of his entourage thought that I was gay because we really liked each other and he would hug me dearly. Because he was so unruly, a sweaty, grunting wild boar crashing through the underbrush, the media mistakenly labeled him a world revolutionary. When I was in pre-production of *Aguirre* in Peru I took two of his films down there along with some of my own and held a mini-retrospective. I think I did a live translation and he kind of liked me for things like that. But often when we would meet there was nothing to say to each other except something like, 'I like your tie.' When it came to his films I had the feeling that two or three films in a row would not be so good – he released them so quickly, sometimes five films a year – and I would almost lose heart. And then all of a sudden he would come out with a great one. I had to keep on telling myself, 'Never lose faith in the man.'

I like Wim Wenders very much. He has been a good comrade and companion and even though we meet very intermittently, it is good to know that there is someone else out there ploughing a similar furrow to my own.

The television system in Germany seemed to play a major role in reinvigorating the country's film industry in the 1970s.

The *Film/Fernsehen Abkommen* [Film/Television Agreement] opened up opportunities for co-productions with the networks[8] because the rule was that films that opened in cinemas could not be screened on television for at least two years. For *Aguirre*, not having any money left, I sold the television rights and they showed it on television the very same evening it was released in the cinemas. Of course, it was not a box-office smash in Germany. For *Kaspar Hauser* I made sure that the contract stipulated there would be this two-year delay between the cinema release and the film's première on German television.[9]

How do you feel about 'customizing' your films to fit television schedules?

It is a question of discipline, and if I sensed that a format of exactly fifty-nine minutes and thirty seconds just would not be adequate, I would probably not make the film for television. In some cases, like *Little Dieter Needs to Fly*, I had to deliver a film that was exactly forty-four minutes and thirty seconds, and so I decided to produce the film for the TV network knowing that it would be only a shorthand version of the film. The real film is actually over eighty minutes long. Of course, most people saw the film in its truncated version on television. I did not mind changing the title to *Escape from Laos* for the TV version because essentially it is a different film. When I made *The Great Ecstasy of Woodcarver Steiner* it was exactly an hour long. But I wanted to have the film televised in Germany so I said to them, 'Let me try to cut it down to forty-five minutes.' 'If you do that,' the network said, 'please try to make it forty-four minutes and ten seconds long, because we absolutely need another fifty seconds for station identification and the introduction for the film.' So I went back to the film and I made it exactly forty-four minutes and ten seconds long. In doing this, I did not feel I had compromised my vision because I consider filmmaking a craft, and as a craftsman

I have to be very aware of the way my work is received by audiences.

Unfortunately the situation with the television stations has changed a great deal in recent years. The only God that the TV networks venerate these days is the ratings figures. That is the Golden Calf for them, a development that is certainly not particularly German. It has to do with developments in worldwide media per se. May I propose a Herzog dictum? Those who read own the world, and those who watch television lose it.

There's always been a certain amount of antagonism between you and the German critics. Why do you think your films have never been as well received in your home country as they have in England, France and America?

And Algeria or Moscow or Argentina. And we are talking about both critics and audiences here. Germany is just not a country of cinema-goers. It has always been a nation of television viewers. The Germans have never liked their poets, not while they are alive anyway. It is an old tradition which goes back centuries. Eventually there is a chance, years after you are dead, that you will be accepted, and maybe this will be the fate of my work. Compare this to a place like Ireland. I once stayed at a tiny guest-house in Ballinskelligs. The landlady asked me what I did, and off the top of my head – I don't know why – I said, 'I am a poet.' She opened the doors wide and gave me the room for half price. At home they would have thrown me out into the street. And in Iceland there exists the *Codex Regius*, the showpiece of antique literature like the Dead Sea Scrolls in Israel or perhaps the *Nibelungenlied* in Germany. It was finally returned to Iceland by the Danes after 300 years. Half the Icelandic population awaited this little wrinkled parchment book, drinking, singing and celebrating for five days. When the islanders discovered that, upon my special request, I had held the actual manuscript in my very hands, I was treated like a king.[10] Something like this is just not conceivable in Germany. Around the time of *Aguirre* I was at a press conference at Cannes talking about the renaissance of German film. There was a loud laugh from one corner of the room. It was the Germans.

There is a great insecurity among German audiences, which is perhaps understandable as Germany was the cause of the two biggest catastrophes of humanity of the past hundred years. This has continued to make post-war generations very cautious indeed. Whenever somebody sticks his head out too far from any kind of obscure or marginal trench – trying in even some small way to draw attention to himself or show his work to the world – the rest of Germany is immediately suspicious. Such people need to be levelled down in Germany, where they were very suspicious of *Aguirre*, *Fitzcarraldo* and *Kaspar Hauser*. I got *very* bad reviews for those films in Germany. It is somewhat strange for me that only very recently has one of my films – *My Best Fiend* – been truly embraced by the German critics and audiences. It really stunned me. Maybe it is because I do not live in Germany any longer and so am considered a foreigner.

Signs of Life, inspired by a short story by the German writer Achim von Arnim, was your first feature film. The film isn't a straight adaptation though. In what ways were you influenced by von Arnim's writings?

There were three primary influences that pushed me to write the screenplay of *Signs of Life*. I took only the most basic outline of von Arnim's story 'Der Tolle Invalide auf dem Fort Ratonneau'.[11] It is a wonderful piece where an old colonel is sitting by the fireplace and gets so involved in telling a story that he does not notice his wooden leg is on fire. It is the only time, with the exception of *Woyzeck* and *Cobra Verde*, where a piece of literature triggered a screenplay in my mind. What I gather may have been an influence on von Arnim himself also weighed heavily on my mind: a newspaper report of a real event during the Seven Years' War which I stumbled across where a guy became insane and locked himself up in a tower.

But certainly the strongest influences on the film were my travels when I was fifteen to Greece, where I spent some time following in the footsteps of my paternal grandfather, seeing what he had done years before as an archaeologist on the island of Kos. At a very young age – he already had a university chair in Classics – he just ditched everything, got hold of some spades and set off to become an archaeologist. He had done his life's work on the island starting around 1906, carrying out important excavations. Later on he went mad, and it is only as a madman that I really got to know him. Whilst in Greece I walked around the mountains of Crete where I came across a valley. I had to sit down because I was sure I had gone insane. Before me lay 10,000 windmills – it was like a field of flowers gone mad – turning and turning with these tiny squeaking noises. I sat down and pinched myself. 'I have either gone insane or have seen something very significant indeed.' Of course, it turned out that the windmills were for real, and this central image became a pivotal point of the film, a landscape in complete ecstasy and fantastic madness. I knew as I stood there that I would return one day to make a film. Had I never seen the windmills, I would not have made the connection between this fantastic landscape and the von Arnim story, which I read only later on. In *Signs of Life* there are long shots of the incredible landscapes of Crete. The opening credits, for example, hold for an unusually long time with a single shot of a mountain valley. It gives you time to really climb deep inside the landscapes, and for them to climb inside you. It shows that these are not just literal landscapes you are looking at, but landscapes of the mind too.

Why did you choose to set the film during the Second World War?

The film is set during the Nazi occupation of Greece, and inevitably some people will want to suggest that the film is something like a 'historical drama'. Of course, it is nothing of the sort. If I had wanted to make a historical or political point by choosing this setting I would have written a speech and stood up with a microphone in my hand instead. The historical facts of the occupation never interested me in this context, and there is absolutely nothing in the story that makes any reference whatsoever to the Second World War. If a historian were to look at the film he would doubtless find many historical falsehoods. For example, when I show the soldiers they are almost always barefoot or shirtless, they never salute, and when the captain has them fall in, one of the soldiers is munching on a roll. This certainly has nothing to do with the Third Reich. And I went out of my way to use a van from the mid-1950s in the film.

The story concerns itself not with a particular time, nor a particular war, but rather with this idea of putting the instruments of war into the hands of individuals. When you watch the scene when they meet the gypsy at the front door, you really do not notice that these men are wearing German army uniforms. How often do you see German soldiers acting as decently as this in a war film? I think that using the war as a backdrop enables the audience to see the absurdity and total violence of what went on during the Second World War in a different light, one we are not used to seeing. It is not a metaphor, but like *Invincible* which is set just before the era of the Third Reich, *Signs of Life* uses the absurdity of this situation – showing the interactions between an occupying army and the locals – to make what is a more 'existential' point.

Was Signs of Life *an easy shoot?*

One thing that happened whilst I was making the film was I understood that somehow I possessed a certain quality which means I attract real disaster during the making of my films. I know

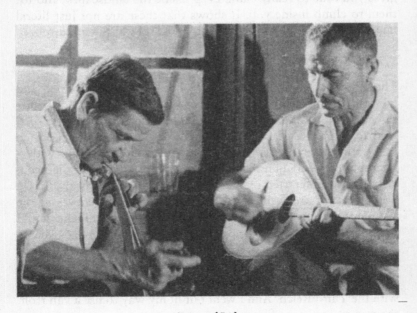

Signs of Life

it sounds crazy, but there were so many problems during the production of *Signs of Life* that seemed to pave the way for what happened on *Fata Morgana* and *Fitzcarraldo* and other films.

Signs of Life started very unfortunately, because everything was prepared, I had secured permission to shoot where I wanted to, and then three weeks before we started shooting there was a military *coup d'état* in Greece. I could not reach anyone, airports were closed and trains were stopped at the border. So I drove by car non-stop to Athens and discovered that I was not allowed even to shoot on Kos because the authorities were so afraid of the colonels. My shooting permits had become invalid overnight. Then, well into the shoot, the leading actor, Peter Brogle, had an accident and broke his heel bone which meant a six-month pause during which he was in a cast and afterwards needed a device to help him walk. Brogle was originally a tightrope walker and I wanted to shoot a sequence in the fortress from one wall to a small tower. He needed to fix the rope himself – no one else could do it – and he fell from something like eight feet, and that was that. A very absurd accident. So we had to suspend shooting for six months and after that I could shoot him only from the hip upwards. And when it came to the final sequences of the film I was forbidden to use fireworks. I told the army major that it was essential for the film. 'You'll be arrested,' he said. 'Then arrest me,' I said, 'but know that I will not be unarmed tomorrow. And the first man who touches me will drop down dead with me.' The next day there were fifty policemen and soldiers standing watching me work, plus a few thousand people from the town who wanted to see the fireworks. Of course, I was not armed, but how were they to know? Nobody complained or said anything. So through all these incidents I learned very quickly that this was the very nature of filmmaking. It hit me harder than it did many of my colleagues around me. A very valuable lesson: things never go as you hope, and there is no point in fuming about it. For a filmmaker, dependent on so many things outside of your control, it is an important lesson.

What exactly is it that causes the main character, Stroszek, to go mad?

Actually, I have always felt that Stroszek really is quite sane, even when he locks himself in the fortress and shoots fireworks at the town. I think he is reacting in an almost necessary way, meeting violence with violence, absurdity with absurdity, certainly when he sees the valley of windmills and then discovers that Meinhard and his wife have reported him. Up to the point where he shoots into the crowd the film has suffered from a kind of inertia. Stroszek has merely been an observer, sitting for weeks under the sun doing nothing, and his actions are perhaps an attempt to break out of this inactivity. But never in the film did I aim to concentrate on Stroszek's psychological state. I wanted instead to focus – with real sympathy – on the physical events that are going on, certainly in the later scenes of the film. Before Stroszek's change, the film is really only an accumulation of scenes spread over several weeks. After his madness kicks in, the story is told in straight chronological fashion and moves through only a couple of days with Stroszek holding out in the fortress. From this point on, the film loses complete interest in his inner personality. We do not have anything like a close-up of him from this point on, and most of the time he is not even on screen. His *actions* take over as he fires rockets across the bay and shoots a donkey dead.

How did the short Last Words *come about? Was it shot at the same time?*

One thing to say about *Signs of Life* – and maybe other filmmakers feel this way about their first films – is that I have always had the very strong feeling that it was made somehow as if there were no history of film preceding it. As such it is my only really innocent film. Something like this happens only once in your lifetime because, once this innocence has been lost, it can never be recovered. I felt this was happening as I was shooting the film, which is maybe one reason why I made *Last Words*, a short produced while we were shooting *Signs of Life*. I wanted to continue venturing out further and further into new terrain, and the film is very much the first stepping stone into totally unknown areas. Today *Last Words* has such a boldness for me in its narrative form and an utter disregard for the narrative 'laws' that cinema traditionally uses to tell stories. Compared to *Last Words*, *Signs of Life* is very conventional.

And without *Last Words* I do not think that *Fata Morgana* or *Little Dieter Needs to Fly* would have happened, nor would certain narrative stylizations that I went on to develop subsequently. I shot the film in two days and edited it in one. Everything about it was so perfectly clear and right, and it has been a source of courage for me ever since.

The idea for the film was that there is an abandoned, decaying island where there were once lepers. It is completely evacuated apart from one man who has lost his mind and refuses to leave. Deprived of his rights, he is then forcibly brought to the mainland by the police. Back living a so-called decent and respectable life, the man has so far refused to speak or to go out, except at night when he plays on a lyre. You get glimpses of all this, but the story itself is not ever explained exactly. It is carried along by compulsive repetitions. For example, the man who tells the tale of the last Turk's last footprint. He had jumped from a cliff into the sea and leaves a footprint behind him, and the Greeks erect a chapel above it. The man has scarcely finished telling this tale when he starts it again from the beginning, and at the end once again he immediately retells it a

Last Words

43

third time. Then there are the two policemen who obviously understood what they were saying over and over again, but to whom I said, 'In cinema you always repeat a scene to find the best one, so why don't you repeat the words ten times. I'll find the best one afterwards.' All at once, despite the compulsion they are locked into, through all the torment, you get an inkling of who this lyre player is. This man is really close to me, he fascinates me. I feel that he talks quite normally, even though for minutes on end he says: 'No, I'm not saying a word. Not a single word. I won't even say no. You won't hear a word from me. I'm saying nothing. If you tell me to say no, I'll refuse even to do that.'

Precautions Against Fanatics was your first colour film, a bizarre comedy set at a racetrack where various individuals feel it necessary to protect the animals from local 'fanatics'. Any comments?

The film was made out of the blue, though like *Last Words* it is quite a bold film in its narrative. Something I should point out is that it has a very strange humour to it, though that might not be immediately evident to those who do not understand German. Recently one of the big magazines in Germany did a feature on me with the headline 'This Man Never Laughs', and a photo with the kind of seriousness that is somehow expected of me, even when you can hear roars of laughter in films like *My Best Fiend* and *Even Dwarfs Started Small*. The photographer had been snapping me with this long lens from a very close distance and saying, 'Laugh! Laugh! Why don't you laugh?' I grew more and more uncomfortable and said, 'I never laugh once a camera is pointed at me.' But of course they left out the second part of what I said.

For *Precautions Against Fanatics* I went to the racecourse on the outskirts of Munich because prominent media figures and actors were taking part in an annual race. When I saw them in training I immediately decided I would do a film. I talked Kodak into giving me some raw colour stock for free; it had been returned to them after it had been in Africa for some time and apparently had been exposed to heat extremes. The stock was also long beyond its expiration date. Under no circumstances can companies like Kodak sell raw stock like this. They keep it to see if it is still usable because they want to discover if the raw stock can survive such disadvantageous circumstances. I talked them into giving me ten or so rolls, which they did so long as I signed a release saying they had warned me this was unusable footage, that it had not been sold to me and that they were not responsible for the results. I gladly took it and basically made this film not even knowing if I would ever end up with anything, so it was a gamble. But dammit, I thought that if decades after Scott had died near the South Pole his negatives could be developed to produce photos, this footage was bound to be OK, and in the end we lost not a single frame. Since then I have often thought about getting my hands on all the wasted stock that companies like Kodak dump and making a film or two.

You then went to Africa where you interwove the filming of three very different films: Fata Morgana, Even Dwarfs Started Small *and* The Flying Doctors of East Africa, *the last of which seems a very atypical Herzog film.*

The Flying Doctors of East Africa, filmed in Tanzania and Kenya, is what I call a *Gebrauchsfilm* [a film for practical use]. I was asked to make it by colleagues of the doctors themselves, and though I do like the final result, it is a film that is not particularly close to my heart. In fact I do not even call it a film, it is much more a *Bericht*, a report. When I was out with the flying doctors they were distributing preventative medicine, in this case treatment against trachoma, the eye disease which leaves tens of thousands of people blind every year. Prevention is very easy and cheap; the disease is caused simply by a lack of hygiene.

The most interesting scenes stemmed from my interest in vision and perception. One of the doctors in the film talks of showing a poster of a fly to the villagers. They would say, 'We don't have that problem, our flies aren't that large', a response that really fascinated me. We decided to take some of the posters the doctors used for instruction to a coffee plantation to experiment. One was of a man, one of a huge human eye, another a hut, another a bowl, and the fifth – which was put upside down – of some people and animals. We asked the people which poster was upside down and which was of an eye. Nearly half could not tell which was upside down, and two-thirds did not recognize the eye. One man pointed to the window of the hut, for example.

For the locals these five objects apparently just looked like abstract compositions of colours. It was clear their brains were processing images in a different way. I still cannot completely figure it out; I can only state that they see differently to us. We know so little about vision and the process of recognizing images and how the brain sorts through and makes sense of them, and after making *The Flying Doctors* it became very clear to me that perception is in some way culturally conditioned and in different societies functions in different ways.

You filmed Fata Morgana *before* Even Dwarfs Started Small *but waited a couple of years before releasing it. Why?*

At the time I never felt *Fata Morgana* was inaccessible, quite the opposite in fact. The film is not there to tell you what to think. I did not structure it to push any ideas in your face. Maybe more than any other films I have made it is one that needs to be completed by the audience, which means all feelings, thoughts and interpretations are welcome. Today, thirty years later, the film is very much alive to audiences. It is like nothing they have ever seen before, and I think everyone comes away with their own understanding of the film.

But immediately after making it I felt that people would ridicule the film. I felt *Fata Morgana* was very frail – like a cobweb – and I did not consider it a robust piece of work that could be released. One reason for this was probably the horrific time we had making the film. I have always felt that sometimes it is just better to keep your work under wraps, handing it on to friends just before death, asking that it be passed on from friend to friend, never allowing it to go public. Only after it has passed down many generations might the film be released. I kept the film for almost two years without showing it, and then I was deviously tricked by my friends Lotte Eisner and Henri Langlois[12] who borrowed a print and gave it to the Cannes Film Festival. When it was finally released it was a big success with young people who had taken various drugs and was seen as one of the first European art-house psychedelic films, which of course it has no connection with at all.

Amos Vogel called the film 'a cosmic pun on cinéma vérité'. Did you go down to the desert with a script, or were your intentions just to document what you found?

46

I never look for stories to tell, rather they assail me, and I knew there was something I needed to film down in Africa. Those primordial and archetypical desert landscapes had fascinated me since my first visit to the continent. But *Fata Morgana* soon became an extremely difficult ordeal, something that I know rubbed off on the general feel of *Even Dwarfs Started Small*, which was made almost immediately after we had finished *Fata Morgana*. Even though I was very cautious in Africa, it always seemed to go wrong for me there. I am not one of those Hemingway Kilimanjaro nostalgia people who love to track animals through the underbrush with an elephant gun while being fanned by the natives. Africa is a place that has always somehow left me frightened, a feeling that I will probably never shake off due to my experiences there as a very young man. What I experienced on the shoot of *Fata Morgana* was sadly no different. My plan was to go out to the southern Sahara to shoot a kind of science-fiction story about aliens from the planet Andromeda, a star outside of our own galaxy, who arrive on a very strange planet. It is not Earth, rather some newly discovered place where the people live waiting for some imminent catastrophe, that of a collision with the sun in exactly sixteen years. The idea was that after they film a report about the place, we human filmmakers discover their footage and edit it into a kind of investigative film akin to a very first awakening. With this completed film we would be able to see exactly how aliens perceive the planet.

But from the first day of shooting I decided to scrap this idea. The mirages that had taken hold of me and the visionary aspects of the desert landscape were so much more powerful than any single idea for the film I had previously had, so I junked the story, opened my eyes and ears, and just filmed the mirages of the desert. I did not ask questions, I just let it happen. My reactions to what I was seeing around me were like those of an eighteen-month-old baby exploring the world for the first time. It was as if I woke up after a night of drunkenness and experienced a moment of real clarity. All I had to do was capture the images I saw in the desert and I would have my film. There are still some aspects of science fiction that remain. For example, the way that, even though obviously shot on Earth, the film does not necessarily show the beauty and the harmony and horror of our world, rather some kind of a utopia – or dystopia – of beauty and harmony and horror. When you watch *Fata Morgana* you see the embarrassed landscapes of our world,

Fata Morgana

an idea that appears repeatedly throughout my work, from *The Enigma of Kaspar Hauser* to *Pilgrimage*.

What actually is a 'fata morgana'?

'Fata morgana' means mirage. The first scene of the film is made up of eight shots of eight different airplanes landing one after the other. I had the feeling that audiences who were still watching by the sixth or seventh landing would stay to the end. This opening scene sorts out the audiences; it is a kind of test. As the day grows hotter and hotter and the air becomes drier and drier, so the images get more and more blurred, more impalpable. Something visionary sets in – something like fever dreams – that remains with us for the entire length of the film. This was the motif of *Fata Morgana*: to capture things that are not real, not even actually there.

In the desert you can actually film mirages. Of course, you cannot film hallucinations which appear only inside your own mind, but mirages are something completely different. A mirage is a mirror reflection of an object that does actually exist and that you can see, even though you cannot actually touch it. It is a similar effect to when you take a photograph of yourself in the bathroom mirror. You are not really there in the reflection but you can still photograph yourself. The best example I can give you is the sequences we shot of the bus on the horizon. It is a strange image; the bus seems to be almost floating on water and the people seem to be just gliding along, not really walking. The heat that day was beyond belief. We were so thirsty and we knew that some of the buses had supplies of ice on board so right after we stopped the camera we rushed over there. But we could not find a single trace of anything. No tyre tracks, no tracks at all. There was just nothing there, nor had there ever been anything there, and yet we had been able to film it. So there must have been a bus somewhere – maybe 20 or 100 or 300 miles away – which was visible to us because of the heated strata of air that reflected the real existing image.

How was it filming in the middle of the Sahara with hardly any money and such a small crew?

On the way down to Africa we drove out of Marseilles and all slept in the two cars we had because we could not afford a hotel. And there were real technical problems shooting in the desert. The emulsions on the raw stock would start to melt away in the heat, and during the sand storms it was absolutely impossible to keep the cameras totally sealed and free of sand. We spent whole days cleaning them afterwards and finding ways to keep the raw stock cool.

The tracking shots past all these embarrassed landscapes were done from the roof of our VW van. Some of it took real work because we would spend days smoothing the terrain out before we started filming. We needed vast areas smoothed out – something we had to do in this incredible heat – because I felt that one six-minute tracking shot would say much more than three two-minute shots. So Jörg Schmidt-Reitwein would be shooting and I would do all the steering myself. I felt it was important for me to learn how to move with the rhythm and sensuousness of the landscape because I quickly learned that what you might call 'mechanical' camerawork just did not work in the desert.

All the machinery you see in the film was, I think, part of an abandoned Algerian army depot. I liked the desolation and the remains of civilization that were out there, things that added to the science-fiction idea. We would find machinery lying in the middle of the desert – a cement mixer or something like that – a thousand miles from the nearest major settlement or town. You stand in front of these things and are in absolute awe. Was it ancient astronauts who put these things down here? Or are they man-made and, if so, what the hell are they doing here? So much absurdity we encountered there. But you know, there is something very primordial and mysterious and sensuous about the desert. It is not just a landscape; it is a way of life. The solitude is the most overwhelming thing; there is a hushed quality to everything. My time in the desert is part of a quest that has not yet ended for me, and even though we were in a car, the spirit of our journey was like one made on foot.

Once you'd junked the script, did you have any plans at all for the shoot? Any structure at all?

None, we just filmed whatever we wanted to with no coherent idea about what we might do with all the footage once we got home. During the filming of *Flying Doctors* I had started shooting some sequences for *Fata Morgana* in Tanzania and Kenya with cameraman Thomas Mauch. Then we went to Uganda with the intention of filming John Okello, the man who a few years before had staged a rebellion in Zanzibar and at the age of twenty-eight declared himself Field Marshal. He was also the mastermind behind the atrocities committed against the Arab population there. I was actually in contact with Okello for a time. He wanted me to translate and publish his book,[13] something thankfully I never did, though I did name a character Okello in *Aguirre, the Wrath of God* a couple of years later. Okello would deliver incredible speeches full of his hysterical and atrocious fantasies over the loudspeaker system from his aeroplane, the climate and taste of which were a strong influence on the language that Aguirre uses. One of them was something like, 'I, your Field Marshal, am about to land. Anyone stealing as much as a piece of soap will be slung into prison for 216 years.' It turned out Okello had been imprisoned in Uganda for the past year and a half and the police there became interested in our footage. We only just managed to hold on to it and fled the country.

I went home after *Flying Doctors* and then set out across the Sahara in two vehicles, initially with this science-fiction idea and three men: Hans Dieter Sauer, who had studied geophysics and had crossed the Sahara several times, the photographer Günther Freyse, and cameraman Schmidt-Reitwein. I ended up doing all the sound recording, but our first day on the road, barely out of Munich, we had to open the hood of the van and accidentally I banged it down on Schmidt-Reitwein's hand. I smashed the bones of his finger in fourteen pieces and he needed some special steel wire to fix it all into place. The whole thing started very unfortunately.

The first place we filmed was the salt flats of Chott Djerid and then we went south to the Hoggar mountains in the middle of the Algerian desert before heading due south for the Republic of Niger. By the time we reached the southern Sahara, conditions were very difficult because it was the start of the rainy season with mud, sandstorms and even worse dangers. But it was also the hottest season, which was the only time we could film the mirages, so we had no choice but to accept these fierce challenges of nature. After that we drove over to the Ivory Coast to film in a lagoon, which is where the procession and the chants I later used in *Even Dwarfs Started Small* were shot. Then I wanted to go back to Uganda to film up in the Ruwenzori mountains where there is a sort of prehistoric landscape. Three or four thousand metres up there is mysterious vegetation that you might compare to that of the dinosaur era. We were not able to cross through Nigeria because of the civil war that was raging there so it became clear that we were not going to make it to Uganda. Eventually we decided on the Congo, and ended up travelling to Cameroon by boat and then heading south-east overland. Almost immediately after arriving in Cameroon things got completely out of hand.

I gather that just before you got there five Germans had got caught up in the troubles between the Central African Republic and the Congolese eastern provinces and were shot dead near the Ugandan border.

Yes, there had been an abortive *coup d'état* in Cameroon a few weeks before we arrived. All four of us were arrested because Schmidt-Reitwein had the bad luck of having a similar name to a German mercenary the authorities were looking for and who had been sentenced to death *in absentia*. We were all thrown into a tiny cell with sixty other men. We were very badly mistreated. I do not want to go into details, but the situation was out of control and Schmidt-Reitwein and I both contracted malaria and bilharzia, a blood parasite. When we finally got out, there was still a warrant out for us all over the country, either on purpose or out of slovenliness the officials forgot to cancel it, so every time we passed through a town we were arrested. We stopped shooting only when we became totally exhausted, and after arriving in Bangui, in the Central African Republic, we took a plane back to Germany. We had been in the desert for three months. Just two months later I was back in Lanzarote in the Canary Islands to start work on *Even Dwarfs Started Small*, which is where I finally finished shooting *Fata Morgana*.

Today *Fata Morgana* seems very frenzied to me, as if a major catastrophe is round the corner of every scene. I am sure that our experiences forced real life into *Fata Morgana*, but unlike the feelings of anger and bitterness I took to the location shooting of *Even Dwarfs*, I do not feel that what happened to us in Africa affected the general feel of a single frame of *Fata Morgana*, at least not in a dark way. Rather, I learned how to wrestle something creative out of the worst set of circumstances I have ever encountered, coming up with something clear and transparent and pure.

Who are all the people in the film? Did you just meet them along the way?

Nothing was planned, we just stumbled across them, including the woman playing the piano and the guy with goggles on the drums. We shot that in a brothel in Lanzarote during *Even Dwarfs Started Small*. She is actually the madam, he is a pimp. He was in charge of discipline and would not stop hitting the prostitutes who had not sufficiently pleased the clients. Looking back now I probably included this sequence because the film is about ruined people in ruined places, and the shot spoke of a terrible sadness and despair. I think it was in the Republic of Niger where we found the nurse who stands in the puddle with the children, teaching them to say '*Blitzkrieg ist Wahnsinn*' ['War is madness']. I always thought the man who reads the letter he pulls from his pocket was very moving. He was a German who lived in great poverty in Algeria. He had been a foreign legionnaire fighting on the side of the French against the Algerian revolutionaries but at one point during the war had deserted and changed sides. I really liked the dignified attitude of the villagers who would feed him and take care of him; the Muslim world deals with people like this with great dignity. By the time we met him he had basically lost his mind and he carried with him a letter that had been written fifteen years previously by his mother. When I asked him, he very proudly read the letter to us on camera. You can see it is in tatters; he kept it under his shirt all this time. The man with the reptiles was from Switzerland and clearly had been out in the sun too long. He owned the little hotel where we stayed during the shooting of *Even Dwarfs Started Small*. At the time it was the only hotel on the island, inconceivable now when you see what the place has become. It is utterly destroyed and ruined by tourism. For me it does not even exist any more.

So the three-part structure of the film was conceived during editing?

Yes, we just brought the footage back and started to see what we had. Of course, we had no opportunities to look at rushes while we were making the film, so the editing of *Fata Morgana* was a much more important process to me than it usually is on my films.

The three-part structure – 'The Creation', 'Paradise' and 'The Golden Age' – was established once all the filming had been done. I looked at the footage and, for example, said, 'Yes, this belongs to the first part and this to the last.' Some of the images I organized, some just seemed to organize themselves. I cannot really explain it.

For the voice-over of 'The Creation', I adapted a text taken from something I had stumbled across when I was living in Mexico, the sacred book of the Quiché Indians, *Popol Vuh*, one of the most beautiful works I have ever read.[14] It consists of long passages on the heroic exploits of the first migrations. The episodes dealing with the Creation explain that it was such a failure the Gods started again – I think it was four times – and by the end they had entirely wiped out the people they themselves had created. Florian Fricke, a trusted collaborator over the years who did the music to many of my films, started a group called *Popol Vuh* as a kind of homage to the book. As I sat watching the footage, I felt that the text of *Popol Vuh* corresponded to the images I was looking at, so I took the creation myths of the books and altered them slightly for the voice-over of the first third of the film. The other two sections have texts that I mostly wrote myself.

Fata Morgana is a film very close to my heart because two remarkable people assisted me. One was Lotte Eisner, who did the original German voice-over and about whom I will talk later. I travelled to her Paris apartment with a Nagra and recorded it in one single take with no rehearsals. The other was Amos Vogel,[15] who refined the English translation I did of the voice-over. Amos is a remarkable man, a true visionary and great film scholar who has been a mentor and advisor over the years. He escaped from Vienna before the Holocaust and went to New York, where he has lived ever since. I even named my son after him, Rudolph Amos Ahmed Herzog. Ahmed comes from a Turkish friend of my grandfather with whom I spent time when I was on Kos at the age of fifteen. He was so overjoyed that the grandson of Rudolph – my grandfather – had come all this way, he opened all the empty drawers and cupboard doors in his house and proclaimed, 'This is all yours!' He even wanted me to marry his granddaughter. I politely refused but promised that I would have children one day and would like to name one of them after him. So the boy has three names.

Let me also say one thing about voice-overs in general. In my 'documentaries' you will often hear my voice. One reason for this is that I would rather audiences who do not understand German listen to *my* voice in English rather than hear me in German and read the subtitles. I think the result is a stronger connection to

54

what I originally intended for the film. I have also never liked the polished and inflected voices of those overly trained actors.

How different do you think Even Dwarfs Started Small *would have been if your experiences in the desert had been less unpleasant?*

Impossible to say. As usual the script was written very quickly, in maybe four or five days. I saw the whole film like a continuous nightmare in front of my eyes and wrote it all down. I distinctly remember being extremely disciplined whilst typing so I would not make any errors in the text. I did not change a single word, rather just let it all pour out. I do not think I made more than five typos in the entire screenplay. I just hammered it out. When I returned to Lanzarote to start shooting *Even Dwarfs Started Small* I was full of bitterness, affected by sickness and the film became a more radical film than I had originally planned. *Aguirre* looks like kindergarten against this one. Somehow I had the feeling that if Goya and Hieronymus Bosch had the guts to do their gloomiest stuff, why shouldn't I?

This was the late 1960s, revolution was in the air, yet you seemed to ignore the political fervour. Is that why you were branded a fascist after the film came out?

I was basically accused of ridiculing the world revolution with *Even Dwarfs* rather than proclaiming it. Actually, that is probably the one thing they might have been right about. The film was made in 1968 and 1969 at the height of the student revolt, and several over-zealous left-wingers told me my film was fascistic because it showed a ridiculous failed revolt with dwarfs. They insisted that when you portray a revolution you have to show a successful revolution, and as *Even Dwarfs* does not do this, for them it was clearly made by a fascist.

I actually find the film very funny; it has a strange comic effect, even though I ache when I laugh. In a way, the revolt of the dwarfs is not a real defeat because for them it is a really good, memorable day; you can see the joy in their faces. Look at the last shot of the film with the kneeling dromedary and the laughing dwarf. If I had gone back three weeks later to where we had been filming, they would still be there, the midget laughing away. Anyway, I told these agitators that the film had absolutely nothing to do with the 1968 movements, that they were blinded by zealousness and that if they looked at the film twenty years down the line they might just see a more truthful representation of what happened in 1968 than in most other films. I think that annoyed them even more. It comes quite simply down to this: nightmares and dreams do not follow the rules of political correctness.

Why were you so resistant to late 1960s politics?

The ideas and actions sweeping the world in 1968 were not for me because at that time, contrary to most of my peers, I had already been much further out into the world. I had travelled, I had made films, I had already taken on responsibilities that very few people my age had. For me, this rather rudimentary analysis that Germany was a fascist and repressive prison state, which had to be overpowered by a socialist utopian revolution, seemed quite wrong. I knew the revolution would not succeed because it was rooted in such an inadequate analysis of what was really going on, so I did not participate. And because I have never been into using the medium of film as a political tool, my attitude really put me apart from most other filmmakers. As there were very few reviewers and journalists who were not wildly into revolutionary jargon at the time and who did not put ridiculous political demands on filmmakers, my films suffered at the hands of many of the critics.

Why dwarfs?

German culture is full of dwarfs and midgets, from the earliest fairy tales through to Wagner and *The Tin Drum*.[16] The dwarfs in the film are not freaks, *we* are the dwarfs. They are well proportioned, charming and beautiful people. If you are only two feet tall that means the world around you is totally out of proportion. Just look around us: the worlds of commerce and consumer goods have become such monstrosities these days. For the midgets, even door knobs are huge. There was a clear decision to shoot from the dwarfs' point of view because then everything, apart from the people themselves, would be out of proportion.

Even Dwarfs Started Small

So if the film is 'saying' anything, it is that it is not the midgets who are monstrous, it is us and the society we have created for ourselves.

We all have a dwarf inside us. It is as if there is something of an essence or a concentrated form of each of us that is screaming to get out and that is a perfectly formed representation of who we are. It is like the laughter we hear at the end of the film. It is laughter *per se*; laughter can go no further than this. It is a very real nightmare for some people who wake up at night and know that basically, deep down, they are just a midget. Sometimes when I was working on the film, I would wake up in terror at night and had to feel about with my arms and legs: was I still as big as I was when I went to sleep? I have found that people essentially react to the film depending on how they react to the dwarf in themselves, which is the reason why the film drew such mixed responses from people: they either loved it or hated it.

Where did you find all the midgets?

Casting was not easy and took a whole year. But generally when you find one midget you find several, so I just went from one midget to the next, hiring their friends. They were very happy to make the film and we would always ask their opinions about what was or was not suitable to do. For the first time in their lives they were able to show their real personalities at work. If the dwarfs are good in the film, it is because they express true humanity and by doing so affirm their own dignity. A really deep relationship formed between the actors and the small crew, and after a week of working with them, I completely forgot they were so tiny. They really got into the spirit of things.

The one who is up on the roof of the car as it is going round and round in circles was truly a very bold little guy. During the shot he was run over by the car. I ran over to him thinking he was dead, but he just scrambled to his feet. He was so proud he did a shot that usually would have been entrusted to a stuntman. Then, later in the film when they burn the flower pots, they actually watered them with gasoline and set them on fire. All of a sudden this same guy caught fire and the crew is just standing there, looking at him like a burning Christmas tree, so I buried him under me and extinguished the fire. His ear was only a little scorched.

All this led to an incident which is reported in almost every little biography of me, a banal little side event. I had the feeling I should be on equal terms with them – a director should not be safe and sound behind the camera while the actors are feeling all alone out there – so that same day I told them all, 'If all of you get out of this film unscathed, if you are unhurt at the end, I am going to jump in the field of cacti.' Some of them were seven feet high. I said, 'You can take your 8 mm cameras and I am going to do the big leap into the plant for you.' So I put on some goggles to protect my eyes and jumped from a ramp. And I can tell you that getting out is a lot more difficult than jumping in. Any old idiot can do the leap in; it takes something else to extricate yourself from something like that. The spines were the size of my fingers. I do not think I have any left embedded in me. It seems that the body absorbs them eventually.

How long was the shoot?

We shot the film in about five weeks. Much of the time was spent on the sound because I knew it was specially important to record direct sound. Take Hombre's voice, the reason why you could never dub a film like this into another language. His voice is very particular and high pitched, and he had this shrill sort of laughter which I discovered on day one of shooting. I found it so astonishing that I decided it would be the element that carried the end of the film with the shot of him and the dromedary as he literally laughs himself to death. That final sequence sums up for me what the film really is. I told him, 'Give it your best laughter, this is your big moment where I am going to end the film. Go wild. We will shoot it only once, but make sure you give the ultimate performance.' And he gave it everything he had. I really love him for that. He started to cough, and just kept on going. I was standing there thinking, 'My God, this really is too much. I should cut.' And just as there really was no mercy in the story I had originally seen in my head, so this shot just went on and on. Eventually the moment came when I just could not take it any longer. 'Just stop the camera, end the film and let's go home. Enough.'

I understand the film was censored in Germany.

In Germany at the time we had something called *Freiwillige Selbstkontrolle*,[17] which is essentially voluntary censorship. After the Nazi era the German constitution refused to accept any sort of censorship, though the film industry had a self-imposed set of rules. You did not have to submit your films, and if you chose to bypass this there were no penalties *per se*, but cinemas would generally not play your films. I submitted *Even Dwarfs* to the censorship board and they banned it from the first till the last minute. There were things in it they felt were very controversial, and I ended up renting cinemas myself to screen it in a couple of towns in Germany. I got several death threats every week during the run. The white supremacists and people like that would call and tell me I was high on their list of people they wanted killed.

Following appeals, the film was finally screened uncut. They said it was 'anarchistic and blasphemous', which I suppose they were quite right about, not that it bothers me. I can certainly see that there is real taboo-breaking in the film. The animal rights people, for example, were furious at the scene where the monkey was tied to the cross and paraded about, even though it was tied down with very soft wool. The religious song they sing meant the Catholics were breathing down my neck too. And the final scene caused problems because a rumour went around that to get the dromedary on its knees for so long I cut its sinews. Very quickly I learned something that was to come in useful years later when I made *Fitzcarraldo*: that you can fight a rumour only with an even wilder rumour. So immediately I issued a statement that actually I had nailed the dromedary to the ground. That silenced them. Of course, in reality the creature was a very docile and well-trained animal whose owner was standing about two feet outside of the frame giving it orders. He was trying to confuse the dromedary by constantly giving it conflicting orders by hand: sit down, get up, sit down, get up. And in despair the animal defecated, something which looks absolutely wonderful on screen.

The only film that has a similar quality to *Even Dwarfs Started Small* is Todd Browning's *Freaks*,[18] which I saw much later and which I think is one of the greatest films ever made. It really fascinated me because I had the feeling all of a sudden that more than forty years before my own film there was somebody who had done something similar. Yet even though the monsters are portrayed with real dignity and tenderness in *Freaks*, it seems that Browning was almost apologetic about the film and maybe never knew what a great piece of work he had created.

Do you ever get bored?

No, never. The word is not even in my vocabulary. I seem to scare and astonish my wife by being capable of standing staring out of the window for days at a time, even when there is nothing happening out there. I may look catatonic, but not so inside. There might be storms raging inside. I think it was Wittgenstein who talked about being inside a house and seeing a figure outside strangely flailing about. From inside you cannot see what storms are raging out there, so you find the figure funny.

You say that you never dream, and yet our conversations have been full of talk about things such as 'dream-like landscapes'. Maybe your films are some kind of substitute to your apparent lack of dream-life?

Every morning upon waking I always feel something of a deficit. 'Again! Why have I not dreamt?' I feel like people who do not eat or sleep enough, who are always hungry or tired, and this might be one of the reasons why I make films. Maybe I want to create images for the screen that are so obviously absent from my head at night. I am constantly daydreaming, however.

My honest belief is that the images in my films are your images too. Somehow, deep in your subconscious, you will find them lurking dormant like sleeping friends. Seeing the images on film wakes them up, as if I am introducing to you a brother whom you have never actually met. This is one reason why so many people around the world seem to connect with my films. The only difference between you and me is that I am able to articulate with some clarity these unpronounced and unproclaimed images, our collective dreams. In no way would I compare myself to the man, but allow me to cite his name to make a point. Many years ago for a whole day I went to the Vatican and looked at Michelangelo's frescoes in the Sistine Chapel. I was overwhelmed with the feeling that before Michelangelo no one had ever articulated and depicted human pathos as he did in those paintings. Since then all of us have understood ourselves just that little bit deeper, and for this reason I truly feel his achievements are as great as the invention of agriculture.

You really never dream? Ever?

I do dream once in a while, maybe every couple of years. But it is always so damned prosaic, usually something like me eating a sandwich. I mean, do they really want to spend time analyzing that?

I have always felt that, to a certain degree, cinema should encourage everyone to take their own dreams seriously and to have the courage to do what they really want to do, even if sometimes it ends in failure. In *Burden of Dreams*, the film Les Blank shot on the set of *Fitzcarraldo*, I tell the story of going back to Germany when things were not going so well in an attempt to hold all the investors in the film together. They all asked me if I was going to continue with the project. 'Do you really have the strength and the will?' I looked at them and said, 'How can you ask this question? If I abandon this project, I will be a man without dreams.' I went on in the face of such opposition, and I finished the film. And today it is the film that everyone knows me for. If you watch *Fitzcarraldo* and you have the courage to push on with your own projects, then the film has truly achieved something. If I find one person who walks out of a cinema of 300 people after watching one of my films and does not feel alone any more, then I have achieved everything I have set out to achieve.

NOTES

1 Wim Wenders (b. 1945, Germany) remains one of the leading film directors working today. His films include the trilogy of *Alice in the Cities* (1974), *Wrong Direction* (1974) and *Kings of the Road* (1976), *The American Friend* (1977) and *Paris, Texas* (1984). See also his volume of collected writings *On Film* (Faber and Faber, 2001).

2 See John Sanford's *New German Cinema* (Da Capo, 1980) and Sabine Hake's *German National Cinema* (Routledge, 2002) for summaries of the state of West German film in the 1950s.

3 Ruy Guerra (b. 1931, Mozambique) trained in Paris and moved to Brazil where he made *The Guns* (1964) and *Gods and the Dead* (1970). He also appeared as an actor in Herzog's *Aguirre, the Wrath of God* (1972). See John King's *Magical Reels: A History of Cinema in Latin America* (Verso, 2000), pp. 105–128.

4 Glauber Rocha (1938–81, Brazil) was the influential director of *Terra em Transe* (1967). See Sylvie Pierre's *Glauber Rocha* (Cahiers du Cinéma, 1987).

5 Established in 1971 by Wenders and Fassbinder, among others, as a production company. 'At the time we started Filmverlag, we were trying to avoid dealing with the mafia of the "percentage producers", who grew fat on the film subsidies scheme,' said Edgar Reitz.

6 Herbert Achternbusch (b. 1938, Germany) is a Bavarian avant-garde writer and director who co-wrote the script for Herzog's *Signs of Life*.

7 Werner Schroeter (b. 1945, Germany) directed the opening opera sequences of Herzog's *Fitzcarraldo* and is the accomplished film director of works such as *Salome* (1971) and *Malina* (1990).

8 For example, Zweites Deutsches Fernsehen (ZDF) is Germany's

second public television station. Throughout the late 1970s ZDF also broadcast a weekly television play under the banner of 'Das Kleine Fernsehspiel'. The series included films by Kluge and Reitz, Werner Schroeter, Theo Angelopoulos, Errol Morris, Bill Douglas and Chantal Akerman. See *BFI Dossier Number 14: Alternative Film-Making in Television: ZDF – A Helping Hand*, edited by Hartnoll and Porter (BFI, 1982).

9 The *Film/Fernsehen Abkommen* was formalized in 1974, after Herzog's *Aguirre, the Wrath of God* but in time to save *The Enigma of Kaspar Hauser* from the same fate. 'The lag time between first cinema release and a television broadcast could be anything between six months and five years.' (Elsaesser, pp. 33–4; see Bibliography).

10 The *Codex Regius* is published by the University of Texas Press as *The Poetic Edda* (edited by Lee M. Hollander, 1998).

11 Translated as 'The Mad Veteran of the Fort Ratonneau' in *The Blue Flower, Best Stories of the Romanticists* (edited by Hermann Kesten, Roy Publishers, 1946).

12 Henri Langlois (1914–77, Turkey), who remains a tremendously influential film historian and curator, helped to educate the French New Wave directors (Godard, Truffaut, Chabrol, Rohmer, etc.) by founding the Cinémathèque Française in 1936 in Paris. Wim Wenders dedicated his film *The American Friend* (1977) to Langlois. As Richard Roud points out, 'The important difference between the Cinémathèque Française and the archives in New York (at the Museum of Modern Art) and London (at the British Film Institute) was that the Cinémathèque began with the idea of showing films as well as preserving them.' (*A Passion for Films*, Secker and Warberg, 1983, p. 11.)

13 Field Marshal John Okello, *Revolution in Zanzibar* (East African Publishing House, 1967).

14 *Popol Vuh: The Mayan Book of the Dawn of Life*, translated by Dennis Tedlock 'with commentary based on the ancient knowledge of the modern Quiché Maya' (Touchstone, 1986). This edition is 'The definitive edition of the Mayan book of the dawn of life and the glories of Gods and Kings.'

15 Amos Vogel (b. 1921, Austria) is an important figure in post-war American film culture. He co-founded the New York Film Festival with Richard Roud and from 1947 to 1963 ran New York's Cinema 16, America's most innovative film club, while his *Film as a Subversive Art* (Random House, 1974) remains an influential book. See Scott Macdonald's *Cinema 16: Documents Toward a History of the Film Society* (Temple University, 2002).

16 *The Tin Drum* was written by German novelist Günther Grass in 1959 (part of his 'Danzig Trilogy').

17 *Freiwillige Selbstkontrolle der Filmwirtschaft* (FSK, Film Industry's Voluntary Self-Censorship) was established in 1949 by Germany's film industry at the behest of the Federal Republic's new government. Though technically 'voluntary', the FSK had a censorship monopoly, i.e. all films released in West Germany had to be given a rating. Were they to flout these recommendations, distributors and exhibitors faced legal and economic pressures from the FSK' (Elsaesser and Wedel, p. 49; see Bibliography).

18 Browning's film *Freaks* is a controversial but recognized classic from 1932. The tagline read: 'Can a full grown woman truly love a midget?'

3

Adequate Imagery

Do you have an ideology? Something that drives you beyond mere storytelling?

Well, I would have to say that 'mere' storytelling, as you call it, is good enough for a film. When I sit down to write a script I never attempt to articulate my ideas in abstract terms through the veil of an ideology. My films come to me very much alive, like dreams without logical patterns or academic explanations. I will have a basic idea for a film and then over a period of time, when maybe I am driving or walking, it becomes clearer and clearer to me. I see the film before me, as if I were in a cinema. Soon it is so perfectly transparent that I can sit and write it all down. It is as if I were copying from a movie screen. I like to write fast because it gives the story a certain urgency. I leave out all unnecessary things and just go for it. A story written this way will have, for me at least, much more coherence and drive. And it will also be full of life. For these reasons it has never taken me longer than four or five days to write a script. I just sit in front of the typewriter or computer and pound the keys.

Whether I have an ideology is not something that I have ever given much thought to, though I do understand where the question might come from. People generally sense I am very well-orientated and know where I have come from, where I am standing now and where I am going. But it is not an ideology as most people think of the term. It is just that I understand the world in my own way and am capable of articulating this understanding into stories and images that seem to be coherent to others. Even after watching my films, it bothers some people that they still cannot put their finger on what my ideology might be. Please, take what I am saying with a pair of pliers, but let me tell you: the ideology is simply the films themselves and my ability to make them. This is what scares those people who try so hard to analyze and criticize me and my work. I do not like to drop names, but what sort of an ideology would you push under the shirt of Conrad or Hemingway or Kafka? Goya or Caspar David Friedrich?

I have often spoken of what I call the inadequate imagery of today's civilization. I have the impression that the images that surround us today are worn out; they are abused and useless and exhausted. They are limping and dragging themselves behind the rest of our cultural evolution. When I look at the postcards in tourist shops and the images and advertisements that surround us in magazines, or I turn on the television, or if I walk into a travel agency and see those huge posters with that same tedious image of the Grand Canyon on them, I truly feel there is something dangerous emerging here. The biggest danger, in my opinion, is television because to a certain degree it ruins our vision and makes us very sad and lonesome. Our grandchildren will blame us for not having tossed hand-grenades into TV stations because of commercials. Television kills our imagination and what we end up with are worn-out images because of the inability of too many people to seek out fresh ones.

As a race we have become aware of certain dangers that surround us. We comprehend, for example, that nuclear power is a real danger for mankind, that over-crowding of the planet is the greatest of all. We have understood that the destruction of the environment is another enormous danger. But I truly believe that the lack of adequate imagery is a danger of the same magnitude. It is as serious a defect as being without memory. What have we done to our images? What have we done to our embarrassed landscapes? I have said this before and will repeat it again as long as I am able to talk: if we do not develop adequate images we will die out like dinosaurs. Look at the depiction of Jesus in our iconography, unchanged since the vanilla ice-cream kitsch of the Nazarene school of painting in the late nineteenth century. These images alone are sufficient proof that Christianity is moribund. We need images in accordance with our civilization and our innermost conditioning, and this is the reason why I like any film that searches for new images no matter in what direction it moves or what story it tells. One must dig like an archaeologist and search our violated landscapes to find anything new.

And there are few filmmakers who are willing to take the necessary risks.

Perhaps, yes. But I would never complain about how difficult it is to get images that are clear, pure, transparent. I would go absolutely anywhere; down here it is hardly possible any more. I did once seriously consider applying to NASA to be on one of their missions. I would like to be there with a camera. I am certain there really would be very good stuff out there to film. Basically, they send technicians up there who are not very inspired and who do not take advantage of the photographic possibilities of travelling to the Moon. On one of the Apollo missions they left a camera on the Moon which for days slowly panned from left to right, then right to left. They transmitted the images and I remember watching it on German television day and night. My God, I was aching for the chance to get up there and grab the damned thing! So many possibilities up there for fresh images. Space travel is unfinished business for me.

Many critics seem to have found themes running throughout your work over the years. Are you able to pinpoint any of these yourself?

Of course, by now you know that I never consciously think about the 'theme' of a film and how the ideas and story might be related in some way to abstract ideas or previous films. Simply, I do not care about themes, I care about stories. Apparently there are running themes throughout my work and, as you say, some writers seem to have identified them. But please do not ask me to name them. You could read to me all these kinds of ideas until you are blue in the face, but I never ask myself specific questions or consciously tackle specific themes when I sit down to write a screenplay. I just write a story. Many of those who write about my films have been trained to think in certain ways, to be able to analyse someone's work and pick out apparent themes, and that is fine. It does not mean they are right, it does not mean they are wrong.

They function in their world and I in mine.

Maybe there are some related ideas in my work, those connecting lines in this tightly woven fabric that is Herzog's body of work. Though I cannot be sure of this, I do know one thing. Let's say you turn on the television and see ten seconds of a film. You would immediately know that this must be one of my films.

Surely you must be able to see some specific connections between at least some of your films?

To answer that, let me say I have always felt my characters all along belong to the same family, whether they be fictional or non-fictional. They have no shadows, they are without pasts, they all emerge from the darkness. I have always thought of my films as really being one big work that I have been concentrating on for forty years. The characters in this huge story are all desperate and solitary rebels with no language with which to communicate. Inevitably they suffer because of this. They know their rebellion is doomed to failure, but they continue without respite, wounded, struggling on their own without assistance.

People often tell me that all my leading characters are so-called marginals and outsiders, but I always felt that a figure like Kaspar Hauser was not an outsider. *He* is at the centre; he manages to retain his unblemished human dignity while everyone around him seems to be so hideously conditioned. These people, transformed as they are into domesticated pigs or members of bourgeois society, are the bizarre ones, not Kaspar. People often say I am a marginal and eccentric filmmaker. When you look at my films you see there is absolutely nothing eccentric about them. When you sit three feet away from me do you see anything eccentric, do you?

No, Werner, absolutely not.

I am dead centre. In comparison to me, all the rest are eccentric. Aguirre, Fini Straubinger, both Stroszek and Kaspar Hauser, they all fit into this pattern. So do Walter Steiner, Hias in *Heart of Glass*, Woyzeck, Fitzcarraldo, the aborigines of *Where the Green Ants Dream* and the people we found in the desert who appear in *Fata Morgana*. Even figures like Reinhold Messner, Jean-Bedel Bokassa, Nosferatu and even Kinski himself, or the 'minor' characters like Vladimir Kokol in *Land of Silence and Darkness*, who can connect with the world only by bouncing a ball off his head and clutching a radio to his chest, much like Kaspar Hauser, who plays with his wooden horse when he is imprisoned in his cellar. Whether they be hallucinating soldiers or the deaf and dumb or dwarfs they are not freaks. These people are not pathologically mad; it is society that is mad. It is the situations they find themselves in and the people who surround them who are mad. It is difficult to put my finger on exactly what binds this family of characters together, but if a member of this family were walking about town, you would intuitively recognize them at once. I cannot really explain it any further, other than to say that all my films appear to be similar in their feeling about life and as such in one way or another form a single whole. They are all close to each other like the parts of a huge body; looked at together, they are a single film with many different dimensions rather than simply a chain of films.

How close do you feel to the characters in your films?

I am sure you can tell that I have a great deal of sympathy for these people to the point where Schmidt-Reitwein used to joke that I should play all the characters in my films myself. I do actually function pretty well as an actor and in many of my films I could have played the leading character if need be. This is something that might answer the question that crops up very often about why there are so few women in central roles in my films. I think one reason is simply because I could not have played these parts myself. I could never make a film about someone – whether I am making features or 'documentaries' – I do not have some sympathetic curiosity for. In fact, when it comes to Fini Straubinger in *Land of Silence and Darkness*, Bruno in *Kaspar Hauser* and Dieter Dengler, these people are points of reference not just for my work, but for my life. I learned so much from my time with them and I think the radical dignity they radiate is clearly visible in the films. There is certainly something of what constitutes them inside me. In Steiner's case, it is some kind of ecstasy and solitude and daring, while in Fini's case, something about her difficulty with communication.

Allow me to say once again: I am not one of those intellectuals who possess a philosophy or a social structure in their mind that from the start guides a film. I have never set out to imbue my films with literary or philosophical references. Film should be looked at straight on, it is not the art of scholars but of illiterates. You could even argue that I am illiterate. I have never read a lot or thought about philosophical themes that I could then shoot through these stories I tell. For me it is much more about real life than about philosophy. All my films have been made without this kind of contemplation. Contemplation always comes after the film.

Land of Silence and Darkness, your film about the deaf and blind fifty-six-year-old Fini Straubinger, is one of my favourites of all your films. Whenever I have presented it to audiences, it has always made a tremendous impact. Why do you think the film strikes such a chord?

In contrast to a film like *Even Dwarfs Started Small*, there is a great deal of softness in *Land of Silence and Darkness*. People generally respond so positively to it because it is a film about solitude, about the terrifying difficulties of being understood by others, something we have to deal with every single day of our lives. In the film one finds the most radical and absolute human dignity, human suffering stripped bare.

Land of Silence and Darkness is a film particularly close to my heart. If I had not have made it there would be a great gap in my existence. Fini Straubinger, a fifty-six-year-old deaf and blind woman, caused me to think about loneliness to an extent that I never had before. In her case, loneliness is taken to unimaginable limits, and I have the distinct impression that anyone seeing the film asks, 'Good God, what would be left of my life if I were blind and deaf? How could I live, overcome loneliness, make myself understood?' And the question of how we learn concepts, learn languages, learn communication is also there. It is a theme that also comes out very strongly in *The Enigma of Kaspar Hauser* and I always felt the two films fit together. Fini is one of those cases where I believe happiness or unhappiness never played a role in her existence. She knew that her life had meaning because she was such a support for so many people, travelling around and

Land of Silence and Darkness

spending time with other deaf and blind people. Of course, she must have experienced unhappiness being bedridden for thirty years, unable to see and hear and being so isolated, so dependent on morphine, but there were things that were just far more important to her.

What's quite inspirational about the film is that basically it was made by three people, wasn't it?

That is right, and the ratio of footage shot to what you see in the final film is probably two to one. The film is an hour and a half, and I think we shot about three hours of footage in total. Not only that, but the film cost only $30,000. It was just me, Schmidt-Reitwein on camera and Beate Mainka-Jellinghaus who edited the film. We had absolutely nothing, yet came up with a film that is still watched thirty years later. This should be a lesson to filmmakers today, especially with the cheaper digital cameras and editing equipment at their disposal. You need only guts to make films, just the sense that you have to make your films. Every able-bodied filmmaker out there should be able to raise the pittance needed to make a film like *Land of Silence and Darkness* today. Do not wait for the system to finance things like this. Rob a bank, for God's sake!

I think the work we did on that film is some of the best I have ever done. You can really feel the very tender approach we took in the camerawork. I wanted the characters to come across in the most direct way possible and told Schmidt-Reitwein not to use a tripod because it would be too static and merciless. I wanted to feel the breathing of the camera and by extension the people he was filming. He had to let the camera beat as if it were part of his own heart. I did not want him to use the zoom but, where possible, move into the crowds using his whole body. Take the sequence at the end with Herr Fleischmann, the deaf man who became blind when he was thirty-three years old and who lived for six years in a cowshed. Remember the shot when he walks over and touches the tree? It is absolutely unforgettable, a whole human drama played out in two minutes. If you had not watched the rest of the film and tuned in just at that point you would just think, 'Well, there's a man who is embracing a tree.' What is happening on screen at that point *is* very simple, but it requires the additional one and a half hours of preceding scenes to make the audience receptive and sensitive enough to be able to understand that this is one of the deepest moments you can ever encounter. I had no preconceived structure to the film before I started making it, but things just fell into place very easily. As soon as I saw Herr Fleischmann under the tree, I knew it was such a striking image that it would probably be the end of the film.

Where did you first meet Fini?

I had been asked to make a documentary about thalidomide victims in West Germany and produced a film called *Handicapped Future*. The reason this film is in no way stylized is because, like *The Flying Doctors of East Africa*, it was proposed by someone else, in this case by a young man whose very best friend was in a wheelchair. I was asked to do a film on him alone, but after some investigation I felt there was more to the subject and I made

Handicapped Future – another example of what I call a *Gebrauchsfilm* – so I could give it to those institutions who take care of the physically handicapped and assist them in raising public awareness of their cause. At the time, treatment of the handicapped was somewhat mediaeval. For example, in Germany there were very few elevators in public spaces or sidewalks that could be used by wheelchairs. It is probably one of my most directly politically aware films because I wanted to explore the development of legislation emerging from the United States – that later trickled across to Germany and other European countries – which was helping the handicapped minority. The film actually helped trigger a change of awareness of these issues in Germany which led to new legislation. I do not know if I like the film; today it seems dangerously conventional. If I was to make a similar film today it would be much harsher. In pursuit of the deeper truths, I would not shrink back from anything, even when telling such a tragic story.

More importantly, *Handicapped Future* was somehow a predecessor to *Land of Silence and Darkness* and directly triggered that film. During filming, Schmidt-Reitwein and I went to hear a speech given by Gustav Heinemann, the President of West Germany, where I met Fini. You can actually see on film the first moment I encountered her: it is the scene that appears about halfway through *Land of Silence and Darkness* when she is at the Heinemann talk and her companion is describing what is going on to her through the tactile language they are using. We were filming the President and I turned and saw this man tapping out something on to the hand of the woman sitting next to him. I immediately sensed this was something big that I should take note of, so I gently nudged Schmidt-Reitwein, who slowly moved his camera around and filmed the two of them.

Let me add something about my work with Schmidt-Reitwein and other cameramen. I have a symbiotic and very physical relationship with the cinematographers that I have worked with over the years. With Thomas Mauch, I would walk step by step in actual physical contact with him, like a pair of ice skaters. More recently, with Peter Zeitlinger, I would put one arm around his chest from behind or my hand on his belt. Each of us knows perfectly the movements of the other, and if I observe something unforeseen and it interests me, I push the cameraman towards it with a nudge or a whisper. In the final sequence of *Land of Silence and Darkness*, I had my arm around Jörg and I just softly turned him. Immediately, he knew that there was something he had not seen, so he turned and straightaway picked up on Herr Fleischmann moving slowly away and zeroed in on him under the tree. I love to work this way.

How easy was it to persuade Fini to allow herself to be filmed?

Fini allowed me to make the film because she understood that it would not be about just her, but would be of some significance for all of us who are in search of clearer forms of communication with others. We groped our way with Fini without really knowing what we were doing, pushing her into areas she would never talk about. It was a case of filming over a period of about half a year or so. For example, we knew it was Fini's birthday and as a present I organized a plane ride, the first time she had ever flown. She really loved it. We waited for events or staged things or would follow her when she would travel out to Lower Bavaria to take care of another deaf and blind person. I truly loved her and did things with her that nobody else would ever do. She had been prevented from making mischief for so long that I decided to take her out into the countryside on my motorcycle where we would poach pheasants. I would take my small calibre rifle with me – she would hide it under her coat as I had no licence – and I would shoot the gun off. It was exciting for her because she sensed the shot, she could feel the power from the muzzle of the gun, and she was exhilarated because for the first time in her life she had the opportunity to do something which was against the law. When she plucked the pheasant later, she was still delighted about the mischief we had done together, and the pheasant tasted twice as good. I even asked her to babysit for my little son Rudolph. He was only a year old, and nobody had ever entrusted her with such responsibility. And my mother who lived in Munich became very close to her after the filming was finished. I was so often away filming, and my mother learned the tactile language so she could speak with Fini. We both learned it quite quickly, about as fast as it takes to learn to type, and by the end I was even tapping into Fini's toes and the sole of

74

her foot and she would understand. So it was much more than just the film for us. Fini died about five years after the film was done.

Why did you want to include the children who had been born deaf and blind?

It came very naturally and I thought it was important to show a different side to the story. Fini went deaf and blind when she was a teenager, which clearly makes a real difference in the kind of contact she had with the outside world. We will never know what these other kids think about the world around them, for there is just no way to communicate with them, and contact rarely surpasses the very basic palpable essentials: 'This is a book. This is heat. Do you need food?'

There are some famous cases like the American Helen Keller, who was born deaf and blind and who actually studied philosophy.[1] Her case raises many questions about what these children think and feel about abstract concepts, to say nothing of innate human emotions. It seems certain they do feel and understand emotions like anger and fear just like anyone else, but it is not possible for us to know truly know how these children cope with the anonymous fears that are within and that can never be explained by the outside world. The children we filmed would have moments of deep fear that seemed to relate only to what was happening inside their own heads, which when you think about it is quite startling.

What was the public reaction to the film?

Land of Silence and Darkness was actually refused by television for two and a half years. I was so angry that I threatened the network executives, telling them that I would buy their television station in twenty-five years when I was rich and fire them all. Of course, they did not take me seriously, but they did finally test the waters by screening it late at night. It got such a favourable response from the public that they repeated it twice very shortly afterwards and the film became a great success. Inevitably, some of the reviews – mainly in Germany – accused me of exploitation. Thankfully, several people jumped to the film's defence, including Oliver Sacks,[2] the neurologist and writer of *Awakenings*. He loved the film so much, and somehow word spread that it was a worthy film. I admire Sacks tremendously for giving the film the backing that it needed.

Aguirre, the Wrath of God was your first international success, a film that is held up today as one of the great achievements of German film of the 1970s. But it took some time before the world caught on.

Even though it was my first international success hardly anyone actually wanted to see *Aguirre* when it got its first very limited release, and it was difficult to find the money to even make the film. It was financed in part by a German television station, Hessicher Rundfunk, which had the right to screen the film the very evening it was released in cinemas in Germany, thus destroying any chances of it succeeding theatrically. The rest of the budget came from the small revenue I had received from previous films, plus a loan from my brother. Everyone else thought it would be a difficult script to film and a difficult sell too, so they backed away. Once finished, we struggled to sell it at first, but it was finally picked up by a French distribution company and played in a cinema in Paris for so long – two and a half years – that the rest of the world took notice.

In a way, by making *Aguirre* I set out to create something of a commercial film, certainly compared to *Signs of Life* and *Land of Silence and Darkness*. The film was always intended for the general public and not the strictly art-house crowd. After looking at my previous films, it was quite clear that I had been serving only the niche market, and with *Aguirre* I made a conscious effort to reach a wider audience. If I could have been absolutely guaranteed an audience for the film I would have made it differently, probably rougher and less genre-orientated. As it is, the film is probably easier to follow than my previous work. The sequence of action, for example, is much less subtle than in a film like *Signs of Life*, and there is a real line of demarcation in the film between the good and the bad, like in the classic westerns, so the audience can choose who they want to root for.

Aguirre could be viewed almost as a genre film, an all-out adventure film that on the surface has all the characteristics of the genre but that on a deeper level has something new and more complex within. At the time I felt that the film was something of a personal test for me. If it failed, I knew I would never be capable of making anything that might be seen widely internationally and I would have to go back to films like *Signs of Life*. The film was a test of my marginality. I do not know how else to qualify *Aguirre*, except to say that it is a very personal film and is still very much a part of my life.

How did you end up making a film about a little known sixteenth-century Spanish adventurer who went in search of El Dorado?

Well, the film really is not about the real Aguirre. As with *Kaspar Hauser* a few years later, I just took the most basic facts that were known about the man and spun my own tale. By chance, at a friend's house I found a children's book about adventurers that had a very short passage on Lope de Aguirre, a Spanish Conquistador who went looking for El Dorado and who called himself 'the wrath of God'. He had initiated a revolt, made himself leader of the expedition, declared the King of Spain overthrown, and set off down the Amazon, only to end up at the Atlantic half starved. These few lines really fascinated me and I tried to find out more about him but very little is known about his life. There remain only a few pages of documents about the man. History is generally on the side of the winners, and Aguirre is one of history's great losers.[3] There are, however, many pieces of literature about him – novels and memoirs that talk about him in rather legendary terms – but no one really knows what is true and what is not. For example, I found a translation of Aguirre's letter to King Felipe II of Spain in which he curses the King, declares him dethroned and stripped of all his rights, and proclaims himself the new Emperor of El Dorado and New Spain. This letter really interested me because of its language, its defiant tone and its absolute madness.

It is difficult for me to explain my feelings about Aguirre as I do not like to analyze characters, but merely present them to the audience. Aguirre fascinated me because he was the first person who dared defy the Spanish crown and declare the independence of a South American nation. At the same time he was completely mad, rebelling not only against political power but nature itself.

In the film he insists that 'When I, Aguirre, want the birds to drop dead from the trees, then the birds will drop dead from the trees. I am the Wrath of God. The earth I walk upon sees me and trembles.' At the end of the story it is not just him who is mad, it is the whole situation that is demented. There is a strong feeling of menace surrounding the characters. You feel them slipping further and further into trouble as the film progresses, and in this respect the movement of time in *Aguirre* is more important than in any of my other films. It is not something explicable in words: you just have to see the film. This is one reason why I was anxious to shoot the film in sequence because the chronology of the story is so linked to its rhythm.

Did the other characters we see in the film really exist?

Many of the characters in the film were invented, or if they did exist they were not actually on the expedition seen in the film. I just made up characters based on the names I had read in the original documents. The entire script is pure invention, the voice-over is a fabricated diary of the monk on the voyage, even though a monk with the same name did exist and wrote a diary of a totally different expedition. Historians are always asking me where I got the documents, and I keep saying that it was in this and that book but regrettably I cannot remember the title.

It does seem that the characters and even the landscapes are moving in a very self-destructive way throughout the film. Aguirre is clearly the cause not just of his own downfall, but that of everyone else's too. And your use of the voice-over seems to give the whole film an almost surreal dimension.

I am glad that is how it appears to you. Unlike the original few pages of documents that still exist from the era, the monk's voice-over is written in a kind of detached language. It is unreal to the point where the film seems to slow down and become almost immobile. In this sense *Aguirre* has a real sense of rhythm to it. The film is about this tremendous military force that steadily comes to a standstill, and towards the end a real feeling sets in that everyone is moving in circles.

What interested me about the story was how these Spanish

Conquistadors set off in search of El Dorado and gradually all drifted to their deaths. At the start, there is an army of a thousand people, but by the end they are a pathetic handful of sick and wounded. The film presents the audience with two opposing thoughts: the seemingly clear sense of direction these people are moving in, and the fact that they are looking for a place that does not even exist. Aguirre's expedition is clearly doomed to failure right from the start. We know this – even before the film has started – when we read that El Dorado is merely an invention of the Indians. So we know that what these people are undertaking is almost the mechanical pursuit of defeat and death. Sometimes it seems to me that Aguirre is deliberately leading his soldiers to their – and his – destruction. It is like a Greek tragedy; at the end it is so obvious that he has brought these horrors upon himself. Aguirre dares to defy nature to such an extent that nature inevitably takes its revenge on him.

Throughout the film real things seem gradually to acquire unreal qualities.

Yes, they move into delirium and become hallucinatory. There is an inner flow to most of my works, one that cannot be followed merely with a wristwatch. It is as if the audience is being taken directly into the interior of things. You see this throughout the film, certainly by the time of Aguirre's revolt against Ursua. Watch the scene of Don Fernando de Guzman's 'coronation' carefully and you will see that there is a tableau, a highly stylized shot where all the characters look directly into the camera, like an old photo from the nineteenth century. It is like the shot during the wedding in *Signs of Life* where the marriage couple and their parents are posing for the photographer, all lined up. They are staring right into the camera, which in this case happens to be our film camera. What I had done was make the actor Peter Brogle race me as fast as he could for two kilometres around Kos. Everyone else was on set ready to roll while we were running back to set at top speed. I quickly tossed Peter a towel for him to dry his face and made him line up with the others, telling him, 'Stare at the lens and try to suppress your heavy breathing.' So he stood there, his face totally disfigured, and when you watch the scene you do not really know what is going on with the guy.

These kind of shots are where the film holds its breath. They feel as mystifying and intense to me as to any other spectator, and I am convinced it is moments like these that truly decide my films. They are the places where the various threads suddenly run together to form a knot. They propel the plot forward, even though I do not really know how. So the story of *Aguirre* is presented very unobtrusively, moving between what is almost documentary-style filming and these highly stylized frozen stills. By the end of the film even the bird noise and the silences on the soundtrack have taken on eerie and illusory qualities. Whenever you hear silence, you know there must be Indians around, and that means death. We spent weeks recording the birds and the soundtrack was composed from eight different tracks. There is not a single bird that has not been carefully placed as if in a big choir. For the music, I described to Florian Fricke what I was searching for, something both pathetic and surreal, and what he came up with is not real singing, nor is it completely artificial either. It sits uncomfortably between the two.

By the end of the film, when Aguirre is staring into the face of the monkey, we're not really sure if this is real or not.

Yes, it might be a hallucination. The surreal qualities and the fever dreams of the jungle have taken over the fantasy of Aguirre and everyone around him. Even the way people die in the film is done in a kind of stylized operatic way, like Aguirre's daughter who dies with no pain, no gore or blood, she just stares up at him. Or Ursua's wife, who throughout the entire film has been wearing a blue dress. When she walks into the jungle, presumably never to be seen again, suddenly she is wearing a beautiful golden royal gown. Logic plays no part in this; grandiose stylizations have taken over. Or take the scene when they find the boat up in the tree. This image might appear unreal, but to the soldiers on the raft – who have already completely lost their sense of reality – it does not seem so strange. For this shot I wanted a slightly stylized feel and so waited for the strange atmosphere that occurs during the rainy season when there are very ominous clouds that appear about an hour before it starts to pour with rain. Incidentally, that is a real boat up there. We built it in five sections, constructed an enormous scaffold of about thirty metres around the tree, and hoisted it up there. It took twenty-five workmen a week to reassemble it. Who knows, it might actually still be up there.

How did you find the locations? When we were talking about Fata Morgana *you said that it was important to find the 'rhythm and sensuousness' of the desert landscape. Can the same be said of jungle landscapes?*

Absolutely. In my films landscapes are never just picturesque or scenic backdrops as they often are in Hollywood films. In *Aguirre* the jungle is never some lush, beautiful environment it might be in a television commercial. Sometimes when you see the jungle in the film it is a reality so strange you cannot trust it, and maybe think it is a special effect. The jungle is really all about our dreams, our deepest emotions, our nightmares. It is not just a location, it is a state of our mind. It has almost human qualities. It is a vital part of the characters' inner landscapes. The question I asked myself when first confronted by the jungle was 'How can I use this terrain to portray landscapes of the mind?' I had never been to Peru before filming but had imagined the landscapes and the atmosphere with real precision. It was curious because when I arrived there everything was exactly as I had imagined it. It was as if the landscapes had no choice: they had to fit to my imagination and submit themselves to my ideas of what they should look like.

I like to direct landscapes just as I like to direct actors and animals. People think I am joking, but it is true. Often I try to introduce into a landscape a certain atmosphere, using sound and vision to give it a definite character. Most directors merely exploit landscapes to embellish what is going on in the foreground, and this is one reason why I like some of John Ford's work. He never used Monument Valley as merely a backdrop, but rather to signify the spirit of his characters. Westerns are really all about our very basic notions of justice, and when I see Monument Valley in his films I somehow start to believe – amazingly enough – in American justice. I think my ability to understand landscapes comes from my grandfather. Like I said, he was an archaeologist and had a real instinct for terrain. People had already spent 800 years searching for the Asklepieion that he discovered. The last surviving workman involved in the dig – the Turk Ahmed who I told you wanted me to marry his granddaughter – took me on a tour of an enormous flat field on Kos. Other archaeologists had carried out excavations in ten different spots there without finding a thing. For reasons that are unfathomable, my grandfather chose to dig somewhere in the middle of the field and promptly discovered a Roman bath.

Landscapes always adapt themselves to the situations required of them. Look at the shots in *Nosferatu* when the coach returns to Wismar with Jonathan. There is a long shot along a causeway and on either side are lakes and trees. There is a real 'serenity' here; it is an image of real peacefulness and beauty, though at the same time there is something very strange about it. And in *Even Dwarfs Started Small*, you can plainly see how important the landscapes on Lanzarote are and how they contributed to the very stark and menacing feel of the film. The island is a totally barren place that was devastated by volcanic eruptions over a hundred years ago. It has this stylized quality of a lunar landscape to it. Back then it looked almost black and white with barely any vegetation.

Or look at the shot of the windmills in *Signs of Life*, where the sound was also vitally important. I started by taking the recording of nearly a thousand people clapping at the end of a concert and distorted it electronically until it sounded like wood banging. Then I added another sound over it: what you hear in the countryside when you put your ear on a telegraph pole and the wind passes through the wires. You hear a humming that we children called 'angel song'. Then I mixed the noise of the banging wood with this 'angel song' and used the sound as if it were the windmills. This does not change the windmills or the landscape physically, but it does change the way we look at them. That is what I tried to render: a new and very direct perspective of things that touch us deeper than more 'realistic' sounds.

Does your understanding of landscapes have anything to do with the fact that from your very earliest works you have often filmed outside of Germany? Films like Signs of Life *and* Aguirre *can hardly be said to be 'provincial'.*

It is difficult to explain why I shoot films so far from home. What I look for in landscapes in general is a humane spot for man, an area worthy of human beings. The search for utopian landscapes is probably an endless one, but I do know that by staying in one place I will never find them. Though I do not like most of his films, it seems that for Ingmar Bergman[4] his starting point is a human face. The starting point for many of my films is a landscape, whether it be a real place or an imaginary or hallucinatory one from a dream, and when I write a script I often describe landscapes that I have never seen. I know that somewhere they do exist and I have *never* failed to find them. Actually, maybe I should say that the landscapes are not so much the impetus for a film, rather they become the film's soul, and sometimes the characters and the story come afterwards, always very naturally.

The landscapes in *Aguirre* are not there as decoration or to look especially exotic. There is profound life there, a sensation of force, an intensity that you do not find in movies of the entertainment industry where nature is always something artificial. To search for locations for *Aguirre*, I travelled down a few of the tributaries because I had to make sure that we had exactly what we needed for the film, and discovered that many stretches of the river were just too dangerous for a film crew and actors in costumes. Finally, I found some very dangerous looking and spectacular rapids – though not *too* dangerous – that could handle the rafts we were going to be filming on.

I gather that the Aguirre *shoot wasn't easy, and the tiny budget and small crew didn't help.*

Pre-production was meticulous. We built a kind of encampment for 450 people near Rio Urubamba, including the 270 Indians from the mountains who were acting as extras. During shooting we then moved on to Rio Huallaga where our encampment was flooded. Filming took about six weeks, a whole week of which was lost when we took the cast and crew from one tributary to another, a distance of 1,600 kilometres. Once we arrived at Rio Nanay, we were living on the rafts themselves, one of which was used as a kitchen. We could not set foot on dry land because in the flat low-lands the jungle had been flooded for miles around. All the rafts had to float about a mile behind the raft we were shooting on to enable us to film the bends in the river without getting any other rafts in shot. There were no riverbanks and at night we had to tie the rafts into overhanging branches.

People should remember that the budget on the film was only $370,000, a third of which went to Kinski, so I really did not have much choice. I could not afford to take too many people with me down the river and the whole crew was less than ten people. We shot only a very small amount of footage in total, so again it was a very low ratio of footage shot to footage that appears in the final film.

Sometimes I had to sell my boots or my wristwatch just to get breakfast. It was a barefoot film, so to speak, a child of poverty. Some of the actors and extras sensed this might be one of the film's virtues and wore their costumes all the time, even though they were full of mould because of the humidity. But you know, I would have spent the entire budget in three days working in a studio. And, of course, there is something authentic about the jungle which cannot be fabricated. You cannot create the jungle in a studio. There was just no alternative to going out there and filming, and sometimes things would happen that I would incorporate into the story. One time while we were shooting, the river rose by fifteen or twenty feet and flooded our locations, sweeping everything away, even some of the rafts. I used these problems at the point in the film when the Spaniards do not know whether to continue or to advance, build new rafts or return to the main expedition.

What about the scenes as the rafts pass through the rapids?

It took only two minutes or even less to get through, but we absolutely had to get the shot first time. In Hollywood films the danger is never real, but in *Aguirre* the audience can really feel the authenticity of the situations the actors are in. Cameraman Thomas Mauch and I were the only people on the rafts running freely. Everyone else, including the Indian rowers of the rafts, were attached by cords to the raft, but this would have been impossible for Mauch and myself because we had to be everywhere at all times, moving around with the camera. There are some shots in the film where you can clearly see the cords that are attached to the actors' wrists.

The first time I went down the rapids was during pre-production to see if it was safe enough for the cast and crew. Our raft split in two and disintegrated, and one half got caught in a whirlpool. What saved us on the other half was getting caught in a strong current that swept us several kilometres away. Of course there were many precautions taken to protect the actors and crew, not least these very solid wooden rafts built by the Indians who were local experts at this kind of thing, and we also had very good rowers. Having said that, sometimes they were drunk and had absolutely no control over where they were going. One time, the water level rose so quickly that a raft was caught in a whirlpool for a couple of days and was then smashed into pieces. The scene when the soldiers get caught in the whirlpool and are found dead the next morning was very difficult to shoot because the flow of the river was so fast and incredibly violent. After a day's shooting we threw cords to the actors, who attached them around their waists in order to get them safely to the riverbank. The next morning the raft would still be there, wrestling with the fierce current. The actors were so proud every evening once they reached the shore, vomiting because of the incessant turning of the raft, ready to go back out there the next day so we could continue shooting.

There were other problems we had to deal with. About halfway through the shoot, it looked as though everything we had shot had been lost in transit to Mexico, where all our exposed negative was supposed to be processed. Only Mauch, myself and my brother Lucki knew about it. We did not tell any of the actors because they already had so much to deal with, keeping themselves dry and warm out there in the jungle. We knew it was an absurdity to continue shooting, but five weeks later all the footage finally showed up, sitting outside the customs office under the scorching sun at Lima airport. What happened was that the shipping agency had bribed customs to stamp the documents so as to prove to us that our negative had left the country.

What about the final sequence of the film with all those monkeys?

85

Months before, I had hired local Indians who had captured the hundreds of savage little monkeys, the ones who overrun the raft with Kinski. I paid only half the money for them because I knew if I paid full price, the guy organizing everything would run off with the cash. The monkeys had been sitting in Iquitos for weeks, but when it came to actually having to use them for the scene it turned out they had all been sold to an American businessman and were already on a plane waiting to go to the US. We ran to the airport and insisted we were veterinarians and that we had to see the vaccination papers for the animals. We shouted so loudly that they admitted they had no papers, and they embarrassedly unloaded the animals from the plane. We just put them into our truck and left. When it actually came to shooting the sequence, the monkeys had some kind of a panic attack and bit me all over. I could not cry out because we were shooting live sound at that point.

Just what is it about the jungle that attracts you?

As a Bavarian I have an affinity for the fertility of the jungle, the fever dreams and the physical exuberance of things down there. For me, jungles have always represented something of an intensified form of reality, though they really are not particularly difficult challenges.[5] A jungle is just another forest, that is all. It is the myth of the travel agencies that they are dangerous places, full of hazards. I really would not even know what hazards are out there. Snakes run away from you as fast as they can crawl and piranhas do not do anything to you unless you do something stupid. I used to catch them with a little hook and eat them. Right after I pulled one out, I would jump into the water and take a swim. As long as you are not in stagnant water there is no danger from these fish.

Where did all the costumes and props come from?

We got them all from a production company that had just shot a film in Peru not long beforehand. We shipped boxes of harquebuses and pieces of armour from Spain where I finally found everything. And jungle transportation was difficult to organize because we had to squeeze everything – armour and technical equipment and the horse – into one big amphibious plane.

Where did you find the Indians who appear as extras in the film?

They all came from the mountain areas. I went to a village and explained what the film was and what I needed from them. We ended up with almost the entire population of the village, a people who were very conscientious as they carried out the sometimes very difficult tasks. They were well paid compared to what they usually earned.

One time, after filming in the mud and swamps, I noticed that the Europeans were exhausted and wanted to call a halt for the day, but the Indians asked me why we were stopping. They said it would be even more difficult to continue later on, so why not just carry on now and finish the job. They understood that what they were working on was not only useful for themselves, but for the Indians' cause as a whole. They were all part of a socialist co-operative at Lauramarca and were very aware of the political situation in Peru. They also had a real understanding of their own history, and why things were as they were today. One time they told me that the Spanish conquest was a real shock for them. It was as if creatures from another planet had landed in spaceships and taken over the whole world. This really was something that every Indian felt inside of them.

I dedicated the film to one of the Indians, Hombrecito. I met him at the main square of Cusco where he was playing the flute. I never knew his real name, but everyone called him Hombrecito, 'Little Man'. I liked him so much that I asked him to come with us for the shoot. I said I would pay him well, more than what he would earn in ten years sitting there playing for people. At first he refused, saying that if he was to stop playing in the square, everyone in Cusco would die. He wore three wool sweaters at the same time which he refused to take off as he thought they would be stolen and which he said protected 'us poor Indians against the bad breath of the Gringos'. A couple of years later I wrote a character called Hombrecito for the circus scene in *The Enigma of Kaspar Hauser*, though I used an actor to play the part.

This was your first collaboration with Kinski. Did you write the script with him in mind?

Most of the screenplay was written on a bus going to Vienna with the football team I used to play for. We were a few hours into the trip and everyone was drunk already because we had some beer barrels to give to our opponents, but the team had drunk half of it before we had even arrived. I was sitting in my seat with my type-writer on my lap. Our goalie was leaning over me and was so drunk that he finally vomited over my typewriter. Some of the pages were beyond repair and I had to throw them out the win-dow. There were some fine scenes, but they are long gone. That is life on the road for you. Later on, in between the games, I wrote furiously for three days and finished the script.

So the screenplay was written so fast and abruptly and sponta-neously that I did not think about who might play the part. But the moment I finished it I knew it was for Kinski and sent it to him immediately. Two nights later, at 3 a.m., I was awakened by the phone. At first I could not figure out what was going on. All I heard were inarticulate screams at the other end of the line. It was Kinski. After about half an hour I managed to filter out from his ranting that he was ecstatic about the screenplay and wanted to play Aguirre.

What was he like on set?

At the time Kinski had just cut short his infamous 'Jesus Tour', scenes of which you can see at the start of *My Best Fiend*. He arrived down in Peru to start filming as this derided, misunder-stood Jesus figure who had identified with his role so strongly that he felt he needed to continue living it. The shoot was very tough and every day Kinski could see the problems I was having. Yet he continued to throw tantrums, create scandals or simply scream if a mosquito appeared.

I had known something of his reputation. Kinski was probably the most difficult actor in the world to deal with. Working with Marlon Brando must have been like kindergarten compared to Kinski. During a play he hit someone so hard with a sword that the actor was in hospital for three months; another time he threw a candelabra into the audience, after having hurled various insults at them first. During the shoot of *Aguirre*, in the middle of a scene, he nearly killed another actor when he struck him on the head with his sword. Thankfully the man was wearing a helmet, but he carries a scar to this very day. And one time the extras had been drinking and were making too much noise for Kinski. He screamed and yelled at them, grabbed his Winchester rifle and fired three bullets through the walls of their hut. There were forty-five of them crammed together and one had the top of his finger shot off. That Kinski did not kill any of them was a miracle. I immediately confiscated his rifle which I still own. It is one of my big souvenirs from him.

During filming he would insult me every single day for at least two hours. Kinski had seen *Even Dwarfs Started Small* and so for him I was the 'dwarf director'. A term of abuse. He cried in a high-pitched shrill voice in front of everyone, insisting that it was an absolute insult that I would even think about directing him, the great actor. I would always just stand there in silence.

How did he react to being in the jungle?

Kinski arrived during pre-production with half a ton of alpine equipment – tents, sleeping bags, ice axes – as he badly wanted to expose himself to the wilds of nature. Actually his ideas about nature were rather insipid. Mosquitoes were not allowed in his jungle, nor was rain. The first night after setting up his tent it started to rain and naturally he got wet, so immediately he had one of his raving fits. The next day we built a roof of palm trees above his tent. Still discomforted, he moved into the one single hotel in Machu Picchu. We would all drink river water, but Kinski had the privilege of mineral water.

We never agreed without a struggle. Temperamentally, he was inclined to hysteria, but I managed to harness this and turn it to productive ends. Sometimes other methods were necessary. There was one occasion on the Rio Nanay towards the end of the shoot when, as was usual when he did not know his lines properly, he was looking for a victim to jump on. Suddenly he started shouting like crazy at the sound assistant. '*You swine! You were grinning!*' He told me I should fire the guy on the spot, but I said, 'No, of course I am not going to fire him, the whole crew would quit out of solidarity.' So Kinski left the set and started packing his things, saying he was going to get into a speedboat and leave. I went up to him very calmly and said, 'You cannot do this. You cannot leave the film before it is finished. The film is more important than our personal feelings. It is even more important than our private lives.

Aguirre, the Wrath of God

It is not acceptable for you to do this.' I told him I had a rifle and that he would only make it as far as the next bend in the river before he had eight bullets in his head. The ninth would be for me. He instinctively knew that this was not a joke any more and screamed for the police like a madman. The next police station was at least 300 miles away though. I would not allow him to walk off the film. He knew that I was serious, and for the remaining ten days of the shoot he was very docile and well behaved.

Yet I'm sure you feel even today that he was the only person who could ever have played the role of Aguirre.

Absolutely, he was an excellent actor and truly knew how to move on screen. I wanted to make Aguirre a man with a vicious little hump. Finally I dropped the idea, but did want there to be a differentiation between Aguirre's movements and everyone else's. The character had to have some kind of inner distortion that could be seen on the surface, so we decided to make one of his arms seem longer than the other. And since his left hand was so short, his sword was never around his waist, but was almost up into his armpit. I introduced these physical aberrations into the film gradually and with real precision, and so at the end of the film Aguirre is even more deformed. And Kinski did it all perfectly. When you first see him, he walks almost like a spider, like a crab walking on sand. As an actor, Kinski really knew about costumes, and I learned a great deal from him as I watched him oversee every single buttonhole and stitch.

No one could have tamed Kinski as well as I did towards the end of *Aguirre*, and even though for a couple of years afterwards he said he hated the film, eventually he ended up liking it very much. Sure, the man was a complete pestilence and a nightmare to work with, but who cares? What is important are the films we made together.

The opening shot of the film is truly spectacular. Was that in the script or did you just stumble across the mountain and decide to film there?

Actually, the original script had a different beginning to the finished film. I had planned a scene on a glacier at an altitude of 17,000 feet that started with a long procession of altitude-sick pigs tottering towards the camera. Only after a few minutes of following this line of animals would the audience realize that they are part of a Spanish army of adventurers, accompanied by hundreds of Indian auxiliaries. Unfortunately, many crew members got altitude sickness for real and I had to abandon the idea.

We filmed it near Machu Picchu, on the side of a mountain that had a sheer vertical drop of 600 metres. It is thick jungle up there, though the Incas had dug out an immense staircase in the rocks, which is the trail the hundreds of people in the shot are using as they come out of the clouds. The scene was very difficult to film. We started transporting everyone at 2 a.m. – the horses, the pigs, the llamas and the cannons up there – and when I finally arrived at the top of the mountain it was pouring with rain, there was dense fog and the whole valley was completely enshrouded in cloud. You could not see anything, except grey clouds. It was indescribable chaos, extremely slippery and quite dangerous to have so many extras up there, something like 450 people. All the native Indians that you see came from the highlands, from an altitude of 14,000 feet, but many of them still got vertigo. We had to somehow secure the extras who suffered from vertigo with ropes along this path until shooting was over. I spent much of the time trying to persuade everyone to stay. I must have run up and down those steps instructing people what to do three or four times. Somehow, I managed to convince them that this was something special and extraordinary, so that a couple of hours later I thanked God everyone was still there as the fog and clouds suddenly opened up on one side of the mountain. We shot it only once, this line of people with the fog on one side, the mountain on the other. As the camera turned, I had a very profound feeling as if the grace of God was with this film and with me. It was as if I were witnessing the start of something extraordinary. It was on this day that I definitely came to know my own destiny.

But Kinski realized that he would be a mere dot in the landscape and not the centre of attention. He wanted to act in close-up with a grim face leading the entire army, so I had to explain to him that he was not yet the leader of the expedition. In the end I just removed him from the shot, because I also had the feeling that the scene would be far more powerful if there were no human faces in it. What's more, our concepts of the landscape differed profoundly.

He wanted the shot to embrace all of scenic Machu Picchu, including the peak, just like a Hollywood-style postcard movie, with the landscape as a beautiful backdrop, exploited for the scene. It would have been just like a television commercial or a postcard. But I wanted an ecstatic detail of that landscape where all the drama, passion and human pathos became visible. He just did not understand this, but for me it was something crucial.

What about the suggestions from several critics that the film is some kind of metaphor of Nazism, with Aguirre inevitably playing the role of Hitler? Or that it is shot through with elements of German Romanticism?

I can answer that question only by saying that in Germany a great many writers, artists and filmmakers are very much misunderstood because their work is seen explicitly in the light of their nation's history. These are misunderstandings that lie in wait around every corner for Germany's artists. Of course I, like most Germans, am very conscious of my country's history. I am even apprehensive about insecticide commercials, and know there is only one step from insecticide to genocide. Hitler's heritage to the German people has made many of us hypersensitive, even today. But with *Aguirre* there was never any intention to create a metaphor of Hitler.

You'd worked with Thomas Mauch previously on Signs of Life *and* Even Dwarfs Started Small. *Was your approach for the jungle shoot any different?*

Not really. For *Aguirre* I wanted to use a hand-held camera for a good part of the shooting. It was the physical contact the camera had with the actors that was one of the keys to the look of the film. Like I said earlier, Mauch and I have had a very close relationship while working, and on this film we were almost like Siamese twins, always moving in sync.

Though we have not worked together since *Fitzcarraldo*, for years after *Aguirre* I did not need even to explain to Mauch what I wanted in certain shots because he just intuitively knew. For the final shot of *Aguirre*, we both got into a speedboat that moved around the raft several times. I manoeuvred it myself, just like when I drove the van through the desert in *Fata Morgana*. When a speedboat approaches a raft at sixty kilometres per hour it creates an enormous wake, which meant we had to move through the waves we were creating. I had to feel with my whole body what the waves were doing as I approached the raft, and the whole process is a good example of what I mean when I talk about filmmaking being a very physical act. During pre-production I was able to develop a strong feeling for the currents of the river – vital if we were going to shoot there – only after helping construct a raft and travelling down the Amazon rapids myself. Aguirre dares defy nature to such an extent that this itself became a central element to the way the film was made, and *Aguirre* became a truly athletic venture. It was a purely tactile and corporeal understanding I was searching for, one that made the entire film possible for me.

The whole of *Aguirre* was shot with just one camera, which meant we were forced to work in a very simple and even crude way during the shooting. I feel that this added to the authenticity and life of the film. There was none of the glossy multi-camera sophistication you find in Hollywood films. In my opinion this is the reason *Aguirre* has survived for so long. It is such a basic film, you really cannot strip it down any more than it already is. The camera was actually the one I stole from the predecessor to the Munich Film School. I wanted them to lend me one but had to endure an arrogant refusal, so I liberated the machine for an indefinite period. They had a row of cameras sitting on a shelf, but never actually gave any out to aspiring young filmmakers. One day I found myself alone in this room next to the unlocked cabinet and walked out with one. It was a very simple 35-mm camera, one I used on many other films, so I do not consider it theft. For me it was truly a necessity. I wanted to make films and needed a camera; I had some sort of natural right to this tool. If you need air to breathe and you are locked in a room, you have to take a chisel and hammer and break down the wall. It is your absolute right.

As a child, ski-jumping was very important to you. What is it about the sport that so excites you, and what gave you the idea to make The Great Ecstasy of Woodcarver Steiner?

I have never made a distinction between my feature films and my 'documentaries'. For me, they are all just films, and *The Great Ecstasy of Woodcarver Steiner* is definitely one of my most important films.

I have always felt very close to ski-jumpers. I literally grew up on skis and, like all the kids in Sachrang, dreamt about becoming a great ski-jumper and national champion. This was until a friend of mine had a horrifying accident. Then, suddenly, with Swiss ski-jumper Walter Steiner there was someone who could fly like a bird, someone who could physically experience everything I once dreamed of: overcoming gravity. I wrote to Steiner, because to me he was absolutely the greatest of his generation. The man is also a woodcarver by profession and has left his art on hidden tree stumps up in the mountains where he lives. He would find a tree trunk and carve something in it; a face filled with horror perhaps. Some hikers apparently once found some of them, but many remain undiscovered, and very few people know where they are. Steiner wrote back to me and kindly suggested we meet at his place in Switzerland. Though he is an introverted, taciturn man I had an instant rapport with him, and he understood my intentions very quickly. I told him that when I saw him as a seventeen-year-old in competitions trailing far behind all the others, I said to my friends, 'I will point out to you the next world champion.' And Steiner became world champion twice just a few years later. Even the network for whom I made the film kept on calling me during the shooting, telling me that in the previous events he ended up in 35th place and asking if I wouldn't rather choose a different jumper for the film. But I knew this man was the greatest of them all. On the gigantic ramp at Planica he outflew everyone and even had to start lower down than everyone else, otherwise he would have landed on the flat and been killed.

Something interesting about *The Great Ecstasy* was that though shooting occurred pretty much without mishap, the film was still not totally clear in my mind. I had found it very difficult to get Steiner to really open up to me in front of the camera, and I really was not completely sure as to what I was going to do with all the footage I had. Then one evening I was with him and the crew and we grabbed him, hoisted him on our shoulders and ran through the streets with him. He looked down at me and said,

'Why are you doing this?' 'Because I know there is no greater one than you in this sport,' I said. I could feel the weight of his thigh on my shoulder. At that moment the film suddenly became quite clear for me because of this immediate physical sensation with the man. I know it sounds strange, but only after this did I truly respond to all these shots we had of him flying through the air and understand how to use them properly. After this, he also seemed to be more comfortable talking on camera. It was as if he had reacted to this physical contact himself. It still was not easy to dig into him with words, but I did feel a newfound connection after this.

What exactly is the 'great ecstasy'?

Ecstasy in this context is something you would know if you had ever ski-jumped. You can see it in the faces of the flyers in the film as they sweep past the camera, mouths agape, these incredible expressions on their faces. Most of them cannot fly without their mouths open, something which gives such a beautiful ecstatic feel to the whole movement.

Ski-jumping is not just an athletic pursuit, it is something very spiritual too, a question of how to master the fear of death and isolation. It is a sport that is at least partially suicidal, and full of utter solitude. A downhill racer might still be able to stop himself if he needs to, but when jumpers start down that track nothing can stop them. It is as if they are flying into the deepest, darkest abyss there is. These are men who step outside all that we are as human beings, and overcoming this mortal fear, the deep anxiety these men go through, this is what is so striking about ski-jumpers. And it is rarely muscular athletic men up there on the ramps; always it is young kids with deathly pale pimply complexions and an unsteady look in their eyes. They dream they can fly and want to step into this ecstasy which pushes against the laws of nature. In this way I always felt that Steiner was a close brother of Fitzcarraldo, a man who also defies the laws of gravity by pulling a ship over a mountain.

We had five cameramen and special cameras which could shoot in extreme slow motion, at something like four or five hundred frames a second. Shooting at this speed on film is a real challenge.

Within a few seconds the entire reel had shot through the camera, which also meant the cameramen had to pan violently to follow the trajectory of the jumpers, at the same time focusing to and fro. An enormous amount of power was needed to control these machines and they all did an excellent job.

Was it difficult to get Steiner to tell the tale of the raven? It is a very powerful story, especially when we remember that earlier in the film he talks of how as a child he 'kept on dreaming of flying'.

I went through his family album and found a picture of him as a kid with a raven. I asked him about it, and he just turned the page over and said, 'Yes, I had that raven once.' And I turned back the page and said, 'There is something about this raven. Tell me.' It took me three more attempts on different days before he agreed to tell the emotional story about this raven. You can see how uncomfortable he is when he explains that when he was twelve his only friend was a raven that he reared on bread and milk. Both the raven and Steiner were embarrassed by their friendship, so the raven would wait for him far away from the schoolhouse, and when all the other kids were gone it would fly on to his shoulder and together they would walk through the forest. The raven started losing its feathers and the other ravens started pecking it almost to death. They injured it so much that Steiner had to shoot it. 'It was torture to see him being harried by his own kind because he couldn't fly any more,' he says. From that scene I cut to Steiner flying in slow motion. It is a shot that lasts more than a minute, and a text appears that is based on words by Robert Walser: 'I should be all alone in this world, I, Steiner, and no other living being. No sun, no culture, I naked on a high rock, no storm, no snow, no streets, no banks, no money, no time and no breath. Then I wouldn't be afraid any more.'

The story with the raven made such an impression on me that a couple of years later I made a little film called *No One Will Play with Me* in which Martin, a young boy, explains to his classmate Nicole that he has a raven at home called Max. The film was made both with and for pre-school children and is partially based on true stories that I heard from the children themselves. Just like with *The Flying Doctors of East Africa*, I was interested in learning more about how young and troubled children perceive things and before filming started I showed some paintings to the children. The results were very revealing and mysterious. I remember one, an Italian renaissance painting which had in the background an entire city with castles and harbours and hundreds of people weaseling around unloading ships, all sorts of things going on. I would project a slide of the picture for maybe ten seconds and then turn it off and ask the children, 'What have you seen?' And four or five of them in one voice shouted, 'A horse! A horse!' 'Where on earth is the horse?' I said to myself. So I put the slide back on and searched. 'Down there!' they all shouted. And yes, in the corner of the picture was a single horse and a single horseman with a lance. It makes me think to this very day.

What's with your use of animals? From the earliest days with the unseen Game in the Sand, *to the kneeling dromedary in* Even Dwarfs Started Small *and the monkeys in* Aguirre, *you have animals all over your films. My favourite is the monkey who gets slapped in* Woyzeck.

Ah, yes! He is a fine one. I knew you were going to ask me this, and I have to say that I do not have a decent answer for you. Please do not ask me to explain. Sure, I like to use animals in the films, and I find it interesting to work with them. I also like to watch those wacky television programmes where people send in videos of their crazy cat or their piano-playing hamster, things like that. But the last thing I have is an abstract concept to explain how a particular animal signifies this or that. I just know they have an enormous weight in my films, and some of the most hilarious performances I have ever seen are from animals.

In almost every one of my films you can probably find animals. The creature that everyone seems to remember is the dancing chicken at the end of *Stroszek*. About fifteen years before I had seen this ridiculous freak show at a Cherokee reservation in North Carolina and the creature stuck in my mind. I knew that I would have to go back there to shoot. At the time when we wanted to film *Stroszek*, all the animals that were usually there had been taken somewhere warm, so three months before we arrived I spoke to the people who trained the birds to dance this barnyard shuffle. Usually the chicken would dance for only about five seconds and pick up a grain of corn after you put a quarter into the machine. I needed it to go on and on as long as possible and this took some weeks of intensive training. Look again at that scene and you will also see a manic rabbit jumping all over a toy fire truck, and a duck playing the drums. No one liked the chicken at the time. The whole crew was disgruntled and did not want to shoot it and asked whether we were really going to shoot such shit after spending so much time on this stupid film. 'Should we really turn the camera on for this rubbish?' Mauch said. I said to him, 'This is something very big. It looks unobtrusive when you see it with the naked eye in front of you, but don't you see that there is something big about it, something that is far beyond what we are?' And perhaps a great metaphor too, though for what I could not say.

You're obsessed with chickens, aren't you?

You might be right. Look into the eyes of a chicken and you will see real stupidity. It is a kind of bottomless stupidity, a fiendish stupidity. They are the most horrifying, cannibalistic and nightmarish creatures in this world. In *Even Dwarfs Started Small* we observed some chickens trying to cannibalize each other. And in a couple of my films, *Signs of Life* and *Kaspar Hauser*, I show how you can taunt chickens by hypnotising them.

Years ago I was searching for the biggest rooster I could find and heard about a guy in Petaluma, California, who had owned a rooster called Weirdo that weighed thirty pounds. Sadly Weirdo had passed away, but his offspring were alive, and guess what? They were even bigger. I went out there and found Ralph, son of Weirdo, who weighed an amazing thirty-two pounds! Then I found Frank, a special breed of miniature horse that stood less than two feet high. I told Frank's owner I wanted to film Ralph chasing Frank – with a midget riding him – around the biggest sequoia tree in the world, thirty metres in circumference. It would have been amazing because the horse and the midget together were still smaller than Ralph, the rooster. But unfortunately Frank's owner refused. He said it would make Frank look stupid.

NOTES

1 Helen Keller (1880–1968, USA) was blinded and deafened aged nineteen months old due to a severe fever. Like Helen Keller, Fini Straubinger used a tactile language tapped out on to her hand, though unlike Fini, Keller learned how to read braille. Keller eventually graduated with honours from Radcliffe College in 1904. After her death the organization Helen Keller International was established to fight against blindness in the developing world. Her book *The Story of My Life* (1902) is still in print.

2 Oliver Sacks (b. 1933, UK) is a Professor of Neurology in New York. He has written several books, including *Awakenings* (1973, the basis of the 1991 film with Robin Williams playing Sacks) and *The Man Who Mistook His Wife for a Hat* (1985). See Chapter 4, footnote 6.

3 See *Aguirre* by Stephen Minta (Jonathan Cape, 1991) for more on the 'real' Conquistador Lope de Aguirre, a Basque adventurer who in the late 1550s went in search of El Dorado.

4 Ingmar Bergman (b. 1918, Sweden) is the director of many films including *The Seventh Seal* (1957), *Persona* (1966) and *Fanny & Alexander* (1982). See *Bergman on Bergman* (Da Capo Press, 1993).

5 See Chapter 5, footnote 2.

4

Athletics and Aesthetics

One idea that has appeared again and again throughout our con-
versations is something you've nicely boiled down to a Herzog
maxim: 'Filmmaking is athletics over aesthetics.'

As I said earlier, I was a ski-jumper when I was a boy. Under normal circumstances, when taking off from a ramp you would hold
your head back when falling, but we would thrust our heads forward like when taking a dive. This is meant to neutralize the pressure of the air which tends to push you backwards. It is like
someone who takes a suicidal jump from a great height, and then
regrets his decision when he realizes, midway through empty
space, that no one can help him. It is the same with filmmaking.
Once you have started, there is no one to help you through. You
have to overcome your fears and bring the project to an end.

Everyone who makes films has to be an athlete to a certain
degree because cinema does not come from abstract academic
thinking; it comes from your knees and thighs. And also being
ready to work twenty-hour days. Anyone who has ever made a
film – and most critics never have – already knows this. I try to do
as much pre-production myself – notably location scouting – when
making my films. I am very good at understanding and reading
maps, and I can figure out from a good map where I would find at
least a good target area for the landscapes and locations I am
searching for. Of course, it is impossible to do everything and I
have a team of very committed assistants and producers when I am
working. But I have learned the hard way that it is important to
know as best I can what might be waiting for me on location.
There are always surprises on a film set, but if I have done my

homework well enough I will always have some idea of what I can expect in the coming weeks. There are *always* great opposing forces on a film set, and if in pre-production I see that my original plans are not possible, I will immediately alter the scene.

I have often said that I like to carry prints of my films. They weigh forty-five pounds when tied together with a rope. It is not altogether pleasant to carry such bulky objects, but I love to pick them out of a car and take them into the projection room. What a relief to first feel the weight and then let the heaviness drop away; it is the final stage of the very physical act of filmmaking. And I never use a megaphone when I direct, I just speak as loudly as I need to be heard, though I am careful never to shout. I never use a viewfinder either and I am careful never to point. I will continue to make films only as long as I am physically whole. I would rather lose an eye than a leg. Truly, if I were to lose a leg tomorrow, I would stop film-making, even if my mind and my sight were still solid.

You talked about your love of ski-jumping and playing for a foot-ball team in Munich. Have you always had this fascination with things physical?

Athletics is something that I have been involved with all my life. Until I had a severe accident, I was a soccer player and skier, yet when I make a film people always seem to think that it is the result of some sort of abstract academic understanding of story develop-ment, or some intellectual theory as to how 'the narrative' should work. When I am directing I feel like a football coach who has given his team tactics for the whole game but knows that it is vital the players react to any unexpected situations. Knowing how to use the space around me really was my only quality as a low-class foot-baller. I played for a bottom division football team for years and would score lots of goals even though technically almost everyone was a better and faster player than I was. But I was always able to read the game and would often end up in the spot where the ball would land. When I would score I would never actually see the goal posts and the bar, yet somehow I knew where the goal was. If I had seriously started to think about what I was doing, my game would have crumbled in a split second and the ball would have been blocked by five defensive players. It is the same with making a film.

If you see something, you should not allow much time for structural deliberation. Just head into it physically, without fear.

When shooting interiors, for example, I always work very closely with the set designer and together we might move a lot of heavy furniture, for example pushing the piano into this or that corner to see if it feels right. If not, I will just move it again. To physically rearrange furniture in a room gives me the physical knowledge necessary to operate within that space. It is this kind of knowledge – that of total orientation within a space – which has decided many an important battle for me. As the director on a film set it is vital to know about the space you are shooting in so that when the cast and crew arrive you already know exactly what lens is needed for the shot and where the camera needs to go. With such things taken care of I can very quickly arrange the actors in front of the camera so no time is wasted.

There is a short scene in *The Enigma of Kaspar Hauser* that was filmed in a garden where we worked for six months during pre-production. Before we got there it was a potato patch. I planted strawberries and beans and flowers myself so that not only did it have a feel for the kinds of landscaped gardens of the era, but when it came to filming I knew exactly where every single plant and vegetable was and precisely how to move through the space. Or take Kaspar's death scene where there are people standing around his bed. There is a perfect balance within the space, a perfect arrangement and tableau of people, but it was staged in seconds with no pre-planned aesthetic. Even if I had given you three days to move people around to find a more balanced image, you would not have succeeded in filling that space more effectively. The final result was borne out of my immediate and total physical knowledge of the room we were shooting in, of exactly what the actors looked like in costume and where they were standing, of where the camera was and what lens we were using.

Do you generally try to avoid working in studios?

For my entire career as a director I have avoided filming in studios, something I feel kills the spontaneity that is so necessary for the kind of cinema I want to create. My kind of filmmaking cannot be created in a constrictive studio atmosphere, and the only day I ever spent in a studio was to film a blue-screen shot for *Invincible* with the boy flying up into the air. The world of the studio rarely offers any surprises to the director; in part, because you run only into people you have paid to be there. There is no environment, only four solid walls and a roof. One other thing that I never do – that inevitably destroys the spontaneity needed on a film set – is to storyboard the action. Coincidences always happen if you keep your mind open, while storyboards remain the instruments of cowards who do not trust in their own imagination and who are the slaves of a matrix.

My approach to every scene is that from the start I know in general what I want, but still allow the action to develop naturally without knowing exactly what camera angles and how many shots will be needed. If a scene develops differently from my original idea because of 'external' elements – the weather, the environment, the actors working with each other, things like this – but does so organically and without major deviation from the original story, I will generally try to encompass those new elements into the scene. As a filmmaker, you must be open to those kinds of opportunities. In fact, I do actively welcome them. My cinema is killed stone dead without the outside world to react to, and it is the same when I work as an opera director. As any stage actor or singer will tell you, each performance has a different form of life to it and room must be given to allow these changes to grow, otherwise the life that is there dies painfully.

What about letting the actors improvise during a scene? Is there any room for that?

Though I have no advance technical vision of the specific shots required for a scene, I always have a very strong idea as to what the scene is about. Normally I start working with the actors, placing them in the scene, seeing how it might work out if, for example, he is standing over here and she is sitting over here, and what would happen if they move about. After placing the actors, I will work closely with the cinematographer to determine where the camera should be and what movements, if any, are required during the scene. In *Invincible* there is a scene in the circus when Zishe challenges the famous circus strongman. The continuity girl kept bothering me by asking over and over, 'How many shots are we going to do now?' I kept saying to her, 'How would I know?' After a while I told her to be quiet and watch the scene along with everyone else. 'Just let it develop. Let's see what they do and how long it takes them,' I told her. I do not want to suggest that I improvise my films, because I do not. But there is a somewhat wider margin for the unexpected in my work than usual. For that scene in *Invincible* we actually shot four and half minutes continuously and it was so good we needed only a couple of cut-aways to the audience here and there to trim it down a little. I knew that the two strongmen were very good friends who knew each other from previous competitions, and I had explained to them exactly what I wanted for the scene. At every stage they knew where each was leading the other and what the next move was going to be, so I just let the scene develop naturally.

When I write a screenplay I am always conscious that things will change – characters might even be added – once we start shooting, so I will never slavishly fill page after page with lines of dialogue. In my early screenplays some of the key speeches were there, but generally no more than that. It is important to allow real life and real images to fill up the film at a later stage. Rather than having the dialogue word for word, the script will 'describe' the dialogue and it might contain scene titles, for example, 'Descent into Urubama Valley'. For *The Enigma of Kaspar Hauser*, much of the dialogue was written as the lights were being positioned and when I was sitting on the set, as the actors simply needed their dialogue. Leaving the writing until the last minute means it is full of life and will inevitably fit much more comfortably into the physical situation that is before us: the actor sitting there in costume amidst the set.

And I gather you don't touch the screenplay until the first day of shooting?

No, because I do not want to engage my mind day after day with the writing. This means that when I pick it up on the set, sometimes months and months later, the material is as fresh for me as it is for everyone else.

More recently I have written screenplays with more dialogue in them, but as usual have changed a good deal en route. I listen to the lines when spoken by the actors and might decide to modify them or ask the actor how he would say a particular sentence in his own words. I trust their judgement on things like this; actors have always been very valuable collaborators. If during this process there are slight mistakes in the dialogue, but the feel and spirit of the scene remains the same, then I can accept such mistakes. Kinski was such a talent that I would give him more space than most to make up lines. Very often he needed this space, for example in the bell tower sequence of *Fitzcarraldo*. I did not tell him how to ring the bells; the only thing I said was that he had to be in complete ecstasy and fury, and that he needed to shout down into the town and explain to everyone the church would be closed until the town had an opera house. But how he would shout it and in which direction, Kinski himself did not know until he did it. Sometimes, of course, he needed very strong restrictions and needed to be reined in.

Let me also talk briefly about working with my cameramen. I hate perfectionists behind the camera, those people who spend hours setting up a single shot. I need people who really see things, who really feel them as they are and not someone so concerned about getting the most beautiful possible images. I always bring the cinematographer with me to the locations before shooting. For *Signs of Life* in Greece I said to the crew, 'For three days we are not going to shoot anything at all.' I told the actors, 'Walk up and down the fortress walls, touch the rocks around you, feel everything there is to feel around you. You have to know the taste of these rocks, feel their smooth surfaces, get to know it all. Only then can we start to film.' And it is the same thing for the cameraman: somehow, he has to feel everything very physically with his whole body even though he never actually touches anything. Of course, occasional shots are obviously planned in advance. A good example is towards the end of *Invincible* when the strongman is dying in hospital. He rises out of bed because he hears piano music and says, 'My ears are ringing. Somebody must be thinking of me.' He looks towards the window, and his kid brother gets out of his chair, pushes the curtain aside and outside, through the window, we see his five-year-old sister who is looking at us.

So there is rarely a pre-planned aesthetic concept behind any of your films?

No, I am not concerned with aesthetics, and when it comes to working with cinematographers there has rarely been any kind of discussion over the look of the film. I always just say to the cameraman, 'Do not worry about centring the image or making it look nice, do not look for good colours.' If you get used to planning your shots based solely on aesthetics, you are never that far from kitsch. Of course, though I have rarely attempted to inject aesthetic elements into a particular scene or film, they might well enter unconsciously by the back door simply because my preferences inevitably impact upon the decisions I make in some way. Somehow I know how to articulate the images on film without resorting to endless discussions about lighting or spending millions on production design. It is just like you 'knowing' how to write a letter. When you look at a completed letter you immediately see your longhand does have a particular style all of its own that has somehow seeped in of its own accord. So the aesthetic – if it does exist – is to be discovered only after the film is finished. And I leave it to the aestheticians to enlighten me about things like this.

On set there is never any discussion about what a particular scene or shot 'means' or why we are 'doing it a certain way'. What is important is getting the shot in the can, and that is all. I think that this kind of approach was a strong influence on the Dogme 95 movement who, like me, would rather work with a tiny crew and low-level equipment.

But I can think of several examples in your films of what seems to be experimentation with the imagery. What about the dream sequences in The Enigma of Kaspar Hauser, *for example?*

Of course there are moments in my films that have been planned in advance or where I have experimented with the imagery. These are moments that I see as absolutely quintessential in the context of the film as a whole, and maybe the best example is the trance-like dream sequences in *The Enigma of Kaspar Hauser*. In these images of this newly discovered foreign world there are certain aesthetic influences. One side would be Stan Brakhage, the other is experimental German filmmaker Klaus Wyborny.[1] When I went to the Spanish Sahara, I took Wyborny along and he shot some of the dream footage. For Kaspar's vision of the people scaling the mountainous rock face, we went to the west coast of Ireland. Every year there is a great procession on this foggy mountain, the Croagh Patrick, with over 50,000 people. The finest of the dream sequences in the film was actually shot by my brother Lucki when he was travelling in Burma as a nineteen-year-old. He filmed what he described to me as a strange and imperfect pan across a huge valley full of grandiose temples but did not like it at all. I thought it was so beautiful and mysterious, absolutely tremendous, and begged him to give it to me. I modified the image by projecting it with high intensity on to a semi-transparent screen from very close distance so that the image on the screen would be the size of my palm. And then I filmed it with a 35-mm camera from the other side so the texture of the screen itself can be seen in the image. The flickering effect and the moving in and out of darkness occurred because I did not synchronize the projector and the camera.

What about a genre film like Nosferatu *where light and darkness play such an important role in the look of the film?*

That film is probably the one major exception to my lack of interest in aesthetics. I felt that a certain amount of respect had to be paid to the classical formulae of cinematic genres, in this case the vampire film. The final shot of the film was on a vast beach in Holland. There was a storm – the sand was flying everywhere – and I looked up to see these incredible clouds in the sky. We filmed them in single exposures, one frame every ten seconds, which means they are moving very fast on screen, and then we reversed the shot as if the clouds were hanging from a dark sky into the landscape. It gave the whole thing a feeling of doom, and in using this process to reverse the shot I can hardly deny that I was attempting to create a specific look – or 'aesthetic' if you would prefer to call it – for the film.

I did spend time talking to Schmidt-Reitwein about how to stylize the images in *Nosferatu* because it was such an essential part of the story itself. I worked with him on *Fata Morgana*, *Land of Silence and Darkness*, *Kaspar Hauser* and *Heart of Glass*. He has a very good feeling for darkness and threatening shadows and gloom, in part I suspect because just after the Berlin Wall went up he was caught smuggling his girlfriend out of the East and was placed into solitary confinement for several months. I think this experience has formed much of what the man is today. Once these guys emerge from underground they see the world with different eyes. Let me say too that Thomas Mauch is the cameraman I go to when I need something more physical. He has a phenomenal physical sense for the rhythm of what is unfolding before him. He was the one who shot *Signs of Life*, *Aguirre* and *Fitzcarraldo*. Sometimes there have been difficult choices to make about which of these fine cameramen to work with on particular films, but I think I have made the right choices over the years. For example, if I had taken Schmidt-Reitwein to the jungle for *Fitzcarraldo* the camera would probably have been a lot more static, and we would have stylized certain scenes with elaborate lighting.

There are very few close-ups in your films. There's the one that opens Cobra Verde, *maybe a couple in* Signs of Life, *but generally you seem to keep away from the actors.*

No, it is not that I strive to keep away from them. It is rather that there is a certain indiscretion if you move too close into a face. Close-ups give a feeling of intrusion; they are almost a personal violation of the actor, and they also destroy the privacy of the viewer's solitude. I can get very close to my characters without using extreme close-ups, probably much closer than some directors who are constantly using them.

Are you careful to take note of the audience reactions to your films? Do you make a point of reading the reviews of your films?

When one of my films is released, generally I do not read many of the reviews. I have never been interested in circling around my own navel. Maybe some of the most important ones, as sometimes they influence the box-office results, but it has never been of much significance for me. The audience reactions have always been much more important than those of the critics, even if I have never been absolutely certain who my audience is. I have never purposely set out to make cloudy and complicated films, or stupid and banal films for tree-frogs.

The opinion of the public is sacred. The director is a cook who merely offers different dishes to them and has no right to insist they react in a particular way. A film is just a projection of light, completed only when it crosses the gaze of the audience, and it was this navel-gazing that was one of the great weaknesses of New German Cinema. When Kleist, afraid of being misunderstood by his contemporaries, sent Goethe the manuscript of his play *Penthesilea*, he wrote in a letter, 'Read this, I beg you on the knees of my heart.' This is how I feel when I present audiences with a new film. Some critics, like the American John Simon, have hated pretty much all my films. But that is OK and I never minded that he dunked me underwater as deep as he could. He is much better than the uninformed idiots who ruminate on some fancy or trendy things that are floating around. Simon is in a league of his own and I actually admire him for his hostility as he actually has something to say. Better to read an interesting and penetrative review by the man criticizing a film for what it is, rather than a gossipy piece about what the film apparently has failed to be. I also like that his vitriol is often all-pervading and dismissive of a film from beginning to end. The man is not apathetic.

One criticism that Simon had about The Enigma of Kaspar Hauser *was one that seemed to be taken up by other critics – perhaps a case of Simon himself starting a trend – that the film was historically inaccurate, the most obvious example of which was getting Bruno S., a forty-year-old man, to play a sixteen-year-old boy.*

But Bruno looks like a sixteen-year-old, Goddammit! And he was so unbelievably good on screen. He has such depth and power, and he moves me so deeply like no other actor in the world. He gave himself completely to the role and was so good doing exactly what the role required, being able to detach himself from every bit of knowledge he had about the world, even how to scratch himself. Bruno is the most co-operative and intuitive actor I have ever worked with. Age itself does not matter in this film at all. It means much more that Bruno radiates such a radical human dignity.

Who truly cares about the man's age? This is the difference between history and storytelling. I am a filmmaker, not an accountant of history, and whether the actor was forty-one or seventy-one and plays an adolescent is in no way important. The film actually never tells you how old Kaspar is, so criticism like this comes from the obstructive presuppositions people so often bring to films, books or paintings that have as their subjects real historical figures. *The Enigma of Kaspar Hauser* is not a historical drama about eighteenth-century Germany, nor does it purport to be the 100 per cent factually correct telling of the story of Kaspar, in the same way that *Lessons of Darkness* is not a political documentary about the Iraqi invasion of Kuwait. They are both just films that tell a particular story. Anyway, historically nobody could tell exactly how old the real Kaspar was, though there are pretty plausible guesses that he must have been about sixteen or seventeen years old when he was pushed out into the open as a foundling without even being able to walk properly.

Historical facts aside, what is the film about?

Kaspar's story is about what civilization does to us all, how it deforms and destroys us by bringing us into societal line; in Kaspar's case this stultifying and staid bourgeois existence. Kaspar was a young man who showed up in Nuremberg in 1828.[2] When the people of the town attempted to communicate with him it transpired he had spent his whole life locked away in a dark dungeon tied to the ground with his belt. He had never had any contact with human beings because food was just pushed into his cell every night when he was sleeping. He never even knew of the existence of other human beings and even believed the belt which forced him to remain seated was a natural part of his anatomy. A couple of years after being taken in by the town, word got out that Kaspar was writing his autobiography. Soon after came the first attempt on his life, followed by his murder. It had been about two and a half years since he was found in the town square, and to this day no one is sure who his killer was.

Kaspar was brutally propelled into the world as a young man who had not experienced society in any way whatsoever. It is the only known case in human history where an individual was 'born' as an adult. He arrived in society having completely missed his childhood and was forced to compress these years into only two and a half years. After this time Kaspar actually spoke quite well. He could write and even played the piano.

For me this is the most interesting element to his story and the reason why *The Enigma of Kaspar Hauser* is not a historical film. It is on a completely separate level to classic historical drama, and the primary issue it deals with is timeless: the human condition. Who the boy really was is neither important nor interesting, and is something that we will probably never know for certain. My film does not deal only with the problems the townsfolk experience because Kaspar is living amongst them, but also with Kaspar's problems with the society in which he finds himself. There is a scene in the film when a young child holds a mirror up to Kaspar's face, the first time he has ever seen his reflection, something which confuses and shocks him. This is actually just what Kaspar is doing to everyone around him: forcing them to confront their day-to-day existence with new eyes.

Is that what the scene with the professor of logic is about?

Exactly. Kaspar is certainly the most intact person in this unnamed town, full of such basic and uncontaminated human dignity. He has the kind of intelligence you sometimes find in illiterates. In terms of pure logic, the only solution to the professor's problem is the one that he himself explains to Kaspar. But, of course, the answer that Kaspar gives is also correct. It is clear that Kaspar is strictly forbidden to imagine and that his creativity is being suffocated and suppressed. We sense that everything spontaneous in Kaspar is being systematically deadened by philistine society, though people like the professor think he is behaving decently with his attempts to 'educate' Kaspar. In the autopsy scene the townspeople are like vultures circling overhead as they feverishly attempt to discover some physical aberration in Kaspar and are overjoyed to finally find that apparently he has a malformed brain. These people are blind to that fact that the aberration is in their own bourgeois society, and finding this physical difference between themselves and Kaspar makes them feel better about how they had treated him when he was alive.

The scene with the professor was difficult to shoot because Bruno had real difficulties in remembering his lines and articulating himself. When we reached the point in the scene when the professor tells him that his answer to the question is wrong, Bruno thought he had actually made another mistake with his lines and became quite angry with himself for the error he thought he had made. So desperate was he that he shifted his whole body round in embarrassment, so contributing to this scene which is very dear to me.

Are any of the lines that Kaspar speaks taken from the autobiographical fragment he wrote?

A few are, like the text of the letter found in Kaspar's hand that is read by the cavalry captain, and Kaspar's own very beautiful line, '*Ja, mir kommt es vor, das mein Erscheinen auf dieser Welt ein harter Sturz gewesen ist*' ['Well, it seems to me that my coming into this world was a terribly hard fall']. But as my recent explorations in my 'documentaries' show, there is a much more profound level of truth than that of everyday reality, for example in the dreams that Kaspar talks of, and it is my job to seek them out. As I said, when it comes to storytelling, I am interested in the verifiable historical facts up to a point. But I much prefer to evoke history through atmosphere and the attitude of the characters rather than through anecdotes that may or may not be based on historical fact. Only the most basic elements of Kaspar's life as we know them are contained within the film and the rest is invented or simplified. Most of the details are my own: for example, as far as we know he was never shown in a circus, he never talked to a professor of logic, and never spoke about the Sahara.

How much historical research did you do?

The Kaspar Hauser archives are in Ansbach, the town where he was killed, but I never went there. There are about a thousand books and more than ten thousand articles and research papers that have been written about Kaspar, but I asked myself whether I really needed to get involved with such extraneous scholarship. Ninety per cent of the literature is about the criminal case, but as I said, what is really interesting about Kaspar is everything beyond this. The vast majority of this material focused on the crime itself or investigating Kaspar's origins, speculating on whether he was

Napoleon's son, or trying to prove that he was an impostor. A recent film version[3] of the story suggested that Kaspar was a prince from the Royal House of Baden, a theory scotched when a German magazine did a DNA test on the blood from the shirt that Kaspar was wearing when he was killed and compared it to blood taken from a living member of the House of Baden. The only volume I read carefully was of original documents and essays that included the poetry and autobiographical fragment that the real Kaspar had written, plus the first part of Anselm von Feuerbach's book. I also read the documents concerning Kaspar's autopsy. At the time of the film, I was frequently asked if I had used Jakob Wassermann's novel[4] as the basis of the film, though I have never read it. I had read Peter Handke's play *Kaspar*,[5] but it is totally remote from my own *Kaspar Hauser* because this very beautiful and important text is all about the origins and distortions of language.

Where was the film shot?

Almost the entire film was shot in Dinkelsbühl, a beautiful small town fifty kilometres from Ansbach in the Franconie region. It is still completely surrounded by mediaeval city walls and is covered in cobbled streets; the only thing we had to do was remove some television antennas. But I particularly did not want to name the town at the start because to tell everyone that this is Nuremberg means to present a precise place and, in a way, make that specific town in some way responsible for what happens in the film. By not naming the town it becomes any town: Paris, Munich, New York. The story is one that is nameless, timeless and could occur anywhere.

You've said that, like Fata Morgana, *the film has elements of science fiction to it. What did you mean by this?*

If you strip the story out of *Kaspar Hauser* and leave just the dream sequences, you would be left with something that feels a lot like *Fata Morgana*, just like if you stripped away the story of *Signs of Life* and left just the shot of the windmills you would have something that feels like *Fata Morgana*. I always felt that *Kaspar Hauser* is almost *Fata Morgana* with a narrative story to it.

Kaspar had no concept of the world, nor of speech or even of what the sky or a tree looked like. In the film he does not even know what danger is. There is a scene where he sits quite calmly as a swordsman lunges at him, and where he burns himself on a flame because he has never seen fire before. When he was first found by the townspeople he spoke only a few words and one or two phrases whose meaning he clearly did not even know, for example, 'I would like to be a rider the way my father was.' ['*Ich möchte ein solcher Reiter werden wie mein Vater einer war.*'] He spoke the sentence like a parrot. There are several different stories about Kaspar and what the boy was capable of at first, but what really interested me was the story of someone who had not been influenced or contaminated in any way by society and outside forces, someone with no notion of anything whatsoever. It is fascinating to read some of Kaspar's own writings because actually he was frightened by the singing of birds; he just could not co-ordinate what he was hearing.

Kaspar was, in the most purest sense, a being without culture, language and civilization, an almost primeval human being. As such he suffered greatly from his contact with people and society. Not an idiot, rather a saint like Joan of Arc, something that I feel really comes out in Bruno's performance. In fact, you can almost see his aureole when you watch the film. So for me the story of this boy is almost a science-fiction tale that takes in the age-old idea of aliens who arrive on our planet, just like those in the original script of *Fata Morgana*. They have no human social conditioning what-soever and walk around confused and amazed. The real question is perhaps anthropological: what happens to a man who has crashed on to our planet with no education and no culture? What does he feel? What does he see? What must a tree or a horse look like to such an arrival? And how will he be treated?

It reminds me of the Oliver Sacks story 'To See or Not To See'[6] about a man blind from birth who finally regains his sight. Yet like Kaspar he has absolutely no concept of the world, and when he is staring into the eyes of his surgeon it just looks like a mass of light and shapes to him.

Exactly, these are the kinds of feelings and questions I want to flow over the audience. And just as we are forced to ask our-selves questions about perception and memory when we see Fini

Straubinger in *Land of Silence and Darkness*, trapped as she is with the images and sounds of years gone by, when we hear about the unique story of Kaspar Hauser we think of someone not deformed or distorted in any way by human civilization. Some of the shots in *Kaspar Hauser* seem to be held for an unusually long time, like the one near the beginning of the rye field blowing in the wind. I felt it was important to hold this image because in some small way I wanted the audience to empathize with Kaspar by looking anew at the things on this planet, seeing them almost with Kaspar's youthful eyes. For some of these kinds of shots I mounted a telephoto lens on a fish-eye lens which gave the image a very strange quality.

The dream sequences and the music used in the film also play a part here. Technically the images remain unchanged when music is placed behind them, but there are certain pieces of music which, when heard alongside particular images, reveal the inner qualities of the scene to the spectator. The perspective changes but not the image itself. A scene might not be logical in a narrative way, but sometimes when music is added it starts to acquire an internal logic. I wanted to use music to show Kaspar's awakening from his slumber, his being shaken awake from his almost catatonic state.

How did you go about casting Bruno S. in the film? And is casting, like location scouting, something that you do yourself?

Casting is such an essential part of my work. When you have a really good screenplay and a very good cast you barely need a director. Whoever said that casting was 90 per cent of the director's job was correct.

Sometimes, however, there are real difficulties in persuading others that your choice is the right one, and Bruno S. is the best example of this. I first saw Bruno in a film about the street performers of Berlin called *Bruno the Black*.[7] I was immediately fascinated by Bruno and asked the director to put me in touch with him. We both went to Bruno's apartment the next week, and when he opened the door and we explained who I was, Bruno would not even look at me in the eyes, just vaguely extending his hand towards me. He did not like talking to people because he was so full of mistrust and suspicion. From childhood he had been locked

The Enigma of Kaspar Hauser

away for so many years and certainly had reason enough to be suspicious. But within a relatively short period of time Bruno and I had established a strong rapport, something that we maintained throughout the shooting, though during that initial meeting it took about half an hour before he would even make eye contact with me.

However, everyone doubted whether he would be able to play the lead character in a feature film. For the first and only time in my life I did some screen tests. I had Bruno in costume with an acting partner and a full crew behind me. I felt absolutely miserable as I was doing it. I knew it was not going to be that good and I was right. The results were like a stillborn child, absolutely dead. What gave me the confidence and the assurance Bruno was the right one for the part was that while I watched this embarrassing footage I was immediately struck by the realization of just exactly what I had done wrong. I knew it was not Bruno who was bad, it was me. Of course, when I screened the test to friends and the television network that was going to finance part of the film I just sank in my chair. After the screening, the network executive from ZDF stood up and asked, 'Who else is against Bruno?' The hands of everyone shot up into the air. But then I sensed that there was a hand not raised just next to me. I turned and it was Jörg Schmidt-Reitwein, my cameraman. I asked him, 'Jörg, is your hand down?' And he just grinned at me and nodded. A great moment.

I have never liked this kind of numerical democracy in voting, and said, 'Bruno is going to be the one.' It was like in mediaeval times when, if a group of monks were against some innovation or a reform of monastic life, just out of indifference and cowardliness or slovenliness and boredom, and only a couple of them had the feverish ecstatic knowledge that these changes had to be made to advance the cause of faith, then out of the enormity of their wish and their insight these two would simply declare themselves the *melior pars* – the 'better part' – and would win the ballot. It makes sense to me: the intensity of your knowledge and insight and your feverish wishes should decide the battle, not strength in numbers. To everyone in the room I said, 'This is the ballot and we have won,' and asked the network executive of ZDF who was putting up much of the budget to declare himself either with me or against me. He looked a long while into my face and said, 'I am still on board.' His name is Willi Segler, and I love him for his loyalty. We went into production almost immediately.

Why did you choose to keep Bruno's identity secret?

We kept Bruno anonymous because he asked us to and I think he was right to do so. When he was three years old his mother, a prostitute, beat him so hard that he lost speech, and she used that as a pretext to put him away in an asylum for retarded children. He escaped and was caught and ended up spending the next twenty-three years of his life in homes, institutions, asylums and prisons. By the time I met him, Bruno's treatment at the hands of the authorities had totally destroyed even the most basic human functions within him, including the desire to take care of himself.

At the start of the film, when Kaspar is in the cellar attached to the floor by his belt, you hear Bruno's natural breathing on the soundtrack. I left this in because I felt it worked well for the character. Working with such an inexperienced actor meant that we had to record all the dialogue live on set as it would have been impossible to re-dub the film. The heavy, artificial nature of studio work would not have been something Bruno could have worked under. This meant a lot of extra work for us because we had to capture all the sounds of 1828 there and then. There could not be the slightest noise from the twentieth century so we had to ban all cars from the environs.

Bruno was very aware that the film was just as much about how society had destroyed *him* as it was about how society had killed Kaspar Hauser. Maybe for this reason he wanted to remain anonymous, and to this day I call him the 'Unknown Soldier of Cinema'. *The Enigma of Kaspar Hauser* is his monument. For a while I even thought about calling the film *The Story of Bruno Hauser*. The role really touched him, really got under his skin. I quickly realized he should not be taken out of his environment for a long time nor should he be exposed to the press or regaled as a film star. He did get very excited when he heard about the Cannes Film Festival and said, '*Der Bruno* [*The Bruno*] wants to transmit his accordion play to these people out there.' I was wary about taking him to the meat market out there, but he really wanted to go and had a good time. You know how intrusive and voracious the press is at Cannes, but he was so grounded when confronted by them, pulling out his bugle and giving them a tune. One time he got up in front of an audience with his accordion and said, 'Now I will play all the nuances of the colour red.' He drew so much attention, yet remained totally untouched by it and was not at all frightened by the masses of photographers. At the press conference for the film he impressed everyone with his complete sincerity and innocence. He said he had come to see the sea for the first time and marvelled at how clean it was. Someone told him that, in fact, it wasn't. 'When the world is emptied of human beings,' he said, 'it will become so again.'

How did Bruno acclimatize himself to being on a film set? It must have been a very strange experience for him.

Without the mutual trust quickly established between the two of us I would not have stood a chance. I would hold his wrist a lot; with Bruno there was always physical contact. Not his hand, just his wrist, as if I had my fingers on his pulse. He kind of liked that. Sometimes he was very unruly and would rant about the injustices of the world. All I could do when this happened was to stop everyone and allow him to say whatever he wanted to say. I got quite angry with a sound man who, after an hour of this ranting, opened a magazine and started to read. I said to him, 'You are being paid now to listen to Bruno. All of us will listen to him.' After a few minutes of this Bruno would see that everyone was looking at him, and would say, '*Der Bruno* has talked too much. Let's do some good work now.' I constantly said to him, 'Bruno, when you need to talk and speak about yourself, do it. It is not an interruption for us. It is very much a part of what we are doing here. Not everything needs to be recorded on film.'

In the past, when he would break out from a correctional institution, he would be in hiding and because of this he was always on high alert, always ready to be recaptured by the police. He liked the character of Kaspar so much that he refused to take his costume off and most of the time he even slept in it. One day he did not show up for breakfast and it was obvious he had overslept so I knocked on his door. There was no answer, so I pushed the door open and immediately bumped into an obstacle. It was Bruno, who had slept not in the bed but right next to the door, something I later found out that he had done from the first day of shooting. He just had a pillow and a blanket on the floor so that he could escape immediately if he needed to. And in a second, less than a second, he stood bolt upright in front of me, wide awake, and he said, 'Yes, Werner, what is it?' It really broke my heart when I saw this, and I said, 'Bruno, you have overslept. Did you really sleep here on the floor?' He always referred to himself in the third person. 'Yes,' he said, '*Der Bruno* is always sleeping next to the escape.' That is where he felt safe.

The shooting of film was tiring for him and whenever he was too exhausted he would just say, '*Der Bruno* is going to take that one' and take a nap for a couple of minutes between takes. I think it was his way of removing himself for very short periods of time, something that was necessary every now and then. At the end of each shot I would always record the room's ambient sound on the set. Every room and every set-up has its own level of silence and its own atmosphere, and for continuity in editing we needed to take a register after every take. But with Bruno around it was impossible to do so because five seconds after calling 'Cut', Bruno would be asleep, snoring loudly. This would happen ten times a day. Occasionally, he would want to direct a scene himself. For example, I explained the scene where he is mortally stabbed to him about a week before we needed to shoot it, and he spent that whole time thinking very seriously about it and making lots of notes to himself. A few days later he came up to me and said, 'Werner, finally I know what to transmit [*durchgeben*] out in this scene.' He would never say 'act' or 'do', always 'transmit'. So he stood there and screamed horrifyingly, like a bad theatre actor, then fell on to the ground thrashing about wildly. He told me, 'I will send out the cry of death.' I could see that he clearly wanted to play the scene that way, so twenty minutes before shooting I rewrote the scene. It would have been too difficult to persuade him otherwise.

Another issue to deal with was the fact that Bruno did not speak pure German, or even grammatically correct German, but rather a dialect from the Berlin suburbs. It was hard work to get him to speak not just in *Hochdeutsch* – proper German, something like the equivalent of the Queen's English – but also as if he were discovering language for the first time; his articulation elevated the acting to a very stylized level and in the end we were able to take advantage of this language problem. I think it greatly adds to the power of Bruno's performance because his speaking voice and his articulation produced a very beautiful effect, and it really seems like he is struggling with a wholly new language.

Did Bruno get more confident as the shoot went on?

Absolutely. In general, filming was truly wonderful because Bruno became very used to the process and he worked very hard the whole time. For the scene near the start when Kaspar learns to walk, Bruno wanted to really numb his legs and had the idea of putting a stick in the hollow of his knees and sitting like that for two hours. After this he could not stand up at all and the scene really is extraordinary. I should say, however, that he had moments of real distrust of all of us, especially me. He was always going into bars and throwing his money around, getting drunk, so I suggested we go to the bank and open an account for him. But he was convinced there was a conspiracy going on to steal his money. No one, not even the bank manager, could persuade him that it was absolutely impossible for me deceitfully to take the money from his account and put it into my own unless I had his personal authorization in writing. He actually accused me of hiring a stooge to play the manager so I could steal his money. But the times when he did trust what we were doing were wonderful. He would talk incessantly about death and started to write a will. He said to me, 'Where shall I put it? My brother will kill me, or I will kill him if I see him. I can't trust my family. My mother the whore is dead, and my sister the whore is dead.' I told him to put it in a safe in the bank or to give it to a lawyer. But he said, 'No, I do not trust them.' Two days later he gave me the will and asked me to take care of it. I still have the sealed envelope.

Did Bruno really know exactly what was going on and that he was in a film?

Of course he did. He is a very intelligent man, very streetwise, and not at all defenceless. I made it very clear to him before we started working that on the most primitive level this was an exchange of services: you will act in the film and be paid for it. But there is more to it, I explained, because you will fill this character with more convincing life than anyone else in the world. 'There is a big task on your shoulders,' I said, a challenge that thankfully he accepted without hesitation.

The conversations I had with Bruno were complex but invigorating and beautiful. We had a very old-fashioned autopsy table made of solid marble for the death scene in the film, and Bruno was so fascinated about death and this table that after the film was finished he desperately wanted to have it. In a strange tone of voice he would say, 'The name of this table is justice.' 'What do you mean, Bruno?' I asked him. He replied, 'Yes, this is justice because I had a vision of my own death. One day you will put me on the table and I will die, and you will all die, the rich and the poor. This is justice. And all those who have done me wrong will confront justice here.' He wanted to take the table, but I explained that it did not belong to us, that we had rented it as a prop from an antique shop. I think I even suggested to him that it was not actually the kind of thing that he wanted to own. 'No, *Der Bruno* must have it!' he would say. 'When I saw myself lying on this table I knew that cause of death was *Heimweh* [homesickness].' I really did not take his requests too seriously until one day when he gave me some of the very naïve paintings he had made of the table as a present. In the pictures he is lying on the table with a speech bubble coming from his mouth saying: 'Cause of death: *Heimweh.*' Some months later I asked him if he wanted any photographs of the film or taken on the set. 'The only one I want', he said to me, 'is a photo of the scene of the autopsy. Because it is justice. The table is justice.' After that I felt he should have the table after all and so I bought it from the shop and gave it to him.

Do you think that the film helped Bruno emotionally?

Sometimes during the shooting of the film Bruno would be completely desperate about his life and what had happened to him, and every single day I tried to make it clear to him that working together for five weeks on a film could never repair the damage that so many years of imprisonment had done to him, something I feel certain that he came to understand quite clearly. His isolation was just too profound for us to make major inroads in only a few weeks. But I think, in the long term, working on the film helped Bruno ever so slightly come to terms with what had happened to him. He had never before had an opportunity to reflect in such a unique way on his own life. There were many things that he still did not understand though; for example, why, when he walked down the street, dirty and neglected, the girls had no time for him. He would grab one of them and cry, 'Why don't you kiss me!' I was also very careful to ensure that he would not lose his job as a forklift driver in a steel factory. He had been treated like a freak there. Later though, after the film had been released, I called the factory and asked to speak to Bruno and the secretary would say, 'Sorry, our Bruno is not on the factory floor at the moment.' So after the film he was given a totally different status in the factory; now he was 'our Bruno'. They were genuinely proud of him and after the film came out people started to take him seriously and he was given real responsibilities. We shot the film during his vacation, and because he only got something like three weeks per year, we asked for extra unpaid holiday time for him.

He earned a good sum of money for his work, so on the primitive level of economics Bruno benefited from the experience. I know this for a fact. He earned a good wage which we helped him put to good use, and the apartment where he lives in *Strozek* is actually the apartment he rented after making *Kaspar Hauser*. He also bought himself a piano and collected all sorts of things from the garbage that filled his new home. Of course, the film did not solve the problems his catastrophic life had showered on him, but it helped him within his own social environment. People who lived in those Berlin streets where he lived would drag him into the pastry shop and buy a cake for him, and the barber would give him a free haircut. They were all very proud of him, something which did him some good.

What about the accusation that your working relationship with Bruno was exploitative?

Just like with Fini and *Land of Silence and Darkness*, I was criticized for abusing an innocent and defenceless man. What can I say about this other than I know I did the right thing. For many people my hiring a man like Bruno was simply too far out of the ordinary.

How was the film received?

As usual, not very well in Germany. Some critics compared it to Truffaut's film *L'Enfant Sauvage*,[8] which is about a doctor caring for the Wild Boy of Aveyron, a young child found in a forest who could not speak or even walk properly. I feel that any comparisons with the Truffaut film are incorrect. There is so often a tendency to compare and contrast one film with another just because the stories they tell appear to be similar, but in fact are completely different. This is mainly because many of the critics have such intellectual backgrounds and they are very much accustomed to making such comparisons, categorizations and evaluations. But it is not helpful at all. There is certainly something to be said about the way the western European critics approach things. Their writings are packed full of comparisons and references to anything and everything they can think of, including literature and other films, of course. When *Aguirre* opened in France, for example, it was compared to Borges, John Ford, Shakespeare and Rimbaud. I was very suspicious about such heavy name-dropping.

In Truffaut's film – which I saw after I made *Kaspar Hauser* – there is a child who has the nature of a wolf and is taught how to act as a member of so-called civilized society. Yet Kaspar has no nature whatsoever, not that of bourgeois society, nor of wolves. Simply, he is human. On the surface the subjects of the two films appear similar, but on closer inspection it becomes clear that there are real tangible differences between them. It is misleading to even talk about this. Truffaut[9] is also concerned with eighteenth-century pedagogy, which is not the case with my film. I would prefer that *The Enigma of Kaspar Hauser* be compared to Dreyer[10] than to Truffaut. The film is really *The Passion of Kaspar Hauser*. Many people have told me that the scene when the three villagers come into Kaspar's cell to hypnotize the chicken reminds them of the scene in Dreyer's *La Passion of Jeanne d'Arc* when the soldiers taunt Jeanne in her cell. Over time there have been several documented cases similar to the one in Truffaut's film, while Kaspar's case remains totally unique.

At the time of post-production, I had the feeling that *Kaspar Hauser* was something like a self-assessment after so many years of work. It was like drawing a line, figuring out what I had done up to that point and seeing where I should go from there. Many of the characters from earlier films appear in the film: Hombrecito from *Aguirre*, Walter Steiner has a small part, and the composer Florian Fricke, who played the piano player in *Signs of Life*.

For your next film, Heart of Glass, *you hypnotized the actors. How could you have been sure that your 'experiment' wasn't going to sabotage the whole production?*

Well, cinema *per se* has a secret hypnotic quality to it. Often when I am on the film set I have to ask the continuity girl what scenes we have already done and what is left to do. I am almost unconscious and get a shock when I am told it is the third week of filming already. 'How is this possible?' I ask myself. 'Where has all the time gone? What have I actually achieved here?' I feel as if I had been at a drunken party and somehow got home without being aware of it. As if the police stood at my bedside the next morning accusing me of having killed someone during the night.

There were two films that were a strong influence on me during the lead-up to *Heart of Glass*. One was *The Tragic Diary of Zero the Fool*,[11] which was made with a theatre group from a lunatic asylum in Canada. The other was Jean Rouch's *Les Maitres Fou*,[12] shot in Ghana and featuring the annual ceremonies of the Hauka tribe who, when heavily under drugs, enact the arrival of the English colonial governor and his people. The reasons for the experiments with hypnosis are quite simple. The script was loosely adapted from a chapter of Herbert Achternbusch's novel *The Hour of Death* which was, in turn, based on an old Bavarian folk legend about a peasant prophet in Lower Bavaria who, like Nostradamus, made predictions about the cataclysmic end of the world. In the film Hias – a shepherd with prophetic gifts – has apocalyptic visions and foresees an entire town becoming halfway insane and the destruction by fire of its glassworks. At the end of the film the factory-owner burns his own factory down, as foreseen, and the prophet is then blamed for the fire.

At the time I knew very little about hypnosis and it never crossed my mind to use it in a film until I started to think about the story I had before me, one about collective madness, one that calls for these characters to be aware of the catastrophe that is approaching, yet one they continue to walk straight into. I wondered how I could stylize everyone who, almost like sleepwalkers with open eyes, as if in a trance, were walking into this foreseeable disaster. I wanted actors with fluid, almost floating movements, which meant the film would seem to depart from known behaviour and gestures and would have an atmosphere of hallucination, prophecy and collective delirium that intensifies towards the end. Under hypnosis the identities of the actors would remain intact, but they would now be stylized. Maybe the title *Heart of Glass* makes more sense in this light. It seems to mean for me an extremely sensitive and fragile inner state, with a kind of transparent glacial quality to it.

Back then, like today, did some people suspect the whole thing was just a kind of circus gimmick?

Oh sure, but there really was a very clear purpose to it. Everyone but the lead character – the only clairvoyant one amongst them – was hypnotized before playing their scenes. I stress that the hypnosis was for reasons of stylization and not manipulation. I certainly did not want a bunch of performing puppets for the film. For years people have accused me of wanting to have more control over actors in my films. In the context of what we were doing in *Heart of Glass*, I assure you that as a director I would have been much better off having actors who were not in trance. And it is a common mistake to assume there is complete control over people under hypnosis. That is not so, for whatever is the hard core of your character remains untouchable under hypnosis. For example, if I ask a hypnotized person to take a knife and kill his mother, he would refuse.

What I did with *Heart of Glass* was, for me, part of a very natural progression. My attempts to render inner states that are transparent from a certain viewpoint were realized in a kind of nightmarish vision in *Even Dwarfs Started Small*, in ecstatic states in *The Great Ecstasy of Woodcarver Steiner*, and even in the state of non-participation of social activities with the children in *Land of Silence and Darkness* and Bruno in *The Enigma of Kaspar Hauser*. In all these films none of the people are deformed, not even the dwarfs.

The film has a profound poetic quality to it, even when there is no dialogue.

I wanted to provoke poetic language out of people who had never before been in touch with poetry. During pre-production I put an ad in the newspaper asking for people who wanted to take part in a series of experiments involving hypnosis. There were sessions once a week for about six months, and we ended up selecting those people according to the types that were needed for the story, and also, crucially, based on their receptivity to hypnosis. We were also careful to choose people who were emotionally stable and who were genuinely interested in what we were doing. Out of about 500 people, we chose thirty-five. Once we had the actors, the aim of rehearsals was also to work out a catalogue of suggestions which would result in the kind of stylized somnambulistic absent-mindedness that you see in the film.

As director I would not say, 'You are a great poet' or 'You are now the most gifted singer in the world', but rather 'You move as if in slow motion because the whole room is filled with water. You have an oxygen tank, and though under water usually you can move only with great difficulty, you feel very light right now. You are just drifting, almost flying.' Or something like, 'You see your partner, but you look through him as you look through a window,' and 'You are an inventor of great genius, and you are working on an insane, beautiful invention. When I come to you and put my hand on your shoulder, you will tell me what you are inventing.' What counted was the way things were suggested to the actors, and soon they were able to feel non-existent heat so intensely that they would break out in a sweat. They were able to hold conversations with imaginary people, and two hypnotized actors could even talk to a third imaginary person. The timing of movements and speech were often very peculiar, and once the actors had been

brought out of their states, many had only a vague recollection of
what they had been doing.

Did you do all the hypnosis yourself?

Initially I had a hypnotist during rehearsals. I knew that he had to
be prepared to play the role of assistant director during the shoot,
but eventually I had to take over because I did not like his
approach. He was a New Age creep who made claims that hypnosis was a cosmic aura only he, with his powers, could transmit
on to specially gifted mediums. He was just too much into the
supernatural aspects, many of which ended up in the script of
Invincible when Hanussen is on stage. After two sessions I found
myself all alone having to hypnotize the cast myself. During the
shooting this meant having to speak to the cast and crew in two
different pitches of voice. I had to whisper instructions to the
cameraman because if I had asked him out loud to move a foot to
the left, the entire cast would have done the same. The only character in the film who was not put into trance is Hias, the prophet.
Also workers in the glass factory were not under hypnosis because
it would simply have been too dangerous, as liquid glass has a
temperature of 1,100 °C.

*How different is it directing actors who are hypnotized from deal-
ing with performers not in trance?*

Normally I would tell them what to do and how to react after I
had put them into trance, but I would give them a lot of space
because so much of what happened was so unpredictable. Imagination functions very well under hypnosis. I would not just ask
someone to write a poem. I told them: 'You are the first one who
has set foot on a foreign island for centuries. It is overgrown with
jungle, full of strange birds. You come across a gigantic cliff, and
on closer inspection this entire cliff is made of pure emerald where
hundreds of years ago a Holy Monk had spent his entire life with
a chisel and hammer engraving a poem into the wall. It took him
his entire life to engrave only three lines of a poem. And you open
your eyes and are the first one to see it. You read out what you see
to me.' One actor in the film tended the stables of a Munich police
station. He had no formal education and I asked him to open his

eyes and read this inscription to me. He stood there and said he did not have his glasses, so I told him to move a little bit closer and everything would be in focus. He moved closer and in a very strange voice said, 'Why can we not drink the moon? Why is there no vessel to hold it?' And it went on, a very beautiful reading. The next guy – a former law student – stepped up. I told him the same story, he took a look and said, 'Dear Mother, I am doing fine, everything is all right. I'm looking to the future now. Hugs and kisses, Your Son.'

Did you think it was important for audiences to know that the actors were hypnotized?

No, I never did, not least because hypnosis really is an ordinary phenomenon, just like sleep. It is surrounded by an aura of the mysterious primarily because science has not yet furnished us with sufficient explanations of it. Hypnosis is similar to, let's say, acupuncture, though we do not yet know enough about the physiological processes of the brain in either phenomenon. It has nothing to do with metaphysics or any kind of evil powers, even if the country-fair hypnotist tries to convince his audience otherwise. The way hypnosis really works is with the hypnotist giving life to the act of self-hypnosis via mind and speech rituals. When I spoke to audiences who said they had no idea about the use of hypnosis in *Heart of Glass*, many of them spoke of the film's 'dreamy atmosphere'.

Actually it is possible to hypnotize someone from a screen, and the original idea was for me to appear on screen in a prologue explaining to the audience that, if they wanted to, they themselves could experience the film under hypnosis. 'If you follow my voice now and look at the object I am holding and focus on it you could become hypnotized, but so deeply that you will have your eyes open and will see the film on a different level.' Of course, at the end of the film I would reappear and softly wake them up without any anxieties. I would have advised everyone in the audience who did not want to participate to avert their eyes. 'Do not listen, do not follow my advice.' I did not follow through with this plan as it would have been wholly irresponsible to do so.

Heart of Glass

*The film is also one of your most beautiful to look at. It is simply
filmed amidst what are very archetypical Herzog locations.*

There are no gimmicks in the film on any level, and for kids today
used to fast-moving editing, a slow-moving drama like this might
be difficult to take. Schmidt-Reitwein and I looked at the work of
seventeenth-century French painter Georges de La Tour.[13] I
wanted to capture something of the same atmosphere you find in
his canvases. Some of the finest shots I have ever done are at the
start of the film when you look down into a valley and a river of
fog floats by. It took twelve consecutive days of the crew sitting on
this mountain top to capture this image. I had people clicking
frame by frame by hand until I got what I wanted, and the shot has
a very strange style to it as if we are looking at a moving canvas.

One of the things I like about *Heart of Glass* is that though it
seems to be set in something like the late eighteenth century, you
are never absolutely certain. It is a very loosely defined past, certainly pre-industrial, and these indefinable landscapes do not help
you place the story of the film in a solid historical past. Most of the
film was shot in Bavaria, some in Switzerland and some in Alaska
near Glacier Bay. But in the film I declare all landscapes Bavarian,
for these other parts of the world share a real affinity to the Bavarian landscapes that I have a very deep connection to. Some filming
was done very close to Sachrang where I grew up, and I was
always surrounded by very familiar-looking terrain. Stories like
Heart of Glass were always being told when I was growing up.
There were mythological heroes that we had; there were idols we
had, the incredibly strong lumberjacks who would brawl in bars.
There was a mythical waterfall in a ravine behind the house, and
on our way to school in the village we had to pass a forest we
thought was haunted by witches. When I pass this spot today I still
get the feeling that there is something different about the forest.

The final sequence was filmed on Skellig Rock, a truly ecstatic
landscape out there in Ireland. It is a rock almost like a pyramid
that rises almost 300 metres out of the ocean where in the year
1000 AD the marauding Norsemen threw the inhabiting monks off
into the sea. It took hours and hours of sailing in small boats
through the rain and the cold just to get there, and only during the
summer is it possible to land there as it is otherwise too windswept.

The breakers rise thirty or forty metres vertically up the sides of it. Up at the top there is mist, steam and a sloping plateau. You have to climb hundreds of steps, carved out of the stone by the monks. Hias has a vision of a man standing up there, one of those who have yet to learn that the Earth is round. He still believes that the Earth is a flat disc that ends in an abyss somewhere far out in the ocean. For years he stands staring out over the sea until several more men join him. One day they resolve to take the ultimate risk: they take a boat and start to row out to sea. In the last shot of the film you can see the ocean growing dark, deep heavy clouds and long drawn-out waves, and the four men rowing their boat out into the totally grey open sea.

The last thing we see in the film are the words 'It may have seemed like a sign of hope that the birds followed them out into the vastness of the sea.' Did you write that?

I did. And somehow, maybe, I want to be that man who looks to the horizon and decides to set out to discover the shape of the Earth himself.

NOTES

1 Klaus Wyborny (b. 1945, Germany) is one of Germany's leading 'alternative' filmmakers (he works almost exclusively on 8 mm) and film theorists.

2 Jeffrey Moussaieff Masson's *The Lost Prince* (Free Press, 1996) is a good summary of the story of Kaspar Hauser and includes the complete translation of Anselm von Feuerbach's 1832 book *Kaspar Hauser: Beispiel eines Verbrechens am Seelenleben des Menchen* (*Kaspar Hauser: A Case of a Crime Against the Soul of a Human Being*) along with the 1828 autobiographical fragment that Kaspar himself wrote.

3 *Kaspar Hauser* (1996), written and directed by Peter Sehr. 'The man, the myth, the crime' reads the video box.

4 Jakob Wassermann (1873–1934, Germany) was a leading novelist of the 1920s and 30s. His *Caspar Hauser* was published in 1908. Michael Hulse's translation was published in 1992 by Penguin.

5 Peter Handke (b. 1942, Austria) is a leading German-language novelist and playwright whose work includes the play *Kaspar* (1968). His novel *The Goalkeeper's Fear of the Penalty* (1971) was made into a film by German director Wim Wenders, with whom he

has worked as a screenwriter (including *Wings of Desire*).

6 'To See and Not See' from *An Anthropologist on Mars* (Picador, 1995). See Chapter 3, footnote 2.

7 *Bruno der Schwarze – Es blies ein Jäger wohl in sein Horn* [*Bruno the Black – One Day a Hunter Blew His Horn*] (1970), directed by Lutz Eisholz.

8 Truffaut's *The Wild Child* was made in 1969. See Roger Shattuck's *The Forbidden Experiment: The Story of the Wild Boy of Aveyron* (Quartet, 1981).

9 François Truffaut (1932–84, France) was one of the leading directors of the French New Wave. His many films include *The Four Hundred Blows* (1959), *Jules and Jim* (1961), *Fahrenheit 451* (1966) and *The Last Metro* (1980).

10 Carl Theodore Dreyer (1889–1968, Denmark) was the director of *La Passion de Jeanne D'Arc* (1928), *Vampyr* (1932), *Day of Wrath* (1943) and *Gertrud* (1964). See his book of writings *Dreyer in Double Reflection* (edited by Donald Skoller, Dutton, 1973).

11 *The Tragic Diary of Zero the Fool* (1969), directed by Morley Markson, a Toronto-based filmmaker, who explains: '*Zero the Fool* was an experimental improvisation. I felt the story would be more interesting approached as a kind of documentary, with real and unscripted interactions plus a probing camera style. The film progresses until it kind of dissolves into a truthful insanity. The actors were all unprofessional, though we didn't actually shoot in a lunatic asylum. The house we filmed in was actually a gathering place for lots of artistic and creative people. I called it the Sunset Asylum in the film because I thought it would help people get into the right frame of mind when they watched the film. *Zero the Fool* played at various film festivals back then. I do remember entering it into the Toronto Film Festival where it failed to qualify for entry because, they said, it's simply "not a movie." I liked that a lot.'

12 Jean Rouch (b. 1917, France) is generally considered the father of modern ethnographic filmmaking. His work includes *Moi, un noir* (1958) and *Chronicle of a Summer* (1960). See Mick Eaton's *Anthropology – Reality – Cinema* (BFI, 1978).

13 See *Georges de La Tour and his World* (edited by Philip Conisbee, Yale University Press, 1996).

5
Legitimacy

We talked earlier about how German romanticism may or may not have influenced your work. Who are the writers, poets and film-makers – German or otherwise – that have been most influential on your own art?

First of all, I am *not* an artist and never have been. Rather I am a craftsman and feel very close to the mediaeval artisans who produced their work anonymously and who, along with their apprentices, had a true feeling for the physical materials they were working with.

Years ago I was in Paris right after a huge exhibition of the work of Caspar David Friedrich.[1] It seemed like every single French journalist I spoke to had seen the exhibition and insisted on seeing my films – especially *Heart of Glass* and *Kaspar Hauser* – within the context of this new knowledge he suddenly had. Then, after a similar exhibition of German expressionism a few years later, everyone told me how many elements of expressionism they could see in my work. One year it was inconceivable to them I had not planned to imbue my films from start to finish with elements of German romanticism, the next year they were even more incredulous that I had no preconceived notion of expressionism within my work. When it comes to the French, it is either romanticism or expressionism I am tainted with, simply because those are the only two movements in German art anyone has ever heard of, so surely I must fit comfortably within one or the other. Please have a look at what I said to Les Blank about the jungle.[2] Anyone who understands romanticism will know that those were not the

135

words of a romanticist. And when it comes to the Americans, who have generally been very good to me and my films over the years, but not having much knowledge of either romanticism or expressionism, for them the only question is, 'Is this film in line with Nazism or not?'

When it comes to being influenced by the work of others, one experiences, maybe only five or six times during a lifetime, the incredible feeling that illuminates and enlightens your own existence. It might happen while reading a text, listening to a piece of music, watching a film or looking at a painting. And sometimes – even if centuries are being bridged – you find a brother and instantly know that you are no longer alone. I experienced this with Kleist, with Bach's *Musikalisches Opfer*, with the scarcely known poet Quirin Kuhlman, with *Freaks* by Todd Browning and Dreyer's *Jeanne d'Arc*. If I had to give you the names of the painters who have influenced me, I would name Grünewald, and above all, Bosch and Brueghel. Leonardo da Vinci too. I am thinking of the Madonna with a window in the background that looks out over a kind of vast ideal landscape. These are the kinds of landscapes I try to find in my films, the landscapes that exist only in our dreams. For me a true landscape is not just a representation of a desert or a forest. It shows an inner state of mind, literally inner landscapes, and it is the human soul that is visible through the landscapes presented in my films, be it the jungle in *Aguirre*, the desert in *Fata Morgana*, or the burning oil fields of Kuwait in *Lessons of Darkness*. This is my real connection to Caspar David Friedrich, a man who never wanted to paint landscapes *per se*, but wanted to explore and show inner landscapes.

There is a painter who I feel even closer to, a virtual unknown called Hercules Segers.[3] He was a Dutch painter who made very small-sized prints. The man was an alcoholic and was considered insane by those around him. He was so poor he painted on anything he could find, including the tablecloth, and when he died many of his prints were used for wrapping sandwiches. Thankfully Rembrandt was the only one who took him seriously and it is known that he owned at least eight of Segers' prints. He also bought one of Segers' oil canvases which is now in the Uffizi in Florence and immediately improved the painting by adding some clouds and an ox-cart in the foreground. It is not stupidly improved, but the resulting painting is not a typical Segers painting. I feel a real connection to his art. He was one of those clairvoyant and totally independent figures hundreds of years ahead of his time. Encountering Segers was as if someone had reached out with his hand across time and touched my shoulders. His landscapes are not landscapes at all; they are states of mind, full of angst, desolation, solitude, a state of dreamlike vision. I often think about what an extraordinary cultural upheaval would have taken place throughout the world if cinema had been discovered a hundred years earlier, and if the writers and artists I draw on – Segers, Kleist,[4] Hölderlin[5] and Büchner[6] – had had cinema to express themselves.

What about musical and literary influences?

Musical influences have always been very strong, maybe the strongest. People think it strange that music could be the most important influence on a filmmaker, but to me it seems quite natural. The early composers like Monteverdi, Gesualdo or Roland de Lassus I like very much. Or let's go back even earlier to Johannes Ciconia, Martim Codax or Pierre Abelard. I would have to say musical figures have been more of an influence on me than literary ones.

Like I said, I do not read that much, but when I do read it is always a very intense experience for me. There are works of literature about which I can only speak of in awe – and I speak particularly of German writers here – like Büchner's *Woyzeck*, Kleist's short stories, Hölderlin's poetry. It is these men who were truly exploring the farthest borders of the German language. More recently I like Peter Handke and Thomas Bernhard, though of course they are both Austrians. And I would rather read the 1545 Bible translation of Martin Luther than any of the German romantics. Joseph Conrad's short stories, and Hemingway's first forty-nine stories, who can walk past them? And of course the first real modern writer in English, Laurence Sterne, particularly his wonderful *Sentimental Journey*. His *Tristram Shandy* does not seem to be read much these days, but I strongly recommend it to all writers out there. It is such a thoroughly modern novel; the way it is narrated still looks so fresh. Let us bring Harmony Korine back again; he loves the book because it does not have a linear narrative, and of course Harmony is not the man to tell his own stories as a normal movie story flows. His approach, like Sterne's, has much more to do with associations and strange jumps and contradictions and wild ravings and rantings.

If I was caught on a lonely island the book I would want with me, without a doubt, is the *Oxford English Dictionary*, all twenty volumes. One of the greatest cultural monuments that the human race has ever created, such an incredible achievement of human ingenuity.

Are there any particular filmmakers with whom you have really connected?

Of the filmmakers with whom I feel some kinship, Griffith,[7] Murnau,[8] Pudovkin,[9] Buñuel[10] and Kurosawa[11] come to mind. Everything these men did has the touch of greatness. Griffith I always thought of as the Shakespeare of cinema. There are individual films that have been very close to me like the Taviani brothers' *Padre Padrone* and, of course, Dreyer's *La Passion de Jeanne D'Arc*. Figures like Tarkovsky have made some beautiful films but he is, I fear, too much the darling of the French intellectuals, something I suspect he worked a little bit towards. For me there are what I call 'essential' films: kung fu, Fred Astaire, porno. 'Movie' movies, so to speak. Something like *Mad Max* with those car collisions or *Broadway Melody of 1940* with Fred Astaire. I love Astaire, the most insipid face speaking the most insipid dialogue you will ever hear up there on the screen, yet it works beautifully. And Buster Keaton. Just thinking about him moves me. He is one of my witnesses when I say that some of the very best filmmakers were athletes. He was the quintessential athlete, a real acrobat.

It is the moving image *per se* that is the message in these kinds of films, the way that the film simply moves on the screen without asking you questions. I love this kind of cinema. It does not have the falseness and phoniness of films that try so hard to pass on a heavy idea to the audience or have the fake emotions of most Hollywood films. Astaire's emotions were always wonderfully stylized. Someone like Jean-Luc Godard is for me intellectual counterfeit money when compared to a good kung fu film.

So you certainly don't subscribe to the belief that your films are in any way 'art films'?

Absolutely not, they are no such thing. I dislike intensely even the concept of artists in this day and age. The last King of Egypt, King Farouk, completely obese in exile, wolfing one lamb leg after another, said something very beautiful: 'There are no kings left in the world any more, only the King of Hearts, the King of Diamonds, the King of Spades, and the King of Clubs.' The whole concept of being an artist is also somehow outdated today. There is only one place left where you find artists: the circus. There you can find the trapeze artists, the jugglers, even the hunger artist. Film is not analysis, it is the agitation of the mind; cinema comes from the country fair and the circus, not from art and academicism. I truly feel that in the world of the painter or novelist or film director there are no artists. This is a concept that belongs to earlier centuries, where there was such a thing as virtue and pistol duels at dawn with men in love, and damsels fainting on couches.

Michelangelo, Caspar David Friedrich and Hercules Segers: these men are artists. 'Art' is a legitimate concept in their respective eras. They are like the emperors and kings who remain the crucial figures in the history of humankind and whose influence is felt even today, something that certainly cannot be said of monarchies today. I am speaking not about the death of the artist; I just feel that creativity is perceived with something of an outdated and antiquated perspective. That is why I detest the word 'genius'. It too is a word that belongs to an earlier time and not to our own era. It is a sick concept nowadays, and this is why with utmost caution did I once call Kinski a 'genius'. My use of the word comes close to my feelings about the man, but the expression itself and the concept behind it is something that heralds from the late eighteenth century and just does not fit comfortably today.

So if your films are not art, what are they?

I often ask myself how I would like my work to be perceived. I would prefer that the films are seen rather like the work of artisans of the late mediaeval times, people who had workshops and apprentices and who never considered themselves as artists. All the sculptors before Michelangelo considered themselves stonemasons;

no one really thought of themselves as an 'artist' until maybe the late fifteenth century. Before that they were master craftsmen with apprentices who produced work on commission from popes or Burgermeisters or whoever. This reminds me of the story that I speak of with director Heiner Müller in *The Transformation of the World into Music*. After Michelangelo had finished the Pietà in Rome, one of the Medici family forced him to build a snowman in the garden of the family villa. He had no qualms about it; without a word he just went out and built the snowman. I like this attitude and feel there is something of absolute defiance in it.

What I also like are the late mediaeval painters, many of whom were anonymous; for example, the anonymous master of the Köln triptych. To remain anonymous behind what you have created means that your work has an even stronger life of its own, and the work is all that is important. I have always felt that the creator is of no intrinsic importance, and this counts when it comes to my own work too. Of course, in practical terms this is impossible because the ramifications of today's media mean that when you make a film there are so many collaborators, and it is inevitable that people will know who wrote the screenplay and who directed. Look at the Dogme films: one rule is the directors remain anonymous. But this is ridiculous, we all know who directed the films simply because they cannot resist being appearing on every TV station from here to Tokyo and back again.

Your next film was a wonderful little piece shot in the United States, How Much Wood Would a Woodchuck Chuck. *How did you end up in New Holland, Pennsylvania, at the World Championship of Livestock Auctioneers?*

I was fascinated by livestock auctioneers and always had the feeling that their incredible language was the real poetry of capitalism. Every system develops its own sort of *extreme* language, like the ritual chants of the Orthodox Church, and there is something final and absolute about the language the auctioneers speak over there. After all, how much further can it go from there? It is frightening but quite beautiful at the same time; there is a real music in the delivery of the speech, the sense of rhythm these people have. It is almost like a ritual incantation.

I went out to make the film during the Championship of Live-stock Auctioneers competition because I was in touch with some of these great masters of speech. The criteria for the jury were not just how wildly the winner would accelerate his speech. It was actually a real auction and within two or three hours two and a half million dollars and a thousand head of cattle changed hands, and so the jury had to note if the auctioneer was able to spot all the secret bidders. Another element is how trustworthy will the auctioneer be, how well will he raise the price of the cattle, and how good a broker is he. My dream ever since has been to go back and do a version of *Hamlet* in under fifteen minutes. All of the world champions of this livestock auction speaking Shakespeare. It would be great poetry.

Some years ago you said that America was the most exotic country on the planet. What did you mean by that?

I truly love places like the midwest of America, for example Wisconsin, where we filmed *Stroszek*. These are the kinds of areas you would normally expect the greatest talents to come from. Orson Welles was from Wisconsin, Marlon Brando was from Nebraska, Bob Dylan from Minnesota, Hemingway from Illinois, these 'middle of nowhere' kinds of places, to say nothing of the South which spawned the brilliance of Faulkner and Flannery O'Connor. I really like this kind of country. For me it is the very heart of America. You still see the self-reliance and camaraderie out there, the warm open hearts, the down-to-earth people, whereas so much of America had abandoned these wonderful and basic virtues.

One thing I do like about America is its spirit of advancement and exploration. There is definitely something bold about America. I very much like this idea of giving everyone an equal chance to succeed no matter who you are. If a barefoot Indian from the Andes had invented the wheel the patent office in Washington would have assisted him securing his rights. I have been to a huge scientific corporation in Cleveland, Ohio, with something like 2,000 people working there. The boss of the whole place was twenty-eight years old. That really impresses me. It is absolutely unthinkable in Germany.

Stroszek

You went back to America to shoot Stroszek. *Do you agree with those people who felt the film was some kind of humorous critique of American capitalism?*

To a certain extent the film is about the American way of life, but that is absolutely not the reason I made *Stroszek*. Originally, at the time I wanted to make *Woyzeck* and had promised Bruno that he could play the title role. He did not know the play, but I explained it to him and he kind of liked the whole idea. But all of a sudden I realized that this would be a massive mistake. It was clear to me that it was Kinski who should play the part, so I immediately called Bruno to let him know. You must have the courage to say these things without hesitation. There was a kind of stunned silence at the other end of the line. 'I have already booked my vacation. What am I going to do?' he said. It was very clear that it had meant a lot to Bruno to be in the film, and I felt so ashamed and embarrassed that out of the blue I said, 'You know, Bruno, we will do another film instead.' And he said, 'What film?' I said, 'I do not know yet. What day is it?' 'Monday,' he said. So I just said, 'By Saturday you will have the screenplay. And I will even give it a title now which sounds like *Woyzeck*. It will be called *Stroszek*.' I felt a kind of relief at the other end of the phone, but after hanging up found myself on Monday at midday with a title and the task to write a story for Bruno. I delivered it on Saturday. I still think it is one of my best pieces of writing and one of my finest films. The title comes from the name of the lead character in *Signs of Life*, which in turn came from a guy I vaguely knew years before. I was enrolled at university in Munich but hardly ever showed up for class and asked this guy to write a paper for me. 'What will you give me in return?' he asked. 'Well, Mr Stroszek,' I said, 'one day I will make your name famous.' And I did just that.

It seems that the character of Stroszek is much closer to the real Bruno than that of Kaspar Hauser.

Stroszek is a film very much built around Bruno. It reflected my own knowledge of him and his environment, his emotions and feelings, and also my deep affection for him. In that way it was easy to write the screenplay. Sometimes filmmaking is all about stylization, but with *Stroszek* we were dealing with real human suffering. This is not like the suffering you find in a theatre, acted out and turned into gross melodrama. With Bruno you always see true suffering on the screen. His character in the film is very close to the real Bruno, and even today it is difficult for me to watch some scenes of the film. The sequence in the apartment when the two pimps beat Eva Mattes up and throw Bruno over the piano pains me so much because it was probably the kind of treatment that had been doled out to him for years when he was a child. There is such magnificence in his performance. 'I'm going to be a good soldier, and I've been hurt much worse before,' he said before we shot the scene. Though the film was scripted from start to finish, some scenes were improvised; for example, when Bruno speaks to Eva Mattes about his solitude and pain as a child in an institution, when he wet his bed and was forced to hold his bedsheet up for hours until it was dry or he was beaten. That really happened to him. Eva was so good in the scene as she just kept listening and encouraging him. She always knew exactly how to trigger certain responses from Bruno and to push the scene in the right direction. And the scenes in Berlin of him singing and playing the accordion in the city show exactly what he would do every weekend. Bruno knows every courtyard and alleyway of Berlin, and some of the songs he sings in the film he wrote himself. The place where he goes immediately after leaving prison is his local beer cellar where everyone knew him, and all the props he uses in the film, all the musical instruments, were his own.

So the idea of in some way writing a critique of capitalism just did not enter my head. Lines like Bruno talking about being in America originated because we were in America. Of course, the film does reflect something of what I experienced when I lived in Pittsburgh where I saw the underside of America, though I say that with real affection. The film does not criticize the country; it is almost a eulogy to the place. For me *Stroszek* is about shattered hopes, which is clearly a universal theme, and it would not really matter if they had moved from Berlin to France or Sweden. I simply felt familiar enough with America to set the second part of the story there.

The apartment in Germany that Stroszek lives in is actually Bruno's own Berlin apartment, isn't it?

Yes, and after getting the apartment with his salary from *Kaspar Hauser* Bruno bought a piano. He loves music and liked *Kaspar Hauser* very much in part because of the music. I remember watching the film with him and he kept squeezing my fingertips whenever the music came on. 'This is into *Der Bruno*'s heart,' he would say. 'Yes, this is feeling strong in *Der Bruno*'s heart now.' He was very proud at being self-taught at the piano, so I told him I would write some scenes for him in *Stroszek* where he could play the piano. You can also see him play in *Kaspar Hauser*, and even today I feel that Bruno's ability to play the way he did, and to express such profound thoughts in the kind of dilettantish way he did, is true culture. After all, how often do you *really* see such agitation of the mind?

Bruno was a very inventive man. He had started to paint – I suppose you would call them 'naïve paintings' – and years ago showed me a great discovery that he wanted to be submitted to the Academy of Sciences in Germany. He would always rummage around city garbage cans and so his apartment was always full of these 'found' objects. One time he found two dozen old ventilators, a couple of which still worked. So he painted one ventilator blade yellow, one blue, one red and so on, and when the ventilators spun around all of a sudden the colours would disappear, and it would look white. He was convinced he was the first person who had discovered such a thing.

What did Bruno think of America?

He loved it. New York was just stunning for him, just like it is for everyone who sees the city for the first time. The sequences in the city were all filmed in a single day as we had no shooting permit and spent the day trying – and failing – to dodge the police. We were improvising the whole day. For example, when we saw from the top of the Empire State Building a boat arriving in the pier, we decided to have the three of them arrive like real European immigrants and went down to the pier. The shot of them driving in a car was done with Thomas Mauch and me strapped to the hood of the car. We got stopped by the police, I think it was the third time that day, and I was handcuffed. The second time it happened I told the policeman, 'We're just a bunch of crazy Kraut film students,' and they let us go. Then half an hour later the same cop caught us again.

One thing to add is that the whole crew somehow found *Stroszek* pretty stupid and embarrassing, I do not know why. It was very difficult to keep the shooting out of the range of these bad moods that were inhabiting the set; there was no way to free it from this all-pervasive mood. You do not sense it in the film, but it was quite a hidden achievement to finish the film. It had nothing to do with Bruno; we all liked him. The only one who did not like him was Herr Scheitz, who plays the old man. He was always complaining that Bruno smelt. But Eva Mattes and Bruno got on very well; it was the small crew of about ten people who were the problem.

Where did you find Clemens Scheitz, who was also in The Enigma of Kaspar Hauser *and* Heart of Glass?

I needed extras for *Kaspar Hauser* and was looking through the card index of extras. I had gone through about 200 of them and got stuck on his face. The agency suggested I choose someone else. 'Even though we work in the interests of our clients,' they said, 'we should warn you that Herr Scheitz is not completely right in his head any more.' I said I did not mind, I want him anyway. He was a charming old man, who in between two sips of coffee could describe to you the function of the rocket he had just built, or who could prove to you by writing a few numbers on a restaurant table-cloth that Einstein and Newton were absolute fools. He was also a piano player who was always in the process of writing a magnificent oratorio. The scene when he talks about animal magnetism in *Stroszek* was my idea, but it comes very close to what his own ideas were. We were out in a tiny place in the middle of nowhere on the highway. It was hunting season and a couple of hunters pulled up. I asked them if they wanted to be in the film, and told them to just listen to Herr Scheitz talking and when they'd had enough to just get into their car and drive off. Of course, they did not understand a word he said but they played along wonderfully. The whole scene was shot basically in real time. There is only one quick change of camera position while we ran around to the other side of the car, but otherwise what you see is exactly what happened. The two guys just drove off. I never knew their names and never saw them again.

Herr Scheitz was always full of fantasies and said he was working on a universal study which was already in his mind but that he would never write down in case the FBI stole it. He was always talking about how he would never dare fly a plane into Berlin, which at the time was deep inside East Germany. 'The KGB will kidnap me and torture my secrets out of me,' he insisted. He had constructed a rocket which would hit a target dead on even after a 30,000 mile flight. I liked him so much in *Kaspar Hauser* that I kept on asking him to stay for another scene, to the point where he basically appears throughout the film. I even rewrote the end of the film so he would have the final word. In *Stroszek*, in particular, I tried to develop his character a little bit around his real 'madness' or whatever you call it. For me he always made sense.

Why did you thank Errol Morris in the opening credits?

Around the time of *Stroszek*, Errol Morris[12] had been deeply involved in researching mass murderers. He had collected unbelievable material, thousands of pages of the most incredible material, and planned to put it all into a book. He had spent months in a town called Plainfield, Wisconsin, and kept talking to me about the place. It was a tiny place in the middle nowhere with 480 inhabitants. What is so extraordinary about Plainfield is that within the space of five years something like five or six mass murderers emerged from the town. There was no apparent reason for this. I know it sounds crazy, but this is all true. There was something very gloomy and evil about Plainfield, and even during filming two bodies were found only ten miles from where we were filming. I certainly felt it was one of those places that are focal points where every thread converges and is tied into a knot. You have these points in the United States – for example, Las Vegas, or the Stock Exchange on Wall Street, or San Quentin prison – where the dreams and nightmares all come together. And I count Plainfield, Wisconsin, amongst them.

Errol was attracted to the place because it was the town where Ed Gein, the man who had inspired the Norman Bates character in *Psycho*, had lived and committed his murders. Errol had spoken to the sheriffs and townspeople and even to Gein himself and had hundreds of pages of transcripts of his interviews. But he was stuck with one very puzzling question: Ed Gein had not only murdered several people, he had also dug up freshly buried corpses from the cemetery and had preserved the flesh by building a throne and a lampshade out of it all. Errol somehow discovered that the graves he had dug up actually formed a perfect circle, and at the very centre of the circle was Gein's mother. He was puzzled by the question of whether or not Gein had actually dug up his own mother, and one day somewhere out of the blue I said to him, 'Errol, you will only know if you go back to Plainfield and dig there yourself. If the grave is empty, Ed Gein was there before you.' We decided we would go there and dig together and we were both quite excited about it. I was shooting a couple of sequences for *Heart of Glass* at the time in Alaska and on my way back to New York crossed the border from Canada and headed down to Plainfield. I was actually there waiting for Errol, but he chickened out and never showed up. Later on I realized that it was the best thing. Sometimes it is much better to have a question and no answer.

Later I went back to film in the town. I loved shooting in Plainfield. The scenes of Eva working in the truck stop were filmed in a real truck stop in the middle of the day. I just went in there and asked if we could film. 'Sure!' the owner said. 'We just love having you Krauts around!' So we told the truckers to be themselves and

Eva just went around pouring their coffee. Ed Lachman, the second cameraman, was a very important part of the production in this respect. He would be the one to explain to the townsfolk and the truckers what was going on and what they should say. We called the town Railroad Flats in the film because Plainfield was still kind of Errol's terrain. He had 'discovered' it and was really pissed off at me, accusing me of stealing his landscapes. Such a fine spirit he has, and a truly visionary filmmaker. So in a pathetic attempt to appease him I thanked him at the start of the film. I think he has forgiven me by now.

I've always found La Soufrière, *filmed on a Caribbean island about to explode, one of your most entertaining films. It has a kind of ridiculous and bizarre profundity to it with the shots of you and the cameramen Ed Lachman and Jörg Schmidt-Reitwein running from clouds of toxic gas wafting down the mountainside as you wait for this 'unavoidable catastrophe'.*

There is certainly an element of self-mockery in the final film. Everything that looks so dangerous and doomed ultimately ends up in utter banality. That is fine, I had to accept it as it was, and of course, in retrospect, I have to thank God on my knees that it was not otherwise. It is a good job the film is missing its potentially violent climax. It really would have been absolutely ridiculous to be blown to pieces by a volcano with two colleagues whilst making a film.

For *La Soufrière*, since we really did not know if the island we were standing on was about to be blown apart by a volcano, each of us had to make his own decision. As soon as I heard about the impending volcanic eruption, that the island of Guadeloupe had been evacuated and that one peasant had refused to leave, I knew I wanted to go talk to him and find out what kind of relationship towards death he had. I immediately called up the television executive with whom I had a working relationship going back to *The Great Ecstasy of Woodcarver Steiner*. I really needed to speak with to him because if I did not leave quickly the whole thing might be over. The volcano would explode and the film would be dead. He was in a meeting at the time so I asked his assistant to drag him out of there for only sixty seconds no matter where he was, what he

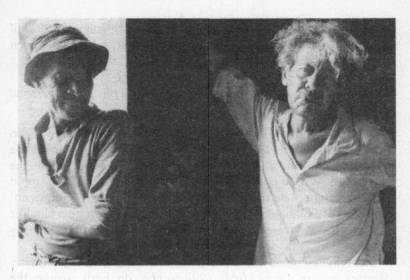

La Soufrière

was doing or how important the people he was with were. 'Tell him Herzog needs to talk to him for sixty seconds.' I think in fifty seconds I explained the situation to him and he said, 'Just get out of here and do it.' And I said, 'How do we do the contract?' All he said was, 'Come back alive and we do the contract.' And he was gone, as simple as that. And we did the contract on our return. I love the man for his faith, a true believer. Let me name horse and rider: Manfred Konzelmann.

Ed Lachman came from New York, and I flew from Germany with Schmidt-Reitwein and we met up in Pointe-à-Pitre in Guadeloupe. Before we arrived on the island – and then even as we were driving past roadblocks up the side of the volcano – I repeatedly asked them if they really wanted to do this. I told them: 'I am definitely going, but you have to make this decision yourself. I need a single camera and can shoot it all myself if necessary.' Schmidt-Reitwein immediately said yes; there was no doubt he was always going to come along. Lachman had some initial hesitations, quite understandably so. He needed to take a leak, so he stepped out of the car and then meekly asked me, 'What will happen if the island blows up?' 'Ed, we are going to be airborne,' I said. It kind of encouraged him and he immediately picked up his camera. We left a camera in the far distance which would click single frames all day long, so if we had been airborne there would at least have been some frames of us making it upwards.

I'm sure you can see how films like this got you this public persona as a risk-taking madman.

I can laugh about it now, but of course what we wanted to do was to get out of there with a film in our cameras. I am not in the business of suicide and there was nothing of bravado about the experience. We did not go there to get blown up. Blind and stupid risk-taking is not something I generally practise. I am simply not that kind of a filmmaker. But I do have to admit that with a film like *La Soufrière* we were playing the lottery. But please note: it really was one of the few occasions I have done something like this.

The film's commentary and the full title of the film, *La Soufrière: Waiting for an Unavoidable Catastrophe,* do both suggest the absurd nature of our task, but this was based on the experts who said that the explosion of the mountain was guaranteed with almost 100 per cent certainty. It was calculated the volcano was going to blow with the force of several Hiroshima-sized atomic bombs, so if it had gone up and we were within a five-mile radius there would be absolutely nothing we could do. And anyway, we were standing on a deep fissure that had been ripped open right on the rim of this steaming volcano that was emitting toxic gases. We had to approach the thing from the leeward side, and we had a real fright one morning when the wind changed and all of a sudden these toxic fumes came drifting down towards us. The day after, Ed Lachman realized he had left his glasses up there and so was really helpless. I decided to go back for the glasses and the others followed, but we soon discovered that there had been so many shockwaves – some of them quite serious – that the whole landscape had been ripped apart yet again and everything looked different.

I knew that if I could escape from this one alive then I would be able to joke about it afterwards. I saw myself as the captain in the joke that I like about Italians in the trenches during the First World War. For weeks they are being bombarded, day after day, until one day their captain grabs a rifle and shouts, 'Up men! Attack!' And before he has gone two steps he is mowed down by enemy fire and falls back into the trench. All the Italian soldiers who have been quietly sitting smoking applaud and say, 'Bravo, Captain, bravo.' Thankfully, *La Soufrière* was one of those moments when we were not mowed down.

Do you see your version of Nosferatu *as a remake of Murnau's film or something much more than that? And for you is it a genre film?*

I never thought of my film *Nosferatu* as being a remake. It stands on its own feet as an entirely new version. It is like both Dreyer and Bresson,[13] who made films about Joan of Arc: one is not a remake of the other. My *Nosferatu* has a different context, different figures and a somewhat different story. It is a very clear declaration of my connection to the very best of German cinema, and though I have never truly functioned in terms of genres, I did appreciate that making a film like *Nosferatu* meant understanding the basic principles about the vampire genre, and then asking, 'How am I going to modify and develop this genre further?' It was kind of what I did with the 'adventure' genre when I was making *Aguirre*.

The images found in vampire films have a quality beyond our usual experiences in the cinema. For me genre means an intensive, almost dreamlike, stylization on screen, and I feel the vampire genre is one of the richest and most fertile cinema has to offer. There is fantasy, hallucination, dreams and nightmares, visions, fear and, of course, mythology. What I really sought to do was connect my *Nosferatu* with our true German cultural heritage, the silent films of the Weimar era[14] and Murnau's work in particular. If his *Nosferatu* is a genre film then mine inevitably is one too. In many ways, for me, this film was the final chapter of the vital process of 're-legitimization' of German culture that had been going on for some years.

Is this where your friendship with Lotte Eisner became even more important?

Yes. Lotte Eisner[15] proved to be crucial in this respect. I have said many times that as children growing up in post-war Germany we had grandfathers but no fathers to learn from. Many men had been killed in the war or were in captivity. My own father was alive but not around for much of the time, and Fassbinder's father abandoned his family very early on. As filmmakers coming of age in the early and mid-1960s, we were the first real post-war generation, young Germans with no one around who could give us points of reference. We were orphans who had no teachers and no masters to learn from and in whose footsteps we wanted to follow, unburdened by any traditions or rituals. For a time in the 1960s and 70s, West German cinema was fresh and exciting, encompassing many different subjects and styles, for just this reason. The father generation had either sided with the barbaric Nazi culture or was chased out of the country. With a few exceptions, before the 1960s – directors like Staudte[16] and Käutner[17] – there had been no 'legitimate' German cinema since 30 January 1933, the day Hitler came to power. Lotte Eisner left the country the very same day, and Fritz Lang left soon afterwards.[18] A gap of thirty years opened up. As a filmmaker you clearly cannot work without having some coherence with your own culture. Continuity is vital. So it was our 'grandfathers' – Lang, Murnau, Pabst and others – who became our points of reference. Incidentally, I have already mentioned my own archaeologist grandfather, who was much more important to me than my father.

For me, *Nosferatu* is the greatest of all German films, and feeling as strongly as I did that I needed to connect to this 'legitimate' German culture in order to find my roots as a filmmaker, I chose to concentrate on Murnau's masterpiece, knowing full well it would be impossible to better the original. It was not nostalgia, rather my admiration of the heroic age of cinema that gave birth to the film in 1922. By this I do not mean I set out to explore German cinema of the 1920s. I never felt I was emulating a particular tradition. What I mean is that many of my generation shared a similar attitude to Murnau and his contemporaries: cinema as legitimate culture. When I had finished *Nosferatu* I remember thinking, 'Now I am connected, I have reached the other side of the river at last.' This might sound rather melodramatic when I speak of it today and might have been incomprehensible to British, Italian or French filmmakers at the time – countries that managed to kick-start film production after the war with relative ease – but was something that impacted on many young German filmmakers back in the 1970s.

Are you saying that when it came to 'legitimacy' you couldn't just proclaim it yourselves? You needed someone to do it for you?

Of course we could not merely issue a self-empowering decree. Just as Charlemagne had to travel to Rome to ask the Pope to anoint him, in the case of New German Cinema we were fortunate to have Lotte Eisner to give us her blessing. She was the missing link, our collective conscience, a fugitive from Nazism, and for many years the single living person in the world who knew everyone in cinema from its first hour on, a veritable woolly mammoth. Lotte was one of the most important film historians the world has ever seen and had personally known all the great figures of early cinema: Eisenstein, Griffith, Sternberg, Chaplin, Murnau, Renoir, even the Lumière brothers and Méliès. And other generations too: Buñuel, Kurosawa, just everyone. So she alone had the authority, insight and the personality to declare us legitimate, and it was vitally important when she insisted that what my generation was doing in Germany was as legitimate as the film culture that Murnau, Lang and the other Weimar filmmakers had created all those years previously.

I first met Lotte because of her voice. At the Berlin Film Festival in maybe 1965 she gave a lecture, the first time she had returned to Germany since 1933. I walked past the open door of the lecture hall and heard her voice. It was so stunning and so special I just walked in and listened. What she said was so extraordinary I felt it was my duty to find out who she was. Later I discovered she had wanted to speak to me after seeing *Signs of Life* but did not dare contact me. A friend finally said to me, 'Lotte speaks so highly of you and she doesn't dare to meet you, and you speak so highly of her and you do not dare to meet her either. I will get you together.' I did not meet her until 1969. One of the most memorable things about the shooting of *Kaspar Hauser* was that Lotte was there for some of the time. For her to show up on the set of one of my films was for me a great honour, something very significant for me. She did not ask anything; she just sat there and had a pleased face the whole time. It gave me a lot of confidence.

Apparently, when Fritz Lang said it was impossible that there were any real German films any longer, Lotte told him to see *Signs of Life*. Her affirmation and support was what gave me the strength to continue battling against the heavy criticism of my work for at least ten years. There were many moments when no one wanted to see my films. I vividly remember sitting with Lotte in her Paris apartment drinking tea and almost casually saying to

Nosferatu

her, 'I just cannot go on.' And in between a sip of tea whilst munching a cookie, without even looking at me, she very calmly just said, 'You are not going to quit. Film history will not allow you.' Then she went on about her noisy neighbours or something like that. It was one of the key moments of my life.

For Nosferatu *did you go back to the original Stoker novel or did you base your own script directly on Murnau's film?*

I could probably have made a vampire film without the existence of Murnau's film, but there is a certain reverence I tried to pay to his *Nosferatu* and on one or two occasions I even tried to quote him literally by matching the same shots he used in his version. I went to Lübeck where he filmed the vampire's lair and found among the few houses there not destroyed during the war those Murnau had used. They were being used as salt warehouses, but where in 1922 there had been small bushes, I found tall trees.

The reason Murnau's film is not called *Dracula* is because Bram Stoker's estate wanted so much money for the rights, so Murnau made a few unsubtle changes to his story and retitled it. My own film was solely based on the original *Nosferatu*, though I knew I wanted to inject a different spirit into my film. In Murnau's film the creature is frightening because he is without a soul and looks like an insect. But from Kinski's vampire you get real existential anguish. I tried to 'humanize' him. I wanted to endow him with human suffering and solitude, with a true longing for love and, importantly, the one essential capacity of human beings: mortality. Kinski plays against his appendages, the long fingernails and the pointed ears. I feel that his vampire is actually a very erotic figure. Moreover, in the film evil does not have only negative aspects; for example, the plague scene where there is real joy.

Stoker's novel[19] is a kind of compilation of all the vampire stories floating around from romantic times. What is interesting is that it focuses so much on new technology; for example, the use of telegrams and early recording machines, the Edison cylinders. Like the changes society was undergoing in the nineteenth century, there may well be something similar taking place today, as for some time we have been living in the digital age. In both cases there is something of an uneasiness in society, and vampire stories always seem to accumulate in times of restlessness. The novel is strangely obsessed with these kinds of things, and in this way Stoker was quite far-sighted by somehow anticipating our era of mass communication. At its heart, the vampire story is about solitude and now, more than a century later, as we witness this explosive evolution of means of communication, Stoker's work has a real and powerful actuality to it. His story is structured in an interesting way, using all these forms of communication to carry the story along, something which does not emerge in film versions.

While we are talking about communication, allow me to add something. It is my firm belief, and I say this as a dictum, that all these tools now at our disposal, these things part of this explosive evolution of means of communication, mean we are now heading for an era of solitude. Along with this rapid growth of forms of communication at our disposal – be it fax, phone, email, internet or whatever – human solitude will increase in direct proportion. It might sound paradoxical, but it is not. It might appear that these things remove us from our isolation, but isolation is very different from solitude. When you are caught in a snowdrift in South Dakota, fifty miles from the next town, your isolation can be overcome with a mere cellular phone. But solitude is something more existential.

There was a great deal of press at the time about the fact that you let thousands of rats loose in the town square in Delft, the town in Holland which substituted for Wismar in the film.

I was looking for a northern German or Baltic town with boats and canals and a Dutch friend of mine suggested Delft. As soon as I saw the town I was fascinated by it. Delft is so tranquil, so bourgeois, so self-assured and solid and has remained unchanged for centuries. Because of this I felt it would be the perfect place to shoot this story. The horror and destruction would show up very effectively in such a clean and uncontaminated town. I have always felt that rats possess a kind of fantasy element in that they are the only mammals whose numbers surpass those of man. The figure is something like three to one, and our fear of the creatures stem in part from this fact. Before we started shooting I explained to the city council in Delft exactly what I had in mind, and got an OK on everything. I had presented to them in great detail the technical plans we had to prevent a single rat from escaping. But many people in Delft were nervous because the town is full of canals and for decades there was a very serious rat problem which had only recently been overcome. So there was a developing feeling of unease.

Where did you get the rats from?

They were from a laboratory in Hungary and it was very difficult to transport them across Europe. At every border customs checked the medical certificates, and one time an official opened one of the boxes to check the contents and fainted. When we bought the rats they were snow white and had to be dyed grey. There was a huge factory in Germany that produced shampoo and hair dye that would test their products on rats because the texture of rat hair is very similar to that of human hair. I went to this factory along with Henning von Grierke, a painter who did the set design of the film, and Cornelius Siegel, the special-effects expert who taught at the University of Bremen. Cornelius was the guy who set the glass factory on fire in *Heart of Glass* and single-handedly built the clock that you see at the start of *Nosferatu*. We asked at the factory how we should go about dyeing 10,000 rats and they gave us the idea of dipping the wire cages for a second into the dye. Cornelius designed this massive conveyor belt for dipping, washing and drying. We had to wash them off with lukewarm water immediately and blow-dry them with a huge system of hair-dryers otherwise they would have caught pneumonia.

What we did before we released the rats in the town was to seal off every single gully, every single side street and doorway. Along the canal we fixed nets to prevent any single animal from getting into the water and even had people in boats down in the canal to collect any creatures that might have escaped. When filming in the town square we had a movable wooden wall just behind the camera, and another in an alley at the end of the street. When the signal was given, both walls moved out of their hiding places and would noisily move towards each other, trapping the rats in an increasingly narrower space so they could then be caged. Fact is, we never lost a single rat.

This was your second outing with Kinski. What was he like to work with this time?

Kinski loved the work and for pretty much the whole time on set he was happy, even though he would throw a tantrum maybe every other day. He was at ease with himself and the world at the time and loved to sit with his Japanese make-up artist Reiko Kruk for hours and hours. He would listen to Japanese music as she sculpted him every morning, putting his ears and fingernails on. We had to do the teeth and ears and shave his head every morning and just seeing him with this enormous patience was a fine sight. I would walk in and sit with him for fifteen minutes. We did not talk, we just looked at each other in the mirror and nodded at each other. He was good with the project, and he was good with himself. Though the film is close to two hours and Klaus is on screen for maybe seventeen minutes, his vampire dominates absolutely every single scene. That is the finest compliment I can give him for his performance. Everything in the film works towards these seventeen minutes. His character is constantly present because of the story and the images which intensify this sense of doom and terror and anxiety. It took fifty years to find a vampire to rival the one Murnau created, and I say that no one in the next fifty years will be able to play Nosferatu like Kinski has done. This is not a prophecy, rather an absolute certitude. I could give you fifty years and a million dollars to find someone better than Kinski and you would fail. And I think Isabelle Adjani is also quite remarkable in the film, the perfect counterpart to Kinski's monster. Her role was an extremely difficult one: she had to be frightened of the vampire and at the same time be attracted to him, something she really managed to communicate to the audience.

Like some of your other features, there was more than one language version of Nosferatu. *What language did you shoot the film in originally?*

As with *Aguirre,* where we had people from sixteen countries on the set, English was the common language. This included Kinski and Adjani. As a filmmaker you have to make a choice, not just to make communication on set easier, but also for the sake of the international distributors, and for them English is always the preferred language. But even though the film was shot in English, we did dub a German version of the film which I have always considered the more convincing version. I do not dare to speak of the 'better' version. I speak of the more 'culturally authentic' version.

Where did you film the scene at Dracula's castle?

Whatever you see of Transylvania was shot in former Czechoslovakia, much of it actually in Moravia at the castle of Pernstein, and in the High Tatra mountains. Originally, I had wanted to shoot in Transylvania proper, in Romania, but was not allowed to because of problems with the Ceauşescu regime. I actually never received a direct refusal from the government, but got word from some friendly Romanian filmmakers who were very supportive of my wishes to shoot in the Carpathians. They advised me to leave the country immediately and not wait for permission, as it would never come as long as Ceauşescu was around. Parliament had bestowed upon him the title of the new Vlad Dracul, the historical defender of Romania. The title had a contemporary meaning: Ceauşescu defending the country against the Soviet Empire. It turned out these local filmmakers were right, though I had a wonderful time in Romania searching for locations, methodically travelling every path of the Carpathian mountains.

Five days after you finished shooting Nosferatu, *you continued with the same crew and, of course, lead actor, and shot* Woyzeck. *Why did you make these films back to back?*

Today *Woyzeck* seems like a little hiccup after *Nosferatu*. It took seventeen days to shoot and only five days to edit, and I would have started shooting the day after we finished *Nosferatu* but we had to let Kinski's hair grow for the role. It was mainly for technical and bureaucratic reasons that we continued with the same crew on a new film. At that time in Czechoslovakia it was an endless saga to obtain shooting permits. We had ended up shooting the second half of *Nosferatu* in Moravia and other places in the eastern part of Slovakia, and I thought it was a good idea to just continue shooting *Woyzeck* but tell the authorities it was still *Nosferatu* we were working on. Actually we did start shooting pretty much the day after *Nosferatu* was completed, and I just shot around Kinski's part.

I don't think that Kinski has ever been better. It is a truly stunning performance.

Kinski was never an actor who would merely play a part. He would exhaust himself completely and after *Nosferatu* he remained deeply in the world that we had created together, something that was glaringly apparent from the first day he walked on to the set of *Woyzeck*. This really gave his performance a different quality and from the opening scenes of the film he seems to be so fragile and vulnerable. Look at the shot of him just after the title sequence where he is just staring into the camera. There is something not quite right with his face. It was actually swollen on one side. What happened was that when he was doing his push-ups during the title sequence the drill major kicks him to the ground. Klaus said to me, 'He's not doing it right, he has to really kick me. He can't just pretend to kick me.' The man who does the kicking is actually Walter Saxer, the man who is being screamed at by Kinski in *Burden of Dreams* a couple of years later. Kinski was kicked so hard into the cobblestones on the ground that his face started to swell up. I saw this and said to him, 'Klaus, stop: do not move. Just look at me.' He was still exhausted from doing his push-ups, but he looks with such power into the camera that it really sets up the feel of the rest of the film.

At the same time he loved playing the part so much and in many ways was very much in balance with himself during the shoot. If something would not go as I had hoped, he would say to me things like, 'Werner, what we are doing here is important, and just striving for it will give it its appropriate size. Don't worry, it will fall in place.' He worked very hard on the text and, unlike so many other times, he generally knew his lines. It was truly a joy to work with him for those days, and I think back on that time with genuine fondness. And yes, he is so good in the role. He truly captured the spirit of the part; there is such a smouldering intensity to him.

This was clearly a project that had been on your mind for a while.

My film of Georg Büchner's *Woyzeck* is probably my simplest connection to what is the best of my own culture, more so than *Nosferatu*, which was more an explicit connection to a world of cinema. Though I have always worked within German culture, making a film of *Woyzeck* meant to reach out to Germany's most significant cultural history, and for this reason there is something in the film that is beyond me. It touches the very golden heights of German culture, and because of this the film sparkles. Yet all I did was reach up and touch these heights.

I had wanted to make a film of *Woyzeck* for some time. For me there is no greater drama in the German language. It is of such stunning actuality. There is no really good English translation of *Woyzeck*, nothing really completely satisfying. The drama is a fragment, and there has been a very high-calibre debate within academic circles as to which order the loose, unpaginated sheets should go in. I used an arrangement of scenes that made the most sense as a continuous story and I think most theatrical productions use this same shape.

Woyzeck is probably my favourite of your features. It is such a tremendously inventive piece of cinema, the way you filmed it in a series of long takes.

We used a series of four-minute-long shots, and so the film is essentially made up of about twenty-five cuts, plus a couple of smaller takes. It was very difficult to maintain this: no one was allowed a mistake. It is a film of such economy that I will probably never achieve again. What made the whole approach exciting is that the film space is created not by cuts and the camera's movement but wholly by the actors, by the force of their performances and their use of the space around them. Look at the scene where Woyzeck tries to flee from the drum major: he heads directly into the lens of the camera and at the last moment is pulled back. In a shot like that Kinski creates a space far beyond that of the camera; he is showing that there is a whole world behind, around *and* in front of the camera. You feel he is crawling desperately towards you, even into you. So the creation of space – and how as a director I used it – became even more important than normal in *Woyzeck*.

I truly like filmmakers who are daring enough to show a whole sequence in one single shot. You really have to let your pants down if you are trying that. What you show on screen has to be *very* strong in order to hold the audience for three or four minutes. Poor filmmakers will often move the camera about unnecessarily and use flashy tricks and an excess of cuts because they know the material is not strong enough to sustain a passive camera. This kind of film-making – full of unnecessary jump cuts and things like this – gives you a phony impression that something interesting might be going on. But for me it is a clear sign that I am watching an empty film.

You seem to have worked with an array of interesting people over the years, very few of them who were actually trained to work in film. I assume that this is a very conscious choice for you?

Many of the people I work with on my films are not professional technicians. One of the keys to filmmaking is surrounding yourself with people who understand exactly what it is you are trying to do, and the only true friends that I have are those I met whilst making my films. Strong men and women, imaginative, dedicated, trustworthy and, importantly, who have faith.

Many of the people with whom I have worked repeatedly over the years are not trained strictly for film work. Yet they are able to bring so much more to the look and feel of a film with their wildly divergent approaches. Ulrich Bergfelder, the set designer on many of my films, is a specialist in old Provençal languages and troubadour literature. Claude Chiarini is a doctor and neurologist in a Parisian lunatic asylum who was on the set of *Heart of Glass* in case one of the hypnotized actors would not wake up properly. He was around for six weeks taking production stills which are still of exceptional quality. Cornelius Siegel, a mathematician and master carpenter, is an ingenious man who can do anything. Peter Zeitlinger, the cinematographer who has shot several of my latest films, used to be an ice-hockey player which means he really understands the physical rhythms that a cameraman needs. Herb Golder, who has been the assistant director on several of my most recent films, is Professor of Classics at Boston University and a karate champion. It is always very important for the people working on a film to know that they are not just employees, but rather part of a team and have a vested interest in doing absolutely the best work possible. For example, on *Fitzcarraldo* the guy at the processing lab had read the screenplay and would look at the footage we were sending him just like a film-maker, to the point where one time I got a message from him asking me where various close-up shots were that he knew I needed.

You said earlier that cinema comes from the 'country fair and the circus, not from art and academicism'. What did you mean by this?

For me, cinema has the same fascination you feel during an eclipse and you see a close-up of the sun with protuberances shooting out that are thousands of times larger than our own planet down here. It is for this reason that I am loathe to address many of the points critics raise about my films, because when everything is explained it gets boring very quickly. It is always the mysterious and those things which do not perfectly fit into a story – the inexplicable images or twists in the tale – that stick out and are memorable. Sometimes I will place a scene or shot into a film that might seem to have no place, yet that is essential to our understanding of the story being told. A good example is in *Kaspar Hauser* with the shot of Croagh Patrick in Ireland that we see after the first attempt on Kaspar's life. It is the same thing in music, these moments of special intensity when suddenly you hear something that rails against the most basic rules you are accustomed to. It is the very nature of storytelling and presentation of images that somehow demand moments like this and that critical analysis cannot penetrate. Really good literature is full of these elements, or maybe is solely these things. All the rest is mere journalism or maybe writing. But not real poetry.

If you truly love film, I think the healthiest thing to do is not read books on the subject. I prefer the glossy film magazines with their big colour photos and gossip columns, or the *National Enquirer*. Such vulgarity is healthy and safe.

NOTES

1 Caspar David Friedrich (1774–1840, Germany) is the painter whose work typifies the German romanticist movement of the nineteenth century. My own favourite is *The Sea of Ice* (1823).

2 'Of course we are challenging nature itself [with this film], and it hits back, it just hits back, that's all. And that's grandiose about it and we have to accept that it is much stronger than we are. Kinski always says it's full of erotic elements. I don't see it so much as erotic, I see it more full of obscenity . . . And nature here is vile and base. I wouldn't see anything erotical here. I would see fornication and asphyxiation and choking and fighting for survival and growing and just rotting away. Of course there is a lot of misery, but it is the same misery that is all around us. The trees here are in misery and the birds are in misery.

I don't think they sing, they just screech in pain. It's an unfinished country. It's still prehistorical. The only thing that's lacking is the dinosaurs here. It's like a curse weighing on an entire landscape. And whoever goes too deep into this has his share of that curse, so we are cursed with what we do here. It's a land that God, if he exists, has created in anger. It's the only land where creation is unfinished yet. Taking a close look at what's around us, there is some sort of harmony. There is the harmony of overwhelming and collective murder. And we in comparison to the articulate vileness and baseness and obscenity of all this jungle, we in comparison to that enormous articulation, we only sound and look like badly pronounced and half-finished sentences out of a [stupid pulp fiction novel], a cheap novel. And we have to become humble in front of this overwhelming misery and overwhelming fornication, overwhelming growth and overwhelming lack of order. Even the stars up here in the sky look like a mess. There is no harmony in the universe. We have to get acquainted to this idea that there is no real harmony as we have conceived it. But when I say this, I say this all full of admiration for the jungle. It is not that I hate it. I love it, I love it very much. But I love it against my better judgment.' (From Les Blank's *Burden of Dreams*.)

3 See John Rowlands' *Hercules Segers* (Scolar Press, 1979).

4 Heinrich von Kleist (1777–1811, Germany) was a playwright and short-story writer whose work includes the plays *Amphitryon* (1807) and *Penthesilea* (1807), and the stories *The Marquise of O* (1808) and *Michael Kohlhaas* (1810).

5 Friedrich Hölderlin (1770–1843, Germany) was a key lyrical poet of the late eighteenth century. He wrote *Hyperion* (1797–99) and published two volumes of Sophocles translations before going insane at the age of thirty-six.

6 Georg Büchner (1813–1837, Germany) wrote the plays *Danton's Death* (1835) and *Woyzeck* (published 1879), and the prose text *Lenz* (published 1839). He was Professor of Anatomy at Zurich University when he died of typhus at the age of twenty-four.

7 D. W. Griffith (1875–1948, USA) was a pioneering Hollywood director who, in the course of his long career which included the features *The Birth of Nation* (1915) and *Intolerance* (1916) as well as hundreds of shorts, revolutionized early narrative cinema. See Richard Schickel's *D. W. Griffith, An American Life* (Limelight, 1996).

8 Friedrich Wilhelm Murnau (1888–1931, Germany) made several films (most of them lost) before directing *Nosferatu – Eine Symphonie des Grauens* (*Nosferatu the Vampire*) in 1922, adapted from Bram Stoker's novel *Dracula*. His later films, including *The Last Laugh* (1924) and *Sunrise* (1927), are equally distinguished. See Lotte Eisner's book *Murnau* (published in French 1964, English translation 1973).

9 Vsevolod Pudovkin (1893–1953, Russia) ranks with Eisenstein as one of the great Russian directors with his film *Storm Over Asia* (1928). His books *Film Acting* and *Film Technique* remain fascinating reading.

10 Luis Buñuel (1900–83, Spain) was perhaps his country's leading twentieth-century film director. His first two films, *Un chien andalou* (1929) and *L'Âge d'or* (1930), both co-written by Salvador Dali, are key works of early surrealist cinema. His later films include *The Discreet Charm of the Bourgeoisie* (1977) and *That Obscure Object of Desire* (1977). See Buñuel's autobiography *My Last Breath* (Vintage, 1994).

11 Akira Kurosawa (1910–98, Japan) remains a strong influence on European and American cinema. His many works include *Rashomon* (1951), *The Seven Samurai* (1955) and *Ran* (1985). See his autobiography *Something Like an Autobiography* (Vintage, 1983).

12 Errol Morris (b. 1948, USA), director of several films including *Gates of Heaven* (1978), *The Thin Blue Line* (1988) and *Mr Death: The Rise and Fall of Fred A. Leuchter, Jr.* (1999).

13 Robert Bresson (1901–98, France) wrote and directed *The Trial of Joan of Arc* in 1962. His other films include *A Man Escaped* (1956), *Pickpocket* (1959) and *L'Argent* (1983). See also his book *Notes on the Cinematographer* (Quartet, 1986).

14 Herzog has described Lotte Eisner's *The Haunted Screen* (published in French 1952, English translation 1969) as the 'definitive and final study' of German expressionist film.

15 Lotte Eisner (1896–1983, Germany) was a renowned historian of German cinema. She fled Germany in 1933, eventually assuming French citizenship, and was the first recipient of the Helmut Käutner Prize for individuals 'whose work has supported and influenced the development of the German film'. See Eisner's autobiography *Ich hatte einst ein schönes Vaterland* (researched and ghostwritten by Martje Grohmann, Wunderhorn, 1984). Wim Wenders dedicated his 1984 film *Paris, Texas* to Eisner.

16 Wolfgang Staudte (1906–84, Germany) directed the first post-war feature (for DEFA, the production company established by the Soviet Union), *The Murderers Are Amongst Us* (1946).

17 Helmut Käutner (1908–80, Germany) made several films banned by the Nazis before and during the war. His post-war work includes *The Last Bridge* (1954) and *The Devil's General* (1955).

18 See Chapter 10 of Patrick McGilligan's *Fritz Lang, The Nature of the Beast* (Faber and Faber, 1997) for more about the German film community who left the country in the wake of the Third Reich's rise to power.

19 Stoker's novel was first published in 1897.

6

Defying Gravity

Les Blank's Werner Herzog Eats His Shoe *is a wonderful short film. How on earth did you end up on a stage in Berkeley, California, munching through your own leather boots?*

I was in Berkeley with Errol Morris, who at the time was a graduate student.[1] Errol is a very talented man, a real comrade in arms. He is one of the people who has started so many projects but never finished them that when you meet him you immediately see this agitation of mind, everything around is aflame. He was one of the great hopes as a cello player until suddenly he abandoned the instrument. Then he said he wanted to make a film but would always complain to me about how difficult it was to find money from producers. I insisted that it was possible to make films without money, that it is faith alone and the intensity of your wishes and not money that result in film. 'Stop complaining about the stupidity of producers, just start with one roll of film tomorrow,' I told him. 'And the day I see the finished work I am going to eat my shoe.' And he did make the film, a wonderful work called *Gates of Heaven* about a pet cemetery.

When I arrived in Berkeley I was wearing the same shoes as when I had made my vow to Errol. The problem was that when I cooked them, that day at the restaurant they had duck as a main course and there was a huge pot of duck fat sitting there. I had reckoned that the duck fat would come to a boiling point at about 140 °C and I would be better off cooking the shoes in the fat than in boiling water. What happened was that the hot fat made the leather shrink and it became even tougher. There was absolutely

166

no way to eat it unless I cut the leather into tiny fragments with a pair of poultry shears and swallowed it down with a lot of beer. I had a whole six-pack of beer which I drank, and I remember kind of staggering out of this place pretty drunk. But don't worry, leather is very easy to digest. And Tom Luddy,[2] who was up there on the stage with me, started distributing small pieces around the audience.

I had a kind of tacit agreement with Les Blank that the resulting film was something strictly for the family album. I had just come from doing pre-production in Peru for *Fitzcarraldo* and had the feeling his footage should not be screened to anyone else. Maybe the film is too private for me to appreciate as something for the public. But Les is such a good filmmaker that I forgive him anything, and today I am kind of glad he captured it on film. A grown-up man should eat his shoes once in a while or do certain things that make equal sense. Today you hear about things like the shoe-eating out of context and it probably seems bizarre, but it is not that I did it as a circus gimmick. It did all make real sense in the context of events. And I did not ever mean to eat my shoe in public. I intended to eat it in the restaurant, but I was pushed a little bit into it.

You stood up there and said that eating your shoes 'should be an encouragement to all of you who want to make films and who are just scared to start'.

Sure, and I wanted to help Errol's film, which at the time did not have a distributor. And anyway, there should be more shoe-eating.

During pre-production in Peru on Fitzcarraldo *you made two shorts in the United States,* God's Angry Man *and* Huie's Sermon. *What was it that attracted you to Gene Scott?*

I could never make a film about or with people whom I do not like, and that includes even the Californian televangelist Dr Gene Scott. As wild as he might be as a public figure, there was something heartbreaking about him, something that moved me. He could never be a friend of mine, but I still liked him a great deal.

I first saw Scott some years before I made my film about him, *God's Angry Man*. Whenever I was in America I would always

God's Angry Man

switch on his programmes and got kind of addicted to them. What I found incredible was the way he would rage at his audience, insisting that 'God's honour is at stake every night' and that it is merely a case of 'Six hundred miserable dollars and you sit there glued to your chair.' He would even threaten the audience, saying things like, 'I'm going to sit here in silence for the next ten minutes, and if there are not $200,000 dollars pledged during that time, I'm going to pull the plug!' And he would just sit and stare into the camera for ten minutes.

I felt he was deeply unhappy. A very intelligent man, but unhappy. There was certainly something of a compulsion to him, and when we made the film he was doing non-stop live shows, six to eight hours a day. He was all alone up there, talking to the camera, day after day and would interrupt his flow a few times by having his singers perform some kind of phony religious song, and this was only because he needed to go to the bathroom. How can you keep something like this up for so many years? I have not seen anything of the man since we made the film, but I hear he has gone completely bonkers and apparently on his television show now he sits in a glass pyramid and talks all about pyramid energies. It seems he has left behind much of his Christian teachings. He somehow appeals to the paranoia and craziness of our civilization, and he is very successful. I know he took issue with the way he came across in *God's Angry Man* and asked me to change the original title, which was *Creed and Currency*.

Huie's Sermon was shot in Brooklyn, New York. I just bumped into Bishop Huie Rogers and asked if I could make a film about him. The film needs no discussion. It is a very pure work about the joys of life, of faith and of filmmaking. There is great joy in the image of Huie as he starts completely harmless and gradually whips himself and his flock up into the most wondrous ecstatic fervour.

Fitzcarraldo is probably the film you're best known for. Yet most discussions centre not around the film itself, but the circumstances under which it was made. When you started work on the film in the Peruvian jungle, did you expect that the media buzz would be so huge?

What I did not expect were things like walking down the street in Munich a few months after *Fitzcarraldo* came out and seeing a man running frantically towards me. All of a sudden he leapt up in the air, kicked me in the stomach, picked himself up from the ground and yelled, 'That's what you deserve, you pig!' The problem was there were very real things going on in the area where we wanted to shoot that had absolutely nothing to do with the film at all. There was a border war building up between Peru and Ecuador and all around us we felt this enormous and increasingly threatening military presence. At every second bend of the river there would be a military camp swarming with drunken soldiers. There were also the oil companies who were exploiting the local oil fields in the areas of the native Indians and who had – with great brutality against the local population – constructed a pipeline across the Indians' territory and across the Andes all the way to the Pacific. During construction they had brought in prostitutes and there were frequent cases of rape.

When we showed up on location in the jungle with the full permission of the local Indians, all the unsolved problems somehow started to revolve around our presence. The media forgot all about the war and the oil because we had *real* media appeal for them. As you know, Mick Jagger was scheduled to be in the film alongside Claudia Cardinale, with Jason Robards as the original Fitzcarraldo. I certainly never wanted to become the dancing bear in the circus of the media, but all of a sudden there was a strange concoction of Claudia and Jagger plus the mad Herzog, a bunch of native Indians, a border war and a military dictatorship. Ultimately, it was not difficult to rubbish the claims the press made, not least because a human rights group sent a commission down to the area and concluded that there had been not one single violation. I had the feeling the wilder and more bizarre the legends were, the faster they would wither away, and this is what happened. After about two years of being criminalized by the press, the whole thing just faded away.

What was the starting point of the story of Brian Sweeney Fitzgerald, the man who loves Caruso so much he wants to build an opera house in the jungle and invite the world-famous tenor to the opening night?

Two things stimulated me to make the film. The first was years before I even thought of the story, when I was looking for locations for another film, and took a drive along the Brittany coast. At night I reached a place named Carnac and suddenly found myself in a huge field of menhirs – huge prehistoric stone blocks – stuck in the ground, some of them nearly thirty feet high and weighing hundreds of tons. They go on for miles in parallel rows inland across the hills, there are something like 4,000 of them. I thought I was dreaming, I just could not believe my eyes. Then I bought a tourist guidebook and read that science still has no clear answer how such big blocks were brought overland to this spot 8,000 or 10,000 years ago and set upright with only stone-age tools. It went on to claim that it must have been ancient intergalactic aliens who put them up. This triggered me and I told myself I was not going to leave until I had worked out a method how – with primitive tools – the stones had been erected. You have to assume that in those days man had only simple hemp ropes or leather thongs. I spent two days thinking about it until I came up with a solution. The method I would use is the following: I would call together

2,000 disciplined men. Let's just assume that I would have to move a menhir over a distance of two kilometres. First I would dig trenches under the stone. Next I would push oak tree trunks into the trenches and move away the rest of the earth, so that the menhir would be resting on the tree trunks. Once this is accomplished the stone could be moved on these wheels with ropes and levers. Give me two months and fifty men and I would be able to move a rock maybe thirty feet high and 200 tonnes two kilometres overland. The reason why I would require 2,000 men is that to get the menhirs into the ground, a ramp of huge proportions with a very slight incline is necessary. It would actually allow an elevation of about twelve metres and would end at an artificial mound with a crater hole. I would move the menhir on its 'wheels' up the ramp towards the mound, finally tipping it into the hole. Once it tilts into the crater with its pointed, light end, you basically have an upright menhir. All that needs to be done is to remove the earth, the mount and the ramp.

Then a friend who years before had helped me raise money for *Aguirre* told me we should go back to the jungle and make another film. I told him that I did not want to make a film in the jungle for the sake of shooting there, I needed a solid story. He told me the true story of Jose Fermin Fitzcarrald, a fabulously wealthy real-life rubber baron at the turn of the century, a man who apparently had a private army of 5,000 men and a territory the size of Belgium. It was all very thin stuff for a film save one detail that he happened to mention: Fitzcarrald had once dismantled a boat, carried it overland from one river to the next and reassembled it once he had reached this parallel tributary. Suddenly I had my story, not a story about rubber, but one of grand opera in the jungle with these elements of Sisyphus. The real Fitzcarrald is not a very interesting character *per se*, just another ugly businessman at the turn of the century, while the history of the rubber era in Peru did not interest me in the slightest. Fitzcarraldo's love of music was my idea, though of course the rubber barons of the past century did build an opera house – the Teatro Amazonas – in Manaus.[3] So the real historical elements of the story were for me merely a point of departure. In my version of events, to raise money to construct an opera house in the jungle, Fitzcarraldo takes a ship up a tributary and, with the help of a thousand natives, moves the boat over a mountain into a parallel river which has millions of rubber trees, but is inaccessible because of the rapids of the Pongo das Mortes further downriver. Thinking back to the menhirs of Carnac, the real question was: 'How do I move a huge steamboat in one piece across a mountain?' Though the film is set in an invented geography, I knew from the start that in telling this story we would have to pull a real boat over a real mountain.

Even before filming started you'd been in the jungle for a couple of years. Why did pre-production take so long?

In the film you see a rusty old boat which Fitzcarraldo repairs. We found it in Colombia, and it was so beyond repair and had such huge holes in its hull that we had to tug it to Iquitos – where we shot the scenes of Molly's brothel at the start of the film – with 600 empty oil drums stuffed into its belly. This ship served as a model for two more identical boats we had to build. While one was being pulled up the mountain, we could be shooting with the other one in the rapids. For a long while Twentieth Century Fox were interested in producing the film, but they proposed we use a model boat and a model mountain, and that was out of the question for me. During these discussions I had already started to build the ships, and it was a very slow procedure since Iquitos does not have a real dock where we could construct them. We also had to build a camp for about a thousand extras and the crew, which took time. Thus pre-production took over three years. Of course, I was doing other things at the same time, but spent a lot of time either in the jungle or travelling up to America or to Europe to pick up things that were needed, or to find more money.

And then, once shooting finally started and we had shot about 40 per cent of the film, Robards became very ill and had to return to the United States, and his doctor forbade him to return. In the meantime Jagger – who played Fitzcarraldo's retarded actor side-kick – had to honour his commitment to a Rolling Stones concert tour and so I decided to write his character completely out of the film because the man was irreplaceable. I liked him so much as a performer that any replacement would have been an embarrassment. He is a great actor, something I feel that nobody had yet seen. And I liked his attitude very much. In Iquitos he had a car we rented for him, and when we had trouble getting people to various places he would chauffeur them for us. I liked that he knew the value of real work; he is an absolute professional in the best sense of the word. Losing Mick was, I think, the biggest loss I have ever experienced as a film director.

Is it true that once Robards had gone you thought about playing the role of Fitzcarraldo *yourself?*

I would have played the part of Fitzcarraldo only as a last resort, and would have been a good Fitzcarraldo simply because what the character has to do in the film was exactly what I had to do as the film's director, and I would not have been undignified in the role. Of course, I would never have been as good as Kinski, and I thank God on my knees that Kinski did it. I met him in a hotel in New York and he was very supportive. I was devastated by everything that had been going on down in Peru, and he opened a bottle of champagne saying, 'I knew it, Werner! I knew I would be Fitzcarraldo! You are not going to play the part because I am much better than you.' Of course, he was right. 'When is the plane leaving for Peru?' he asked. I truly liked him for his professionalism, even though once he arrived at the site where the boat was to be pulled over the mountain and saw how steep the terrain was, his heart sank at once. He was convinced it could not be done and later became the strongest negative force on the film.

In an interview from the time you said that if you were to make a film like Fitzcarraldo *again 'there would be only ashes left of me'.*

People tried to protect me from what they saw as my madness and folly, and at various times I was repeatedly asked, 'Why don't you just rewrite the screenplay and cut out the whole thing of pulling the ship over the mountain?'

There was a lot to deal with. One time a crew member had a strange fit and burnt down my house, a beautiful thatched hut on stilts built by the Indians. About ten days' voyage further up Rio Camisea from where we were working lived the Amehuacas, a nomadic tribal group who had repelled all attempts by missionaries and the military to contact them. That season was the driest in recorded history, and as the river virtually dried out this group

Fitzcarraldo

moved downriver, further than ever before, in search of turtle eggs. They attacked three locals who were extras in the film and who were fishing in our camp, and shot a gigantic arrow right through the throat of one of the men, something you can see in *Burden of Dreams*. His wife was hit by three arrows in her abdomen which left her in critical condition. It was too risky to transport them anywhere, and so we performed eight hours of emergency surgery on a kitchen table. I assisted by illuminating her abdominal cavity with a torchlight, and with my other hand sprayed with repellent the clouds of mosquitoes that swarmed around the blood. The attack had occurred about a day's voyage upriver, and it came silently and in total darkness. Nearly fifty of our best native extras left on a retaliatory raid but luckily never encountered any of the Amehuacas.

Naturally there were also many problems with getting the boat up the mountain, and every spare part had to be shipped in from Miami. Then, once we had actually got the boat to the top, we had to leave it there for six months because there were only two feet of water instead of fifty feet on the other side. I engaged a family with five children and a couple of pigs to live inside it until we got back and finally spent a couple of weeks getting the few shots of the film we needed, those of the ship moving down the other side of the mountain.

And what was it like filming in Iquitos?

Though we constructed an infrastructure there, filming was still very difficult. Phoning long distance was practically impossible, power cuts would occur twice a day, the dirt road from town to our offices was basically a swamp and taxi drivers would refuse to make the journey. I may sound pathetic, but if I would have had to climb down to Hell itself and wrestle a film out of the claws of the devil, I would have done so. It was just not possible for me to allow myself private feelings of doubt whilst in the middle of making *Fitzcarraldo*. When I returned to Germany one time to try and hold all the investors in the film together they asked me, 'How can you continue? Do you have the strength and the will and the enthusiasm?' And I said, 'How can you ask this question? If I abandon this project I will be a man without dreams and I do not want to live like that. I live my life or I end my life with this project.' Had I allowed myself the privilege of hesitating for a single minute, or had I panicked for even a split second, the whole project would have come tumbling down around me immediately.

But you know, the final film was pretty much as I had always hoped it would be, with the exception of the Mick Jagger character. Once the film was finished, Claudia Cardinale said to me, 'Werner, when you came to Rome four years ago, you explained your idea to me and all the difficulties we would have to overcome. Now I see the film and it is exactly as you first described it.'

I can just see the Hollywood version of Fitzcarraldo *with a miniature plastic boat being filmed on a studio sound stage. Were you after realism?*

No, I did not undergo those exhausting things for the sake of realism. When the boat is crashing through the rapids it jerks the gramophone so that suddenly we hear opera music playing, and all the realistic noises fade away to reveal Caruso singing. And at the end of the film, once the boat starts to move, there are fewer and fewer people in shot. It is almost as if the boat were gliding by its own force over the top. Had we shown anyone it would have been a realistic event, an event of human labour. As it is, the whole thing has been transformed into an operatic event of fever dreams and pure imagination, a highly stylized and grandiose scene of jungle fantasies.

Since the Hollywood 'plastic' solution had been ruled out, we ended up with a ship weighing 340 tons that had to be heaved in one piece for well over a mile over a very steep mountain. At the start the gradient was 60 per cent and we levelled it down to 40 per cent, but that is still very steep. And this was in the primeval forest, 1,200 kilometres away from the next real town, Iquitos. We did it all on a budget of only $6 million, much of which had not even been secured by the time shooting began. In the beginning I invested my own money because I knew that no one would be prepared to back a project like this. I started construction of the two ships and the camps for the crew and the actors, though obviously my money would not be enough to pay for everything. But I felt confident that the only way to carry through a project on this scale was just to start moving the train out of the station so that everyone could get an idea of its scale, its speed and its direction. Once this was accomplished, I knew there would be people who would want to jump on board.

Pulling a boat of that size over a mountain would inevitably create situations that nobody had foreseen and so would bring life to the film. For example, I wish we had shot in Dolby stereo because the sound of this boat was so stunning and so amazing no sound engineer could ever have invented what we heard on location. There is a mysterious truth in what we did, and I wanted the audience in a position where they could trust their own eyes. I want to take cinema audiences back to the earliest days, like when the Lumière brothers screened their film of a train pulling into a station. Reports say that the audience fled in panic because they believed the train would run them over. I cannot confirm this, maybe it is a legend, but I do very much like this story. I personally have seen people in a small village in Mexico who kept talking back to the bad guy in a scene in an open-air cinema. One of them even pulled a gun and opened fire at the screen.

I think science-fiction films are wonderful because they are pure imagination and that is what cinema is all about. But on the other hand, all of these films hint that what you see is artificially made in a studio with digital effects. This is the issue of truthfulness in today's cinema. It is not about realism or naturalism. I am speaking of something different. Nowadays even six-year-olds know when something is a special effect and even how the shot is done. I remember when the film was shown in Germany there was shouting from the audiences at the moment when the boat was hoisted up on to the mountain. Little by little they realized that this was no trick.

What about the logistics of pulling the boat over the mountain. Were you certain from the start that it would work?

Of course, there was a certain risk in doing what we did with the boat, and on *Fitzcarraldo* one of the strongest accusations against me was that I risked people's lives during production. Absolute rubbish. The Brazilian engineer who had planned the logistics of moving the boat over the mountain ended up leaving the set of the film because he doubted, once in the jungle, he could actually do it.

As a pretext he pointed out that there was a real danger that the dead post which we had established to take the weight of the boat would be pulled out of the ground if we went ahead with our plans. When he left I stopped production for twelve days with the realization we would have to perform our task without the assistance of a specialist engineer. So we dug a much more stable hole for the dead post – I think it was three times deeper – and sunk a huge tree trunk about thirty feet into the ground, letting it stick out above ground only two feet. It is not difficult to calculate the forces of physical objects like the boat against the post, and I think ten times the weight of the boat could have been sustained by this thing.

We also brought in a heavier and more substantial pulley system. What is so stunning about the kinds of cables we were using is that when they are close to breaking point, they sound unhealthy and sick. From there, the only thing to do is to release the tension and get out of the way, because when a steel cable breaks under such tension it means it is like a gigantic whip, glowing red hot inside from the pressure. With the new dead post there was now a margin of safety that was so massive that there would not be any problems. But even so, I would never allow anyone to get close to the ship – particularly behind it – when it was being pulled up the mountain. The native Indians demanded that if they had to be close to the ship for a shot, the director had to be there as well, which I always felt was a very fair request and acceded to immediately. No one was ever at risk while the ship was pulled over the mountain. No one means no actor, no technician, no extra. The simple reason for this was that the space at the rear of the ship was sealed off from the rest of the set. If the cables holding the ship had snapped, it would have slid down the mountain without harming anyone.

We had about 700 Indians who provided much of the pulling force by moving the winches. Theoretically speaking, I could have pulled the boat over the mountain with my little finger given the fact that we had a pulley system with a 10,000-fold transmission. It would have taken very little strength, though I would have had to pull the rope about five miles to move the boat five inches. I think it was Archimedes who said that you can hoist the whole Earth out of its orbit if you have a pivotal point and a lever sticking far enough out into the universe. So there are very primitive physical laws behind what we did on that mountain. The real Fitzcarraldo moved a far lighter boat from one river system to the next, but he disassembled the boat into little pieces and got some engineers to reassemble it later on. But for what we did there was no precedent in technical history, and no book of instructions we could refer to. And you know, probably no one will ever need to do again what we did. I am a Conquistador of the Useless. The obvious problem was the steep inclination – even though we had flattened it out a little bit – and also that because of the torrential rains there were landslides which meant the boat kept on sinking into the mud.

When I watched Wings of Hope *with an audience recently, one of the questions was about 'how far Herzog is willing to go?', citing the fact that in searching for the crashed plane you cut down a small swath of trees in the jungle to land your helicopter. The portrayal of you as megalomaniacal filmmaker who will stop at nothing is a persona that was probably established during the making of* Fitzcarraldo.

There is no sense of proportion in this kind of criticism. You can see in the shots from *Wings of Hope* that there are hundreds of miles of thick jungle in all direction; it is an ocean of trees. To land that helicopter we cut five trees and some undergrowth, that is all. It was a necessity for the film because otherwise it was a very difficult trek through the jungle for several days. You cannot complain about things like cutting down a tiny swath of trees to land a helicopter. Five trees out of millions and millions of trees. It is like being on a beach and taking a handful of sand home with you. When I made *My Best Fiend*, I went back to the locations we used for *Fitzcarraldo* where we cut the hundred foot wide path over the mountain from one river to the other and there is no trace of us ever having been there. If you did not know where we shot the film, you would never recognize it because twenty years later the side of the mountain looks just as it did before we arrived. There is not one nail, not one scrap of wire left. Absolutely nothing.

The determination with which I work, and my determination to see things through, has nothing to do with so-called megalomania. Some people look at a film like *The Great Ecstasy of Woodcarver Steiner* and accuse me of self-promotion because I appear in the film. But I was actually forced to make an appearance. The German television network for whom I produced the film had a series called *Grenzstationen* [*Border Stations*] which had screened some films that were remarkably good. I had to accept that any film I made for the series would have to conform to the network's rules, one of which was that the filmmaker had to appear in the film as the chronicler of events. It is as simple as that, and because ski-jumping is so close to my heart, I did not find it problematic to film myself as the commentator of events. Regardless, this accusation of megalomania is a good one. Another one floating around was that I was into 'Teutonic mythomania'. So I suppose I got off quite lightly with plain old megalomania.

People still believe that Indians were killed during the pulling of the boat up the mountain.

There is a shot in *Fitzcarraldo* where the boat finally starts to edge up the side of the mountain a few feet before slipping back again, crushing a couple of Indians. I am proud that the scene is so well directed it was claimed these Indians really had died and I had the audacity to actually film their bodies, deep in the mud underneath the boat. Thankfully Les Blank got that shot he used in *Burden of Dreams* – the film he made on the set of *Fitzcarraldo* – where we see the Indians emerging from underneath the boat, laughing, and then washing themselves in the river. I suppose that many of these wild accusations were triggered by shots that looked so convincing.

There were some accidents that occurred during shooting, however. I knew that many of the Indians could not swim – they had come from the mountainous areas – and I would sometimes see some of them taking one of the many canoes we had into the middle of the river. I told them not to do this as I did not want anything to happen to them, and eventually I decided to move the canoes up to higher ground and even chain them together. But one day I was coming round a bend of the river on a speed boat and saw a great tumult on the river bank. I immediately knew something had happened and heard from shouts that a boat had capsized just moments before. I dived down and tried to find these two young men who somehow had managed to steal a canoe. Though one reached the shore, the other drowned, and we never found the body. We also had two plane crashes. Everyone survived, but some people sustained very serious injuries. At our field hospital we were also able to treat many locals who had nothing to do with the film and who might otherwise have been very ill, yet an elderly woman did die of anaemia. Simply, those injuries that occurred on the set of *Fitzcarraldo* were not directly related to the production.

Were there no other less serious incidents directly related to the shooting?

Naturally there are some things that I have to take responsibility for. During the filming of the scene of the boat moving through the rapids, the assistant cameraman Rainer Klausmann was sitting with a camera on a rock in the river covered with moss and surrounded by quite turbulent water. It had not been easy to get to this spot, let alone to stabilize a camera there. We did the shots and the boat smashed against the rocks so badly that the keel was completely twisted around itself. Just past the rapids it ran aground on a sandbank, and we were frantically trying to free it because the dry season was imminent and we knew that the water level would sink even further, preventing any kind of rescue of the ship. So we all had a lot on our minds, and eventually made it back to camp for the night. Next morning at breakfast I look around and cannot see Klausmann. And all of a sudden I ask if anyone had seen him last night, and no one had. We had forgotten him on that rock the day before. I took a boat and went over to the rapids as fast as I could, and saw him just sitting there, hanging on to this rock. He was very angry, and rightfully so. Actually, before that, Klausmann had had bad luck. Near Iquitos there was a dead branch of the river, the kind of place where normally you would find piranhas, but because all the townsfolk and children would go there to swim, we did too. One afternoon we are in the water and all of a sudden I hear a scream and see Klausmann scrambling to shore. A piranha had bitten off the top joint of one of his toes. He could walk only on crutches for the next six weeks.

Weren't most of the claims about your treatment of the locals made during the extended period of pre-production?

That is correct. Months before we had even brought the cameras down into the jungle, the press tried to link me to the military regime in some way and make me out to be a major force in the exploitation of local Indians. In fact, the soldiers were constantly arresting us because for a time I had no official permits to move the ships along the river Marañón. And the reason I did not have the paperwork the military required was that I felt it was better to ask the Indians who actually lived on the river for permission rather than go to the government in Lima. When we got to Wawaim, which was in the vicinity where we wanted to pull the ship over the mountain, we talked at length to local inhabitants, who were happy to help, and I drafted a detailed contract about what needed to be done and how much each person would be paid for this basic exchange of services. They actually earned about twice as much as working for a lumber company.

At that time there was a real power struggle going on within the larger communities of Indians in the general area, which meant there was real opposition to us shooting the film where we had originally planned, even though this opposition came from another completely separate community some distance away. There had been a kind of unofficial tribal council of Aguarunas [the Consejo Aguaruna y Huambisa] that insisted it represented all the communities in the area, even though many Indians where we had established our camp had no idea the council even existed. There was never one voice for the Aguarunas, despite what this group said, and the council was merely trying to make a name for itself by blaming us for having built the oil pipeline and generally being responsible for the military presence. They said we were going to cut a canal between the two river systems which would devastate several of the local communities. They also said we wanted to do real harm to the local population, things like rape their women and use their bodies for grease. It did not help that almost from the start there were rumours from the press that we were smuggling arms and that while we were shooting we had destroyed the Indians' crops. But we were still in the early stages of pre-production and it was many months before a single frame of film was even shot.

Weren't there also attacks from outsiders who came down to the area with the specific intention of inciting the Indians against you?

A political propagandist arrived from France and started showing the local Indians photos of Auschwitz victims, piles of skeletons and corpses. He was one of several activists from other countries who were out there, the kind of people who make up the Diaspora of Shattered Illusions. Most of them were doctrinaire zealots of the failed 1968 revolution who wanted to fulfil their illusions somewhere new. One of the Indian leaders showed me the material given to them and explained that the French guy had tried to convince the Indians that this is how the Germans treat everyone.

After several months of pre-production the military build-up on the border had become very scary. One time we passed by one of the army's encampments on the shore of the river and they fired a shot over our heads. We rowed to shore and were held for a couple of hours. This was the first time I had real doubts about whether we should stay in this area, and finally I made the decision to abandon the camp we had built and find another location for the film. We looked at aerial shots and spoke to pilots and geographers, and concluded that there were only two places in the whole of Peru where the film could be shot. The first one was the site we had just evacuated; the second was 1,500 kilometres to the south, in the middle of the jungle. Actually, I had not yet found the second location before I moved out of the first camp, but could see very clearly that I was the axis of a wheel that was spinning out of control and that we definitely did not belong there. The press jumped on the fact that we were moving deeper into the jungle, away from Iquitos, and they all wondered why I could not just shoot the whole thing outside of the town, which would have made things easier for everyone. Well, naturally it would have made things easier, but I had extreme limitations when it came to suitable locations for the film. I needed two rivers that ran parallel, that almost touched each other, and that had in between them a mountain that was not too big, but not too small either. Most of the tributaries of the Amazon are something like twenty kilometres apart with 2,500 metre-high mountains in between, and for a thousand miles in the vicinity of Iquitos there is no elevation more than ten feet.

Only a few people remained in the first camp, and I maintained the medical outpost there for the local people. I felt that as long as I could pay for a doctor, one should remain there, and I secretly hoped by doing so things would fall into place. It was only after the camp was almost entirely evacuated that some Aguarunas of the tribal council who did not live in the area set the huts on fire. They brought some press photographers along with them. Around that time, I do not recall whether before or after, the border war between Peru and Ecuador broke out in the immediate vicinity.

There was even a tribunal in Germany established to try you in absentia for your crimes. Who were these people?

A group of doctrinaire left-wing ideologues, another sad leftover of 1968, accused me of torturing and imprisoning native Indians, depriving them of their culture, and so on. Their accusations were so bizarre that even some of the press who normally loved this kind of stuff did not listen to what was being said. In fact it was very obvious that we had not invaded a tribe of untouched natives. The Aguarunas were politically the best organized group in Peru. They communicated via short-wave radio, loved kung fu videos, and most of the men had served in the army. In *Burden of Dreams* you can see some of the Indians wearing John Travolta T-shirts, and it was claimed that I had sent a load of these T-shirts into the Amazon.

The only serious allegation lingering was that I had four Indians arrested by the military. I went to the town of Santa Maria de Nieva to uncover the facts for myself, and it turned out all four men actually existed but had never had the remotest contact with the production of the film. One of them had actually been in jail for about a week, but only because he had unpaid bills in every bar in town. Upon my request, Amnesty International looked into the reports of human rights abuses and I think they unofficially spread word that I was not causing any problems. Of course, the media took no notice as this was not a good story for them. Typical of the climate was a big report in *Der Stern* magazine. A photographer was sent to our jungle set where he took at least a thousand pictures, none of which were published. Instead the magazine ran photos from their archives of naked Amazon Indians spearing fish, hinting we had intruded into a sanctuary of 'uncontaminated' natives.

How did Les Blank come to shoot Burden of Dreams? *You said that if it wasn't for the fact that twenty years ago you gave him several discarded scenes from the original version of the film with Robards and Jagger, then you would never have been able to cut them into your film about Kinski,* My Best Fiend, *all those years later.*

That is correct, I did not keep any of the footage of Robards and Jagger, and the only scenes that still exist are those from Les's film. I did not invite Les Blank to the jungle, but he was very eager to come down and make a film down there. I was at first quite reluctant to have a camera around because there is something distasteful about making films about films. When you work, like when you cook a meal at home, and there is someone staring at your hands, watching what you are doing all the time, suddenly you are not a good cook any longer. I have the feeling that we function differently when being observed. But Les turned out to be a good presence. He is very unobtrusive and he certainly does have a good eye. But something to remember is that what he recorded for his film was shot in only five weeks, while *Fitzcarraldo* took four years to make. So he captured only a tiny fraction of what went on during the making of the film.

What I always liked about Les was that he was not some sort of a court jester who would adulate the production. Most of the time he would hang around the camp where the natives would do their cooking. He would cook with them, he would shoot trails of ants, he was as much interested in what was going on with the ants as he was with the film itself. I always liked that attitude. Though in some sequences the film might not project a particularly favourable image of me, I do like *Burden of Dreams*, though it did cause some problems for me. For example, at one point in the film I talk of how people have lost their lives, but Les did not include my explanation of the circumstances in his film. He just cut it out, and so all of a sudden it sounds as if I had risked lives for the sake of a film. This stench followed me for a whole decade.

In Burden of Dreams *there are shots of you and Kinski on the boat as it moves through the rapids. Was it your idea to take a camera crew out there?*

Yes, but I certainly never forced anyone to come with me; they all came on board of their own volition. It was just like when we did

La Soufrière: I made sure that everyone made up their own mind. Kinski was immediately eager to do it. He always had a good knowledge of what would work on the screen and knew this was a moment he should be involved with. Actually, he pushed me because I had some hesitation. What happened was that before we could even set up the cameras, the fourteen steel hawsers broke simultaneously under the enormous thrust of the water and the boat took off through the rapids with nobody to steer it, though there were some people on board: the cook and his pregnant wife. After this incident we set up three cameras and filmed the boat striking against the rock wall river banks. The anchor pierced the hull and the keel twisted up like a sardine-can lid around its key, but the boat was so solidly built, with its steel lining and protective air-chambers, that it did not sink. Once that was done, I had the feeling it would be good for the film if we had a scene with Fitz-carraldo waking up realizing that the boat is careering through the rapids. I wanted to do it for real so asked who wanted to come along. I knew there was a danger, and everyone was left in no doubt that getting on the boat to film the sequence was most definitely a risk that could not be fully calculated.

With great effort – it took about ten days – we managed to winch the second boat through the rapids against the current and we got on board. There were seven people on board with three cameras. We tied Jorge Vignati and his camera with two belts to the back wall of the helm, and when we hit a rock he was jerked so hard that he broke a couple of ribs. And Beat Presser, who was not very attentive, hit his head on the camera which was cemented to the deck and suffered a concussion. And you can see what happened to Thomas Mauch in *Burden of Dreams*; he flew through the air with the heavy camera in his hand and on impact split his hand apart between his fingers. Only two days previously all of our anesthetic had been used during emergency surgery on the two Indians hit by arrows. As we had many Peruvian lumbermen and oarsmen, we had been advised by a local missionary to have two prostitutes stationed in our camp, otherwise the men would chase after the women in the next settlement. As we fixed up his hand without anesthetic, one of these women consoled Mauch in his agony by burying his face between her breasts and telling him how much she loved him.

We all got off the boat once it had passed through the rapids, almost immediately after which it dug itself into a gravel bank. We tried to pry it loose, but in the end had to face the fact that the boat could not be moved until the rainy season, which was months away, because of the low water level. Since we needed it for various shots on the river, especially for the big crowd scenes in Iquitos, and because the other boat was being pulled up the mountain, it was clear we would have to come back later in the year to finish filming. We were prepared for something like this to happen because it was not all that unlikely the ship would sink in the rapids. The speed of the water was more than sixty kilometres per hour and there were large whirlpools all over the place. If it had sunk, we would have had a couple of minutes of material we could use from the four cameras. I would have just edited out the shots where the ship goes down and replaced them with shots of the second ship. No way would we have ever sent the boat through the rapids without having a feasible back-up plan and a second ship.

One thing that always seemed a little unclear in the film to me is exactly why the Indians agree to help Fitzcarraldo in the way they do.

The Indians are just as obsessed as Fitzcarraldo is. While his dream is to build an opera house, they want to rid themselves of the evil spirits that inhabit the rapids, which is why they release the ship into the rapids. They are on a mythic mission, one that Fitzcarraldo himself never quite understands. We spectators are similarly left in the dark about their true motivation and never really understand why they are toiling, why they go into all this trouble to tow the ship over the mountain. Only when they cut it loose and it hurtles through the rapids do we truly understand. By sacrificing the ship, they want to calm the evil spirits who dwell in the rapids. So it is only the Indians who make their dream come true. They win and Fitzcarraldo loses, though ultimately he converts this defeat into a triumph through the power of his imagination and creative spirit.

At the end of the film we know that Fitzcarraldo has bankrupted himself, yet that he will be up to more mischief before long. Who knows, a week later he might decide to finally finish his trans-Amazon railway. This is a guy who will always stand his ground.

And like him, we have all got to try to make our own dreams come true, even if it is against all odds. An image like the ship moving across a mountain seems to give us all courage for our own dreams. This is a film that challenges the most basic laws of nature. Boats just are not meant to fly over mountains. Fitzcarraldo's story is the victory of the weightlessness of dreams over the heaviness of reality. It defies gravity head on, and by the film's end I hope that the audience feels utterly elated and even lighter than when they went in. One reason I used opera music is the strange effect it creates in translating the reality of a boat moving over a mountain into dreams. Everyone always compares the film to *Aguirre* because they both have Peru, jungle rivers and Kinski. But as I explained earlier, it is actually much more like *The Great Ecstasy of Woodcarver Steiner* because both men are dreamers who want to defy the laws of gravity.

Do you know what the lasting effect of your work with the Indians was?

Our presence in that part of the jungle was ephemeral, yet to some degree helpful because so much attention was focused on the problems of native Indians in the Peruvian rain forests. When we shot the film we were conscious that we should do more for the Indians than merely pay them for their services. The younger men dreamt of buying Honda motorcycles as they had loved them ever since their army service, even though there were no roads in the jungle. What had a longer-lasting effect was that we built a boat so they could transport their crops to the next market. Their own dug-out canoes were too small. Normally, travelling merchants would buy things from them for very low prices and make huge profits further downriver. It was also clear that lumber and oil companies were quite a threat, and the Indians wanted us to assist them to get land rights for their territory, so we sent in a land surveyor to chart their land. I even took two Indians to see the President of the Republic, Belaunde, who promised to co-operate. The two delegates wanted to bring proof home that they had been in Lima and had seen the ocean. I remember vividly how they waded with their blue jeans into the surf and filled two bottles with sea water which they took back to the jungle. We assisted them for a couple of years so they would get legal title to their land. By the time I was back there a few years ago to shoot *My Best Fiend*, they had succeeded in obtaining their land title, while on the other side of the river – land that was not part of the Indians' territory – there is a camp and an airfield that belongs to the oil companies. Actually it seems to be one of the largest deposits of gas in the world. But to this day there is absolutely no drilling on the land of the Indians. They really do have control over it, and so I do feel that we assisted them in a small way, even though their moral and historical right to the territory was always absolutely unquestionable.

You said earlier that the best way to fight a rumour is with an even wilder rumour. Is that how you handled the attacks from the media?

At one point the entire Italian press exploded with the story that Claudia Cardinale had been run over by a truck and was critically injured. A hysterical journalist from Italy somehow reached me on the phone in Iquitos – it sometimes took forty-eight hours to place a phone call down there – and I remember this crazed voice asking me about her. I calmly told him that I had just come back from a restaurant in Iquitos with her only a few minutes previously, and that she was quite OK. But it did not stop, it just got worse, and we started to hear that reports of her injuries were spreading all over the world. Two days later this journalist reached me from Rome yet again and I had a flash of inspiration. I said to him, 'Sir, please do not repeat what you have written so far. It is actually much more serious than that. Not only was Claudia Cardinale badly injured when she was hit by the truck, the truck driver was a barefoot drunkard who raped his unconscious victim.' There was a minute of silence, and then he hung up. From that moment on there was never a line about her and this truck.

You said that the rumours followed you for a decade. Was this a real problem for you?

The rumours never concerned me, either back then or later on. There is something about time, how it sorts things out and allocates the right significance to things. Not always, but usually.

189

Hopefully this book will do that.

No, let's not do this book for that purpose. I can argue against all the accusations best, perhaps, with the film itself. There is a moment when Fitzcarraldo tells the story of a Frenchman who was the first white man to see the Niagara falls, at a time when America was hardly settled. Upon relating what he had seen, the man was called a liar. 'What is your proof?' he was asked. 'My proof is that I saw it!' was his answer. I – and many others – were eyewitnesses to what happened during the making of *Fitzcarraldo*, and what is remarkable is that in every story the media came up with, I was able to get acquainted with a Werner Herzog who had very little to do with me. So be it. I feel safe from the world knowing that in between myself and the rumours is a layer of false Herzogs who will protect me. In fact, let's get more of these *doppelgängers*, these stooges, out there. I offer a good wage.

Your next film also caused you some trouble. How did you get involved with Ballad of the Little Soldier, *probably your most political work? It's about the struggle fought by the Nicaraguan Miskito Indians, allies of the Sandinistas in the revolution against Somoza, in their own rebellion against the Sandinistas.*[4]

May I correct you: it is about children who are fighting in a war, not a film about the Sandinistas or Somoza. As it was filmed in Nicaragua, the dogmatic left – for whom the Sandinistas at that time were still the sacred cow – could not accept that I was not working alongside the CIA on the project. But the film is not 'political'. It was made because a friend of mine, Denis Reichle, had started to make a film about child soldiers and got stuck with the project and asked me to help.

Who is Reichle?

He is a photographer and writer who for decades travelled extensively to inaccessible places to cover oppressed minorities from the inside. He is an equally daring and prudent man who has survived civil wars, riots and even five months' captivity by the Khmer Rouge in Cambodia. As an orphan of fourteen, he was drafted into *Volkssturm*,[5] the battalions made up of children and older men that Hitler used in the defence of Berlin in the final months of the war, an experience Reichle was lucky to survive. Because he was originally from Alsace, he became a French citizen after the war and with his military experience was sent off to Indochina, where he survived Dien Bien Phu.

Denis is the most fearless person I know. He arrived in East Timor as the mass murder of hundreds of thousands started, just after the Portuguese had left their former colony. Nobody dared to land on shore, so he swam the last kilometre from a small fishing boat holding his camera above his head. He has unnerving knowledge and finely tuned instincts about danger because he has been in it so much. One time he was driving a jeep in Angola, a country absolutely saturated with landmines. Travelling down a country road he saw some boys sitting under the shadow of a huge tree just outside of town. As he advanced towards them, all of a sudden he spotted them plugging their ears with their fingers. Denis slams on the breaks immediately and stops about six feet away from a landmine. He knew the boys wanted to watch him blow up. He is the most methodical man I know, which is why he has lived so long.

What is the background to the film?

Originally the Miskitos had fought against Somoza as allies of the Sandinistas, and in their social structure they traditionally lived a primitive form of socialism. The Sandinistas wanted to help the Indians take a step forward towards 'real' scientific socialism, and in an attempt to reorganize the village communes a whole strip of Miskito land on the Honduran border was categorically depopulated and sixty-five towns and villages razed to the ground. The excuse the Sandinistas gave was they wanted to transform the region into a military zone of protection against the Contra rebels, and inevitably, after these great abuses had been committed against them, the Indians broke from the Sandinistas.[6]

For some people, showing nine-year-old kids fighting against the Sandinistas meant I was clearly an American imperialist. No one would even contemplate that the Sandinistas could violate the essential rights of native Indians, which even the Sandinistas themselves admitted later on. *Ballad of the Little Soldier* actually turned into a film that really had some practical results because

Ballad of the Little Soldier

afterwards I was invited by the Sandinistas to screen the film in Nicaragua, and a couple of years later practical politics really did change to a certain degree. But the film does not mince its words and when it was released I was immediately labelled as being in the pay of the CIA.

The intellectuals were simply unable to understand that politically dogmatic cinema is not something I practise, and they did not bother to look at what the film is really about; rather, they superimposed their own political views on to *Ballad of the Little Soldier*. At the time it was known to everyone that the United States was actively working against the socialist regimes of Central America, but *Ballad of the Little Soldier* is still in no way any kind of direct comment on American foreign policy or anything like that. For me the human element to the story is the key to the film. During the making of the film, many things became clear to me; for example, when I talked to a young girl who left the village early in the morning with a rifle and returned in triumph because she had traded it for a chicken. This war was about a traditional culture being ripped apart by the introduction of modern instruments of killing, and to talk about it in political or military terms is not useful. I wanted to concentrate on the child soldiers, and as such could actually have filmed in any number of other countries, like Liberia or Cambodia. It does not matter what political content there is when you have a nine-year-old fighting in a war. Child soldiers are such a tragedy that you do not need every single detail of the conflict. I think at the time about twenty per cent of the Miskito army was less than thirteen, and some were as young as nine. What was most interesting about the Miskito children was that they were all volunteers, and a very personal and traumatizing experience had forced every one of them to take up arms. I talked to a young boy in a commando unit who was in a state of shock and who could barely speak. His two-year-old brother, six-year-old brother and his father had all been killed and his mother cut in pieces before his eyes. He had not yet finished his training, but he wanted to go out the next day and kill. In fact, many of the children you see in the film were dead by the time the film was released.

Your next film, The Dark Glow of the Mountains, *contains one of my favourite scenes in any of your films. You stand with Austrian mountaineer Reinhold Messner and talk about how you'd like to just walk and walk until the world ends.*

Messner talks of his desire to walk from one Himalayan valley to the next without ever looking back. He says that 'either my life or the world stops. Presumably it will be that as my life ends, so will the world.' This is something that I have always thought about. I like the idea of just disappearing, walking away, turning down the path and just carrying on until there is no more path to follow. I would like to have Huskies with leather saddle bags and just walk and walk on until there is no road left.

Who is Reinhold Messner?

In the 1970s Messner[7] was one of the young climbers who brought a new approach to the sport. He was determined to climb the peaks of the Himalayas alpine style and succeeded in reaching the peaks of all fourteen mountains over 8,000-metres that exist on this planet, and did it without large-scale expeditions with hundreds of sherpas. He was the first to climb in the Himalayas with just a rucksack and no fixed camps, and also the first to

The Dark Glow of the Mountains

climb Mount Everest without oxygen – what he called 'fair means' – considered a great achievement in the mountain-climbing community. An Italian named Maestri, a very famous climber of the 1950s and 1960s, used to scale peaks by hauling himself up inch by inch with sledgehammers and hooks and machine drills. It would take him weeks and weeks to get to the top. Frankly, an utterly ridiculous thing to do. I could climb the World Trade Center if I had all that equipment and three months to spare. Maestri's approach was another case of the perversion of adventurism in mountain climbing. He shamed and embarrassed every mountain he climbed this way. Messner, by using as little technical equipment as possible, really is the father of modern mountaineering, a man with an incredibly professional attitude. He is a man of fantastic survival skills, truly amazing. Not only technical skills, but also his sense of exactly what is happening and when something is not right. I have learned a lot from him about evaluating danger.

The Dark Glow of the Mountains came from questions I was asking myself. Why did Messner – a man who lost his brother during an expedition – feel the need to climb Nanga Parbat for a second time? What motivates a man like this? One time I asked him, 'Don't you think you're a little deranged to keep climbing mountains?' 'All creative people are insane,' he said to me. I always felt the man had the wisdom of the snake, sitting there coiled up, waiting for the opportunity to strike. One time he said to me that he was unable to describe the feeling that compels him to climb any more than he could explain what compels him to live.

For me the film was also some kind of predecessor to something much bigger that I wanted to do. I wanted to make a feature film in the high altitude zone of K2, the second highest and most beautiful of the Himalayan mountains, and in preparation for this I wanted to make a relatively small film in the extremes of the 8,000-metre-high mountains with Messner and his climbing partner Hans Kammerlander to test the situation, learn about the logistic difficulties of filming up there and what technical problems we might experience. I needed to know how feasible it was to get supplies for everyone up there. During filming we experienced temperatures so low that raw stock in the camera would break like uncooked spaghetti. Later in the filming a gigantic avalanche hit the bottom of the glacier a mile away from us. Like an atomic explosion, the impact sent a cloud of snow towards us, and wiped out our camp. I quickly abandoned my plans.

Did you feel you were pushing Messner too far when you asked him about his brother?

Messner has appeared on every single talk-show that German television has ever aired. He has a very polished media attitude, he is a great showmaster and knows how to handle all kinds of media situations. Messner knew in making the film that I would be digging deep into the untouchable parts of him, and might ask difficult questions about the Himalayan expedition where his brother died. Before we started the film I told him, 'There will be situations in which I will go far. But you are a smart fellow, you know how to defend yourself.' It was difficult to decide whether to keep the sequence with him weeping in the film, but I finally called him up and said, 'You have done these lifeless talk-shows all your life. Now, all of a sudden, something very personal has been brought to light, you are here as someone who is not just another perfect athlete or who conquers every mountain with cold perfection. That is why I have decided to keep the scene.' And once Messner saw the finished work he was glad we went as far as we did.

What was difficult at first was getting him to appear on camera as himself. The first thing we shot was a sequence right in front of Nanga Parbat. We were driving at night and when I awoke the next morning I saw the mountain right in front of me. It was absolutely stunning, not a cloud in the sky. Nanga Parbat is something like Messner's nemesis: it is where his brother died and where he lost most of his toes. So I woke Messner up and got him in front of the camera, and immediately he starts this kind of media-rap that he is so used to giving. I stopped the camera immediately and said, 'That is not the way I want to do a film with you. There is something deeply and utterly wrong to continue like this. Not one foot of film will be wasted that way. I need to see deep inside your heart.' Messner looked at me kind of stunned and was silent most of the rest of the day. Towards evening he came to me and said, 'I think I have understood.' There would be no mercy for him, because film *per se* knows no mercy.

What mountain is it they are climbing in the film?

I should explain that in mountain climbing it is considered a particular feat to climb an 8,000-metre mountain, and Messner has done them all. To traverse a mountain using one route and then climb down the other side of the same mountain is considered an extraordinarily difficult feat. But what Messner and Kammerlander did during this expedition was traverse *two* 8,000-metre mountains – Gasherbrum 1 and 2 – in one go, something never attempted before. And they did it without oxygen and sherpas, a remarkable feat of climbing that has never been repeated. They set off at 2 a.m. in the morning in pitch darkness with lights on their helmets and had to maintain a fantastic speed as they could carry only a small amount of provisions. Of course there was no way for me to follow them with a camera, that was clear from the start, so the shots of the summit are taken by Messner himself. When they took off for the summit Messner said to me, 'Maybe we will not survive this. If you do not hear from us within ten days we must be dead. It would take twenty days for help to arrive, much too long to save us. So if this happens, you take over the expedition and see that the sherpas get paid with the money I deposited in such and such a place.' And then he left without uttering another word. I had not even asked him a question.

I went only as far as the base camp, a little over 5,000 metres up. But then I climbed – without a camera – with a Spanish expedition another 1,500 metres. They had some supply camps they wanted to clear out and I went to help them retrieve things, so they took me along a very difficult and dangerous area of the glacier. Slabs of ice as big as office blocks that keep on shifting. It is easy to perish there because of deep crevasses in the vast shifting masses. The Spaniards moved up very quickly and I realized when we had arrived at the camp that I had signs of altitude sickness. The symptoms are clearly recognizable. You become very apathetic, and I remember just sitting down in the snow with my whole body just slumped. It was very alarming to me and I decided to go down to the camp on my own, which was an utterly stupid thing to do. I almost fell into a snow-covered crevasse. I had a very lucky escape.

One of my favourite photos of you is on the set of Fitzcarraldo *in the jungle, the clapper-board is in your mouth and you're clambering up the hillside while Kinski stands proudly looking down at you. When you were making the film there was much talk in the press of you being an 'adventurer' in the jungle. Are you an adventurer? Or maybe an explorer? I've also read in plenty of places that you're most definitely a masochist too.*

I think I would be the last one who could be labelled a masochist. It comes to this, plain and simple: things have to be done for the sake of the film, personal sacrifices maybe have to be made, and once you decide on a certain project like *Fitzcarraldo*, it just does not matter how many difficulties are encountered and how much pain it costs. I knew full well what the film would involve and knew that I myself was insignificant compared to the work we had to do, regardless of whether it cost many sleepless nights or gallons of sweat or whatever. I always wanted to be a good soldier who wants to win, does not complain and holds the position that others have already abandoned. The hardships encountered do not interest me and they should not interest the public either. The only thing that counts is what you see on the screen.

We have spoken of risk-taking and the accusations that I am a megalomaniac. Another one that comes up is that I purposely make things more difficult for myself and the actors. I assure you I would rather have filmed *Fitzcarraldo* in the middle of Central Park, the only problem being there is no jungle there. I would have directed from a suite on Fifth Avenue, just like a few years later I would rather have filmed *Scream of Stone* in Munich where I could have slept in my own apartment and travelled to the set on a funicular. For years I have been explaining that while maybe mountaineers are motivated to seek out the most difficult routes, this would be wholly unprofessional and irresponsible for me as a filmmaker. You can bet your life I would never have made a single film if I had purposely sought out trouble. Filmmaking is difficult enough already, and it is just plain bad luck that I am drawn to characters like Fitzcarraldo whose mission is to pull a boat over a mountain. I am never seeking adventure; I am just doing normal work.

There is such a vast difference between exploring and adventuring. I am curious. I am searching for new images and dignified places, but I am *not* an adventurer, even though I am often given that contemptible tag. To me, adventure is a concept that applies only to those men and women of earlier historical times, like the mediaeval knights who travelled into the unknown. The concept has degenerated constantly since then and turned into an ugly embarrassment when, in the nineteenth and twentieth centuries, people attempted to reach the North and South Poles. Such acts contradict my definition of adventure, for those kinds of voyages served only the purpose of self-promotion, nothing else. There is nothing interesting about the North Pole; it is just water and drifting ice, and I feel the labelling of these kinds of voyages as the great remaining adventures of humankind was an embarrassment.

Is this something to do with the fact that so many of these kinds of voyagers have attempted to domesticate and conquer nature?

Exactly, and that so many speak of their travels in such military terms. 'We conquered the summit.' 'We returned victorious over Mount Everest.' I just cannot stand it. And what's more, local mountain people do not climb the mountains; they respect them much more than these so-called 'adventurers'. There is some foul philosophy behind this quest of adventure. I would like to make a comparison with a river that is sick. You find dead fish, white, bloated and belly up, floating in the water. Today, the concept of adventure has this kind of rottenness to me. Oh, what a big shot you were in 1910 when you came back from Africa and told the ladies how many elephants you shot! Do the same thing at a party today and you will have the first available glass of champagne tossed in your face. Very soon from now, 'adventurers' should receive the same treatment.

I particularly hate this old pseudo-adventurism where the mountain climb becomes about confronting the extremes of humanity. I had some arguments with Messner about this. For a while he stylized his media persona on the concept of 'The Great Adventurer' and would make pronouncements that he was some kind of vicarious adventurer for the public. Me, I am waiting for the ridiculous act of the first one barefoot on Mount Everest. My God, you can even book an 'adventure holiday' to see the headhunters of New Guinea. Just make sure you follow your tour guide and do not get lost. This is the kind of absurdity pervading the utterly degenerate concept of 'adventurism', one that reveals only its ugly face nowadays.

On the other hand, I love the Frenchman who crossed the whole of the Sahara in reverse gear in a 2CV. And I love people like Monsieur Mange Tout, who ate his own bicycle. I think he also tried to eat a twin-engined aeroplane. What a guy!

He's dead.

Really? Ah well, there will surely be another like him.

NOTES
1 See Chapter 5, foonote 12.
2 Tom Luddy (b. 1943, USA), film producer, co-founder of the Telluride Film Festival and former head of Berkeley's Pacific Film Archive.
3 Construction started in 1882 at the height of the rubber boom and it opened on New Year's Eve 1896. 'No expense was spared to make

Teatro Amazonas the grandest opera house in the world. Everything was brought from Europe: wrought iron staircases from England, crystal chandeliers from France, classical busts and marble from Italy. The wood is Brazilian, but it was sent to Europe to be polished and carved.' (*Daily Telegraph*, 17 June 2001.)

4 See Bernard Diederich's *Somoza and the Legacy of U.S. Involvement in Central America* (Junction Books, 1982).

5 The *Volkssturm* was established in September 1944. All previously non-conscripted men between the ages of sixteen and sixty (totalling 6 million) were called up in this last-ditch attempt to ward off the Allied forces. The battalions were deployed mainly in areas close to where they had been assembled, but remained very poorly trained and led, and were often forced to fight with captured weapons. More often picks and shovels were used.

6 Roxanne Dunbar Ortiz's 'The Miskito Indians of Nicaragua' (Minority Rights Group, 1988) gives political and historical background to the issues raised in *Ballad of the Little Soldier*, while George Paul Csicsery's article '*Ballad of the Little Soldier*: Werner Herzog in a Political Hall of Mirrors' (*Film Quarterly*, Winter 1985/86) describes the political controversy raised by the film.

7 Reinhold Messner (b. 1944, Italy) was for many years considered the world's greatest mountain climber. More recently he has been pursuing his interest in the Yeti, who he allegedly encountered in Tibet in 1986. Since 1999 he has been a Member of the European Parliament for the Green Party. See his book *All Fourteen Eight-Thousanders* (Crowood Press, 1999).

7
The Work of Illusionists

In the 1979 documentary about you, I Am My Films, *you said, 'I could have made my films anonymously and still people seeing the films would know me pretty well.' What did you mean by that?*

It was more than twenty years ago and it all sounds rather heavy to me now. But there is a certain truth in it and I can still accept a statement like that, though with much more caution today. The low-level answer to your question is that the people in my films – particularly the real-life ones – are for me not just mere characters; they are a vitally important part of my life. The more I have progressed as a filmmaker, the more I find it is real life I have been filming, *my* life. I do not sit and write a script about something that interests me and then feel in some way detached from what I have just written, as if I have freed myself from it. Rather, these two procedures – being fascinated by something and then processing it into a film – are simultaneous and inextricably linked. Sure, there are some films that are not as close to me as others, but I really do like *all* my films, maybe with the exception of the first two. I love them as I love my children. Children are never perfect, one might have a limp, the other a stutter, they all have their weaknesses and their strong points. But what matters is that they are all alive; it just does not matter that every single one of my films is flawed in some way. Although I have made many films, they are all present in my being all my time. In this respect I am like some of the African tribesmen who can count only up to ten, but they only need to cast a glance at their herds of 600 cattle to realize whether some of them are missing. Or like a mother of many children who can tell if one is missing when she enters a train compartment in which she has placed them. And like that mother, I know some of my children are missing and that a few of them are still on their way, the films that I have not yet made. The opportunity – or event – of making them has not yet occurred.

I am not like some other filmmakers who, having finished one project, sets about looking for the next screenplay to film or the rights to the next big bestseller to buy. For me, it has always been a question of doing just one single thing: searching for a new grammar of images and expressing this desire through the films I have made. I hope you can see that the films count much more than anything I can possibly tell you as we sit here. I am some strange creature moving on through life and leaving tracks in the sand. The tracks are my films. As a child I never asked myself, 'What shall I do with my life?' It just never occurred to me that I even had a choice. Sure, I can sit here and talk about how and when the films were made, but it is so misleading to have you focusing on me personally because the only thing that really counts is what you see on the screen.

I can only hint at a higher-level answer to your question, and that has to do with an attitude I have towards certain things. I have asked myself why am I different from, let's say, most of the Americans who have goals in life and who strive for happiness. The 'right' to happiness is even in their Declaration of Independence. I keep on asking myself why I do not care so much about happiness. I simply do not have goals in life. Rather, I have goals in existence. I would make a very clear distinction between the two, and I hope that makes sense to you.

A little. Do you consider yourself to be an independent filmmaker?

What does it really mean to be independent? Independent from what? There is no independent cinema, with the exception of the home movie made for the family album. I remember one time I was shooting in New York and showed up with my rental van at the place where I wanted to rent some equipment. The man said, 'You cannot pick it up yourself, a union truck has to deliver it.' I said, 'But my van is ten feet from your door here.' There was an endless debate until I just picked up the cameras and carried them to my van. An absolute waste of time. In Hollywood there are too many rituals and hierarchies, and to be independent means to be free of things like this. I have always known that true independence is a state of mind, nothing more. I am self-reliant. That probably describes me better.

Has it generally been easy to find money for your films?

For my entire working life I have struggled to find money. But the money is really not that important. I knew the second I walked out of the office of those producers all those years ago that I would never shoot a single frame of film if I continued wasting my time with people like that. If you want to make a film, just go and make it. I cannot tell you the number of times I have started shooting a film knowing I did not have the money to finish it. Financing of films only comes when the fire ignites other fires. That is what happens when you are into filmmaking. It is a climate you have to create, one that has to be there otherwise nothing is going to happen. I am not into the culture of complaint. Everyone around the world, whomever I meet, starts to complain about the stupidity of money. It seems to be the very culture of filmmaking. Money has only two qualities: it is stupid and it is cowardly. Making films is not easy; you have to be able to cope with the mischievous realities around you that do everything they can to prevent you from making your film. The world is just not made for filmmaking. You have to know that every time you make a film you must be prepared to wrestle it away from the Devil himself. But carry on, dammit! Ignite the fire. Create something that is so strong that it develops its own dynamic. Ultimately, the money will follow you like a common cur in the street with its tail between its legs.

The best example of this happened many years ago. I wanted to publish my screenplays and prose texts, and by this time I had something of an international reputation, so I approached Suhrkamp Verlag to see if they would be interested in publishing the books. When they turned me down, I immediately realized that there was no point spending time sending out letters to other publishers asking them the same question. So I just set up my own publishing house, Skellig, and published *Heart of Glass* and two volumes of screenplays which included *Aguirre, Fata Morgana, Signs of Life* and *The Enigma of Kaspar Hauser*. I printed a few thousand copies of each title, and whenever I was invited to talk at a cinema would load a box into my car and sell them to the audience. They cost something like 4 DM a copy to produce, and I charged 5 DM per copy, so I actually made a small profit on them. If a big publishing house had produced the book and sold it in a store it would have cost eight times as much, but I just did not need to get involved with that kind of thing. I did not need advertising and a complex system of distribution, the things that make books expensive. The technical costs of a book are actually quite minimal. And then, once it was clear how successful the books had been, Carl Hanser Verlag in Munich contacted me and asked if they could continue publishing the texts. I agreed, but insisted that the cover design had to be exactly the same as the Skellig editions, a very simple design of orange lettering on a black background with no photographs at all except on the front cover.

Have your films made money for you?

That is not a question I can really answer. You know I have never functioned in the way that a traditional movie producer does. It was always a long-range perspective I had, more than just the day-to-day financial arrangements. For ten years in Germany I worked in a vacuum with very few critical or financial returns. When, for example, *Aguirre* was released in the cinema the same day it was screened on television and did very badly, both on TV and in the cinema, the question of survival raised its head yet again. 'How can I survive this disaster? And how can I continue working?' To this very day these are the questions I constantly carry with me, even after forty years. But I always had faith in my films and in the knowledge that one day they would be seen and enjoyed. This is what has kept me going over the years: faith and, just as importantly, perseverance. Things do not happen overnight, and filmmakers must be prepared for years of hard work, even if with filmmaking – compared to something like novel-writing or painting – there is a real financial imminence from day one because it is so expensive. But even though I have invested everything back into my films over the years, I live like a rich man. My forty-five films or so have meant I could do the things I have truly wanted to do throughout my life, which is priceless. There are very few people who can say this. It is more valuable than any cash you could ever have thrown at me. I made films, other people bought houses. Money lost, film gained. Today, for example, I can earn money on films I made thirty years ago by releasing them on DVD, screening them on television and at retrospectives. At a very early age I understood that the key to this business is self-reliance and, crucially, being your own producer.

What also makes me rich is that I am truly welcome almost everywhere. I can show up with my films and am given real hospitality, something you cannot achieve with money alone. At lunch yesterday you saw how that man insisted on paying for our meal. 'Thank you for *Woyzeck*,' he said. For years I have struggled harder than you can imagine for true liberty, and am privileged in the way that the boss of a huge powerful corporation never will be. In fact, hardly anyone in my profession is as free as I am.

You have to eat, though, have a roof over your head.

I never cared about paying myself when I made the films. Early on, I never took a salary for writing and directing because I produced them myself, and also worked a great deal with my brother and my wife. The money we found we cobbled together from revenues of previous films, subsidies and pre-sales, and we used it for only the very bare essentials, like travel costs, raw stock and lab fees, costumes, things like that. In the early days I made a living, but only just. I have always preferred to spend every possible penny I can scrape together for the films themselves, even if I might not know how I will pay my rent next month. Somehow I always manage. I have always lived with few possessions, most of which are the tools of my trade: a camera and a car, a laptop and a Nagra tape recorder. For many years I also had a flatbed editing table.

It is not money that moves ships over mountains, it is faith. And it is not money that makes films, it is these things [*holds up his hands*]. You have to establish just one little heap of money and make it seem big. There is a German proverb: '*Der Teufel scheißt immer auf den grössten Haufen.*' 'The Devil always shits on the biggest heap.' So heap up a little money, then the Devil will shit on it.

Where did the idea of the aborigine drama Where the Green Ants
Dream *come from?*

I had spent some time in Australia in the early 1970s at the Perth
Film Festival, where I read about the battle between some aborigines
and a Swiss company that did bauxite mining in the north-west
of the country. Soon afterwards I wrote the story of a group of
Australian tribal aborigines struggling to defend their sacred site –
the place where the Green Ants dream – against the bulldozers of
a mining company. The courtroom scenes in the film are actually
based in part on the real court transcripts.

I was also fascinated by the fact that only two centuries ago in
Australia there were approximately 600 different languages, and
today there are less than one-tenth of that number left. When we
made the film there were about six people who were believed to be
the very last speakers of their language as there was nobody else
left of the tribe. The tragedy is irrevocable. It was a real pleasure
working with the local aborigines, though there were a couple of
objections they raised; for example, one of the names in the screenplay. Apparently, there was a deceased member of their community
who had the same name, and once a man dies, for at least ten years
afterwards you must never say that name out loud. They would
speak of 'the man who died'. The other objection they made is one
visible in the film: the sacred objects during the courtroom scene.
It actually happened that in a case heard before the Supreme Court
of the Northern Territories, the aborigines produced some sacred
objects which they had dug up that had been buried for about 200
years and asked that all the spectators in the courtroom be
removed so they could show them only to the judge. They were
wooden carved objects, completely beyond the comprehension of
an Anglo-Saxon judge. Yet for the aborigines it was the proof of
why and how they belonged to this special area. For the film they
asked me not to show anything, and even refused my offer to fab-
ricate some duplicates. Therefore they are not visible in the film;
you only see that they have something wrapped.

*Though based on ancient tribal mythology, isn't the idea of the
Green Ants your own invention? And what is the aborigine concept of 'dreaming'?*

Where the Green Ants Dream

I made up the story of the Green Ants. There is a character in the film – some kind of specialist – who spouts all sorts of facts about green ants, but of course it is all invented. Also, I did not want to be like an anthropologist, strictly following the facts, but felt it would be better to include in the film legends and mythology that come close to the thinking and the way of life of the aborigines. I have to be careful when discussing concepts like 'dreaming' because I am no expert. I cannot bear it that there are so many people – missionaries of all kinds, anthropologists and politicians – who claim to understand the aborigines completely. The aborigines come from a stone-age culture that strongly and practically influenced their way of life until only maybe two or three generations ago. There is something like 20,000 years of history that separates us from them. My very limited understanding is that the aboriginal dreamtime stories and myths explain the origins of everything on the planet and were especially important to the pre-colonial aborigines. I can say that the film is certainly not their 'dreaming', it is my own. At the same time, of course, I could not claim to make their cause my cause. That would be ridiculous. One of the tribesmen even told me,

'We do not understand you either, but we see that you have your own dreaming.'

It is very beautiful how the whole continent of Australia somehow is spread over with a kind of river network of dreams or 'songlines'. The aborigines would sing a song when travelling and through the rhythm of the song would identify a landscape. My friend Bruce Chatwin[1] once travelled with them in a car and said they would sing in fast-motion – as if you were running a tape forward at ten times the normal speed – because the car was passing so fast and the rhythm of the song had to keep up with the landscape. There are things about the aborigines we will never comprehend and that are very beautiful. Simply, because I respect them as a people who are in a deep struggle to keep their visions alive, and because my own understanding of them was limited, I wanted to develop my own mythology.

You don't really like the film, do you?

Well, the film is rather blatant about having something of a 'message'. It has such a self-righteous tone to it that I wish I had cut out of the film; it stinks to high heaven. The film is not that bad, it just has a climate to it that I cannot stand. I still like the shots at the beginning and end very much, images as if from the end of the world. Jörg Schmidt-Reitwein spent four weeks in Oklahoma just to chase after tornadoes. It is how I see the collapse of this planet, a tornado that comes and wipes everything away, sucks everything into the clouds. I was very intrigued by hurricane 'Tracy' that destroyed the city of Darwin in northwestern Australia. A few years later I saw some of the destruction, a huge water tank with a vast rectangular imprint on it. What had happened was a refrigerator had flown through the air for a few kilometres and smashed into the tank, a hundred feet above the ground.

You then joined up with Kinski again to make Cobra Verde. *After the filming you made certain pronouncements that it would almost certainly be your final collaboration.*

The production was, simply, the worst in my life and I publicly swore after filming that I would never again work with Kinski.

At the time I thought to myself, 'Will somebody please step in and carry on the work with this man? I have had enough.' There was something about Kinski's presence in the film that meant a foreign stink – his stink – pervaded the work we did together there, and *Cobra Verde* suffers somewhat because of this. I will not say I resent this, but the film does feel rather foreign to me. In some scenes there is a certain stylization that Kinski forced on the film that is vaguely reminiscent of spaghetti westerns. To this very day I have difficulties with certain scenes because they have something in them that I felt very strongly on the set but that I wanted to avoid capturing on film. When Kinski arrived for the early part of the film in Colombia he was falling apart. To hold him together and make him productive, to harness all his insanity, his rage and his demonic intensity was a real problem from day one. Kinski was like a hybrid racehorse who would run a mile and after reaching the finish line collapse. However, at the time of *Cobra Verde* he was in a different film. Kinski had written a confused screenplay of the only film he was ever to direct,

Cobra Verde

the life story of Paganini, with himself in the title role. For years he had implored me to direct it, and I always said no.

Every single day I did not know if the film would ever be finished because Kinski terrorized everyone on set. He would halt filming even if one of the buttons on his costume was too loose. In fact, he terrorized cinematographer Thomas Mauch and I had to replace him within the first week. This was one of the worst things I have ever done in my life. Thomas loved the film but unfortunately caught the brunt of Kinski early in the battle. I chose his replacement, the Czech Victor Růžička, because I had heard he was physically strong, built like a peasant, and very patient. Anyone else probably would have quit within two hours.

Was pre-production in Africa any easier than the shoot itself? You said earlier that the continent never seemed to be very friendly to you.

Logistically, pre-production was problematic. Sometimes it was so hot you could not even step outside. To find a telephone that worked was a major chore, there was hardly any gasoline for our cars, and I had to make sure there was accommodation, transport and food for cast and crew. We even had to build an entire palace – the one you see in the film – in only ten weeks in Ghana, which was constructed in the traditional style. We worked around the clock with nearly 200 workers. Then we had another ten weeks to choose the Amazon army of a thousand young women. We gathered them all together at a football stadium in Accra, the capital of Ghana, where an Italian stunt co-ordinator trained them in the use of swords and shields. They were a truly frightening bunch of ferocious, eloquent, proud, strong women. One time we asked them to line up in front of these huge pots of food we had prepared for them which they did, but after about thirty seconds they all rushed over – hundreds and hundreds of them – and were piled about twelve deep around these vast pots. The food was ruined. Another time we had to line them up in the inner yard of the slave fortress to pay them. We opened only a small gateway through the main door which meant that they came out one after the other, otherwise they would have fallen over the money. What happened from inside was that 800 of them pushed against the door at the same time and were squashing the ones at the front almost to death. Some of them were fainting, and I diffused the situation only by grabbing a nearby policeman and getting him to fire three shots into the air to make them retreat. Often we had to wait to clear the area we were shooting in because so many people were wandering in and out of shots. All the costumes and other props had to be produced in an extremely short period of time, which caused endless headaches because normally in Africa everything takes much longer than it should do. It is not a question of money; even with $25 million I would still have had as many problems. You just have to deviate from your normal way of doing things and try to understand their improvisations and tempo. You cannot be a strict Prussian military type of organizer or you would probably be thrown out of the country after two days.

When did you first come across Bruce Chatwin's novel The Viceroy of Ouidah?

Around the time of *Fitzcarraldo* I had read Chatwin's *In Patagonia* and was so impressed I immediately read his *On the Black Hill* and *The Viceroy of Ouidah*, the nineteenth-century story of the bandit Franciso Manoel da Silva, who travels from Brazil to the Kingdom of Dahomey in Africa and becomes a viceroy and slave trader. I am a great admirer of Joseph Conrad and Chatwin, I feel, is somehow in the same league. He had some sort of touch you rarely see in literature. I contacted Chatwin to let him know about my interest in the book, but added I could not undertake such a monstrous project right after *Fitzcarraldo*. I had to lick my wounds for a couple of years at least, do some easier stuff like *Where the Green Ants Dream*, some operas, some smaller films. I asked him to let me know immediately if someone else wanted to buy the rights to the book, and a few years later he contacted me to say that David Bowie's agents had expressed an interest. Apparently Bowie had read the book and wanted to direct the film, so I bought the rights.

The novel doesn't exactly have a linear narrative, so presumably it took some careful thinking as to how to structure the screenplay.

The first thing I did was explain to Chatwin that the story in *The Viceroy of Ouidah*[2] was not a film story *per se*, which meant there would be certain technical problems in adapting the book. It is narrated in a series of concentric circles, and I knew a film would have to proceed in a more linear way. Rather than having the story and intrigue of a cinematic work, the book captures the inner world of an amazing character, as well as a rich understanding of Africa and the slave trade itself. I told Chatwin I would have to invent a lot of things and narrate the tale in a different way. 'Let's go ahead with it,' Chatwin said. He never wanted to get mixed up with the screenplay or involve himself in the production, though he was on location with us in Africa for a few days.[3]

Did the slavery element play a large part in your wanting to tell the story? Is the film in some way an indictment of the nineteenth-century slave trade?

No, the film is not about the history of colonialism, and nor is Chatwin's novel. And I do not consider it a historical film just as I never saw *Aguirre* as being in any way historical. A film like *Invincible* is much more a film about the era in which it is set than *Cobra Verde*, though I hesitate to push that point too much either. *Cobra Verde* is about great fantasies and follies of the human spirit, not colonialism.

The fact is that in Ghana, where we filmed, slavery is still something of a taboo subject, unlike colonialism. In the United States and the Caribbean there is much debate about slavery, in Brazil too, but in many places in Africa the wound of slavery is so deep and painful that hardly anyone speaks about it in public. It is an almost untouched subject. I have always suspected that one reason for this is the well-established fact that African kingdoms were involved in the slave trade almost as much as the white traders. There was also a great deal of slave trading between the Arab world and black Africa, and even within African nations themselves.

Africa really seems to be the star of this film, not Kinski.

I think so, yes. When writing the screenplay I preferred to let the story move through the action at its own speed and always felt the sequences in South America were quite heavy, while it was the African part of the story that really interested me. The film expands in the second half and the best of the film is when Cobra Verde arrives in Africa. What you see of Africa in the film are things audiences are not used to seeing in films, like the court rituals or the flag signals across the beach. The crowd scenes have real life to them, wonderfully anarchic and chaotic. In most films set in Africa, the continent is portrayed either as a primitive and dangerous place full of savages, or with a kind of *Out of Africa* nostalgia. *Cobra Verde* deviates from that. I always had the feeling this was one of the keys to the film, not the images themselves but rather the sophisticated and complex structures of Africa that are up there on screen. In many of the modern African countries, political and social life is overshadowed by corruption and inefficiency and bureaucracy. But within these kingdoms, social life is paramount, and the clan system is very strong indeed. If somebody is ill, a kind of social-security system ensures that the person who is incapacitated is taken care of.

I even managed to get the part of the King of Dahomey to be played by King Nana Agyefi Kwame II, the real incumbent King of Nsein, a wonderful man who brought 300 retainers of his court with him. Everything and everyone you see around him is authentic, all the court jesters, princes, princesses, ministers, dancers and his musicians and the traditional things that they carry. They were all amazing to work with. The kinds of things that are in the film are not things you could ever write and cast. I could never have found anyone more convincing than him to play the part of the King, for he exercised an incredible authority over everyone.

Do you feel that at least some of your films could be categorized as being ethnographic or anthropological in any way?

My films are about as anthropological as the music of Gesualdo and the images of Caspar David Friedrich. They are anthropological only in as much as they try to explore the human condition at this particular time on this planet. I do not make films using images only of clouds and trees, I work with human beings because the way they function in different cultural groups interests me. If that makes me an anthropologist then so be it. But I never think in terms of strict ethnography: going out to some distant island with the explicit purpose of studying the natives there. My goal is always to find out more about man himself, and film is my means. According to its nature, film does not have so much to do with reality as it does with our collective dreams. It chronicles our state of mind. The purpose is to record and guide, as chroniclers did in past centuries.

I know what you are getting at with a question like that. A film like *Wodaabe* cannot really be considered ethnographic because some of the film is stylized to such an extent that the audience is taken into the realm of the ecstatic. There is no voice-over and even the short text at the start of the film tells you only the barest facts about these people, that they have been around as a tribe since the Stone Age and they are despised by all neighbouring peoples. I purposefully pull away from anything that could be considered anthropological. In the opening scene of the film the tribesmen are rolling their eyeballs, extolling the whiteness of their teeth, making these ecstatic faces, and on the soundtrack over these images you hear Gounod's 'Ave Maria', a recording made in 1901 and sung by the last castrato of the Vatican. And the final shot is a bridge over the river Niger in Niamey, the capital city of Niger. I just happened to see the dromedaries being led across the bridge amongst all these cars. For me this is a shot of real depth and beauty, similar to the last shot of *Pilgrimage* with the women crossing the river that is frozen over. An ethnographic filmmaker would never dare do things like this, but as a filmmaker I do. I do not deny you can learn a great many 'facts' about the Wodaabe from the film, but this certainly was not my primary intention. Using the aria means that the film is not a 'documentary' about a specific African tribe, rather a story about beauty and desire. Though watching these men on their toes might be an odd spectacle to you and me – coming as we do from different cultural traditions – the music helps to carry us out of the realm of what I call the accountants' truth. Without the music, the images of this amazing and bizarre male beauty contest just would not touch us as deeply.

What drew you to the Wodaabe tribe of the southern Sahara?

The Wodaabe are referred to scornfully by neighbouring peoples as 'Bororo', a term of abuse that roughly means 'ragged shepherds'. Wodaabe, the name they call themselves, means 'those under the taboo of purity'. They say that the earth belongs to no one, that it would only belong to human beings if they were the shepherds of the sun. The tribe numbers no more than about 200,000 people who travel around the desert from Senegal on the Atlantic almost right across to the Nile, particularly in Mali and in the Republic of Niger. The tribes have been in the Sahara since time immemorial and have no real concept of the frontiers that exist today. They are in strong danger of dying out because their living space has shrunk as a result of the dramatic spread southwards of the desert.

What is fascinating about the Wodaabe is they consider themselves to be the most beautiful people in the world. During preparations for their beauty contests you see groups of young men in the encampments joking and laughing, trying to make themselves handsome and taking pains to dress themselves up and put on make-up. Some take the whole day to get ready, and some even take herbal aphrodisiacs before the contest starts. It is the men who compete against each other in the contests, and it is up to the young women to pick one of them out in order to disappear with him into the bush for a few nights. For the most part the women are already married, which is why they return their handsome booty to the bosom of his family once they are done. Occasionally they will keep the man wholly for themselves, resuming their nomadic journey with him.

The festival starts at dawn and goes on all night, in fact for the following five nights. The young men form a big circle, standing shoulder to shoulder in tight formation, and sing and clap their hands rhythmically. On each beat they rise up on their toes in order to appear even taller for a moment and then take a step to the right. In this way the large circle of dancers slowly starts to revolve. Outside the circle the women have taken up their positions, able to observe as it passes by them. The men roll their eyes, flash their teeth and click their tongues in order to draw attention to themselves. It is thought to be particularly beautiful to show as much of the white of one's teeth and eyeballs as possible, and some of them roll their eyes upwards as if in ecstasy. But it is also charm, charisma and grand gestures that count too, and the festival includes a complicated succession of different dances and rituals. The young men form straight lines, stride forwards, grimacing ecstatically, then retreat until it is time for the moment of decision when the winner is chosen.

When did you first hear of self-proclaimed Emperor Jean-Bédel Bokassa, the subject of Echoes from a Sombre Empire?

It was during the making of *Fata Morgana* that I first went to the Central African Republic.[4] We had ended up there after being released from prison in Cameroon. Bokassa was in power and I had read a few things about him. He seemed truly bizarre, and the evil sparkling of this incredible character was utterly fascinating to me. There was such a cornucopia of absolutely unbelievable stories surrounding him and his regime. For me, film allows us to reveal the least understood truths of man. It pushes on the floor of dreams or nightmares; in this case definitely nightmares. Bokassa seemed to represent the kind of human darkness you find in Nero or Caligula, Hitler or Saddam Hussein, and *Echoes from a Sombre Empire*, the film I made about him, was an attempt to explore these dark landscapes that lie at the heart of man.

The stories about Bokassa are endless and so unbelievable, most of which are well documented. Things like him having several children killed because they would not wear his school uniforms, or spending a third of the country's national budget to pay for his coronation. He also had people indiscriminately thrown to the crocodiles and apparently fathered fifty-four children. The deeper we dug, the more we discovered these inexpressible tragedies worthy of Shakespeare. There is the tale of the two Martines, a film in itself. What happened was that when he was a soldier in Indochina, Bokassa met a local woman and had a child called Martine. Once in power he decided to find her and bring her to Africa. What happened was that the girl who was found and brought over turned out not to be the real Martine. When he eventually did find the genuine Martine, he generously allowed the 'fake' one to stay. The two girls were married on the same day in a huge celebration, though soon afterwards both husbands were executed. Apparently one of them was involved in the murder of the other's newborn child. Bokassa decided to send the 'fake' Martine back to

Vietnam. She was put on a plane that returned only half an hour later; it was quite clear to everyone that she had just been pushed out over the jungle.

Did you want to interview Bokassa himself for the film?

Bokassa was still alive when we made the film, though unfortunately we never managed to interview him in prison. After he was deposed he fled to France and was condemned to death in absentia, though after a few years he just could not take the French winters any longer and, cold and homesick, boarded a commercial airliner believing he would be received like Napoleon returning from exile, his nation on its knees before him. Of course, he was immediately arrested, put on trial and condemned to death again, though his sentence was later commuted to life imprisonment, then twelve years, then house arrest. At the time of filming, we did have permission from President Kolingba to film him and Bokassa did want to meet us, but just before going to the prison we were arrested and expelled from the country by the Minister of the Interior. From what I understood the Minister was implicated in several crimes from the Bokassa era and was very much against the idea of us coming over and sticking our noses into things. What I did see was some of the secret footage of him in his cell the French had filmed so that in case something happened to him they would have proof they had not murdered him.

And did the man really eat human flesh?

The German Ambassador to the Central African Republic told me that one time, after an execution in front of the press and diplomatic corps, the execution squad rushed forward and ripped the liver from the body and ate it. This was in public, to demonstrate that the power of the dead man had passed over to them now. During production of the film I spoke to a great many people who had stories to tell about Bokassa, and I realized that when there is so much hearsay about a single man, when you hear the same stories from so many different people, then this speculation really does condense into something factual. We have to believe it.

The deeper truth of the situation is outside of our reach, but not the facts. You want a fact? Bokassa was a cannibal, yes. It is as simple as that. The conclusions of the tribunal and the lies of the remaining witnesses are of little importance. However, though it is a fact, I think it is good that something of a mystery remains and will always remain, even though during the trial there were very precise accounts given by Bokassa's cook about what the Emperor liked to eat. There is also evidence that when the French paratroopers who assisted in deposing the Emperor opened up the huge refrigerators in his palace, they found half the Minister of the Interior deep frozen. The other half had been eaten during a state banquet.

When we made the film, even those officials who had been in opposition to the Bokassa regime flatly denied he ever ate anyone. Such behaviour clearly breaks so many taboos, and admitting such things took place in the country in some way casts the whole continent of Africa in a bad light. You see the same kind of behaviour in Mexico where some people still seriously maintain that the Aztecs never sacrificed human beings or never practised cannibalism because they think it is so shameful. They come up with the wildest concoction that it is a fabrication of the Spanish to denigrate the Aztec way of life. But cannibalism is certainly within human nature, and it is a phenomenon that has always interested me because it has a direct link with a part of ourselves that is very ancient and buried deep within us. Maybe we are above such things now, but people like Bokassa show us that cannibalism is still something that can resurface. Look, for example, at the Nazis in Germany. The Germans were a dignified people, the greatest philosophers, composers, writers and mathematicians. And, in the space of only ten years, they created a barbarism more terrible than had ever been seen before.

How did you find Michael Goldsmith, the man in the film who guides us through the story of Bokassa's regime?

I encountered Michael Goldsmith only after I decided to make the film. I do not recall exactly where I first met him, but like those who have crossed the Sahara, people who have been in the Central African Republic during Bokassa's reign and the chaos of the Congo somehow find each other. It is nothing to do with a 'network' or anything like that. The law that connects people like this

I cannot describe; they just recognize each other, like me and Ryszard Kapuściński, the Polish writer and philosopher who has spent many years in Africa.[5] Kapuściński was one of the very few people who survived the horrors of the Eastern Congo in the early 1960s. Within a year and a half he had been arrested forty times and condemned to death four times. He is such a forceful personality, full of such serenity and insight. One day I asked him what his worst experience had been, and in this very soft-spoken voice he said it was when they threw dozens of poisonous snakes into his tiny cell with him. All he said was, 'That was not so good. My hair turned white in five days.'

Michael Goldsmith was a journalist who had been imprisoned and sentenced to death by Bokassa in the 1970s because he insisted Goldsmith was a spy. In fact, he was almost beaten to death by Bokassa himself with the imperial sceptre, and wanted very much to return and explore the country now that Bokassa had been deposed. Right after we finished the film Goldsmith went to Liberia and disappeared. It was known that he had been taken prisoner by a faction of insurgent rebels, all of them child soldiers. Eight-year-old children wearing rags and with Kalashnikov rifles and M16s were shooting everyone that moved. Goldsmith later told me that they were often drunk and stoned. One time they raided a bridal store and dressed up as bride and groom. The 'bride' was an eight-year-old boy, wearing a veil and a bridal gown with high heels much too big for him and firing his rifle wildly. The 'groom' was naked except for a tailcoat that dragged after him. Very strange images. Goldsmith was held captive in a building from where they had shot a passer-by. He said the worst thing was to see, day after day, the decomposition of the body. By the end, dogs were carrying the last pieces of the body away, and only a dark ugly spot on the street was left. Goldsmith had been in situations like this quite often, and even though he looked like a librarian, he was a very courageous man and had real insights into Africa. He managed to get out of there and saw the film when we showed it at the Venice Film Festival. Three weeks later he died.

How did you get involved with the film you shot in India at the Palace of Udaipur?

The origins of *The Eccentric Private Theatre of the Maharaja of Udaipur* lie in the invitation I received from the Austrian director, singer and creator of events, André Heller, to film the mammoth event he had organized at the City Palace of Udaipur on the banks of Lake Pichola in India. Heller, the man who once staged what I think was the largest fireworks display in Europe, had a permit from the Maharaja to stage just one time what became the events of the film. He sent out people throughout India in search of magicians, singers, dancers, snake charmers, fire-eaters and performers, ending up with something like 1,000 performers speaking a total of twenty-three languages. I get sent a lot of screenplays that people want me to make, but I do not get very many requests to make films like this so I agreed because I knew of Heller's work and his vision was, simply, a unique one. The actual event took place in one day, but I wanted to put it all into some context and so I invented some kind of a little story for the film, something about a palace crumbling into the lake, and spent a few days shooting the rehearsals. For Heller it was more of a cabaret show, a gathering of performers and jugglers and jesters and fire-eaters. That was basically it, nothing really beyond that for him. I did it for a friend and I very much enjoyed the work and travelling out to India, somewhere I had not been before.

Do you ever go to the theatre?

I dislike theatre profoundly. The few theatrical productions that I have watched were an affront to the human spirit. Theatre has been so disappointing and revolting for me that I stopped going a long time ago. I find stage acting disgusting and not credible at all, somehow very dead to the world. The overdramatic forms, the screaming, the fake passion, it really pains me to watch. And I do not like to make distinctions between professional and non-professional actors. The only distinction worth making is between who is good on screen and who is not.

Let me say it even more drastically: you would get me into the audience of the World Wrestling Federation before you could drag me into a theatre. The kind of fake, choreographed drama that wrestlers practise and the characters who speak to the audience showing how evil they are, I prefer this kind of fake drama to theatre. Another thing is that I feel profoundly uncomfortable with theatre audiences. I know I do not belong there. I know they feel and think and function in a different way to me, and frankly I would feel much more comfortable with all the vulgarity of the wrestling crowd.

What led you to translate Michael Ondaatje's play The Collected Works of Billy the Kid *into German?*

My sister is a theatre director and saw a performance of the play in Canada. She decided she wanted to stage it in Germany and asked me to translate it. The text is almost impossible to translate; sometimes it almost destroys grammar and uses invented words. Though she never actually staged my version, some time later Carl Hanser Verlag heard about it and wanted to publish the Ondaatje novel of the same title and asked if I could translate the novel for them as there was much overlap between the novel and the stage play. I agreed because I felt it was an important text. I did have to ask Ondaatje himself what certain words meant, but in some cases even he did not know, so I would invent a word, just as he had done in English.

I do sometimes read plays, and I particularly like the work of Brendan Behan.[6] It is much better to read a work rather than see it performed because you can imagine all the characters and faces and voices. Even though I am a great lover of opera, I profoundly dislike going to see other people's productions, with very few exceptions. I often see a whole world when I listen to an opera and inevitably I am always disappointed when I see someone else's vision. Let me put it like this: when I see someone else's opera production I see images out there that are in direct contradiction to those in my head. The whole experience is miserable for me.

What about ballet and dance?

These things are foreign to me. I also do not like concerts because I do not really listen when I see an orchestra. I am too interested in seeing how the bassist's hands shoot up and down; I just never actually hear what they are playing. I am too visually interested in what is going on. I like to listen to recordings; I just hear much better. And I never go to exhibitions. I do not like the world of the *vernissage*. The crowds you find there are the most repulsive of all.

Museums?

I have hardly ever been in museums. It is a huge obstacle for me to go to a museum. You may not believe it, but I have been to Athens fourteen times from a very early age and only on the very last time did I have the guts and the nerve to climb up and see the Acropolis. Incomprehensible to everyone around me: 'Ah, you went to Athens! How did you enjoy the Acropolis?' Once in London I went to the British Museum because I wanted to see the Rosetta stone. Such a monumental achievement to decipher the ancient Egyptian hieroglyphics. Just the size of this achievement and knowledge required to decipher something like that, it is just utterly fascinating to me. But generally museums intimidate me. As do restaurants with very formal waiters. I am deeply scared by the sheer thought that somebody serves me as a waiter, and when it is overly formal then it is total misery for me. I am close to panic. I would rather eat potato chips sitting on the sidewalk than go to one of these chic restaurants. The same thing about hotels. Often I am forced to stay in hotels when I travel, but whenever there is a chance to avoid that world I do. In Berlin, for example, I will sleep on my son's floor rather than stay in a hotel. I did not mind living on a raft for weeks while shooting *Aguirre*. It has nothing to do with money or physical comfort, but keep me away from hotels, please.

We talked about how The Enigma of Kaspar Hauser *and* Nosferatu *were important films for you because they helped create an atmosphere of what Lotte Eisner called 're-legitimate' German culture. You once said that apart from the* Heimatfilm, *German cinema has created only one other genre: the* Bergfilm *or mountain film of the pre-war era. Does your feature* Scream of Stone *attempt to make any connection to these kinds of German films?*

Throughout the 1920s German directors like Luis Trenker[7] and Arnold Fanck[8] were producing a great number of mountain films. Unfortunately the genre later fell in step with Nazi ideology, which is probably the reason why it is somewhat unexplored today. I liked the idea of creating a new, contemporary form of mountain film,[9] like Peter Fleischmann, who used the elements and rules of the *Heimatfilm*[10] in *Hunting Scenes in Bavaria* and brought a new depth to the genre. But I would not push the idea of making a connection between *Scream of Stone* and the Leni Riefenstahl[11] melodramas of the 1920s, which actually I have not seen. I find Riefenstahl's existence as a filmmaker during the Nazi time a very sensitive thing. I cannot figure it out completely, and I would not dare to make a judgement.

I should say at the start that *Scream of Stone* had a very problematic birth. Reinhold Messner, with whom I had worked on my film *The Dark Glow of the Mountains*, had an original idea based on a true story for a screenplay about the first apparently successful attempt on Cerro Torre, a two-kilometre-high needle-like peak in Patagonia. Maestri, an Italian climber who I said earlier would climb mountains with pneumatic drills, had claimed to have reached the summit. However, there had been instant doubt as to whether he actually had, flamed in part by the fact that his climbing partner had never returned and his body was never recovered. Walter Saxer, my production manager on many films, picked up on the story and developed it with a colleague. He really was the driving force behind the film right from the start. I liked the ideas they came up with immediately but also saw the script had many weak points, particularly the dialogue. So at first I hesitated to accept the project because I did not know to what extent I could articulate it in a way I could easily live with. Finally we came to an agreement and I stepped into the project, first doing some work myself on the screenplay. Unfortunately I found myself up against a wall of stone when it came to making real changes, though thankfully I did cast the film myself. The character of Fingerless, played by Brad Dourif, the climber who leaves a picture of Mae West at the top of the mountain, was the only character I was allowed to change in the screenplay. It needed more changes very badly, but because I was prevented from doing so, I cannot even say that *Scream of Stone* is my film.

Scream of Stone

Did your experiences working with Messner on The Dark Glow of the Mountains *help you at all when you were making* Scream of Stone?

Yes, to a certain extent. Cerro Torre is the most dangerous, the most difficult and ecstatic mountain on Earth. There really is nothing like it anywhere. It is more a symbolic image of deadly fear than a mere mountain. It is a 3,300-metre-high needle of basalt sticking straight up into the sky and for years was considered unclimbable. The first verified ascent was somewhere in the mid-1970s. I think about 200 times more people have succeeded in climbing Mount Everest as have ever made it to the top of Cerro Torre. You can only truly understand why it strikes so much fear into climbers when you see it standing before you. There may be higher peaks to scale but what makes Cerro Torre particularly difficult are the sheer cliff faces and weather conditions. Most of the time there is a pandemonium of storms, and you cannot see the peak. I call them storms, but actually we do not have an equivalent in our language to describe this phenomenon. The winds easily reach 200 kilometres an hour at the top and ice fragments the size of my fist come shooting by like bullets. Even if you hang on with nails and crampons you will still be blown off. On a mountain near Cerro Torre I saw one unforgettable sight: a waterfall with the storm hitting the rocks around it so hard that the waterfall literally went up vertically. The water shot straight up into the air and dissipated into mist.

Were you ever at the top of Cerro Torre yourself?

I was twice on the summit, both times by helicopter of course. It was important to go up in the helicopter so I could establish the pattern I needed to get the shots I wanted. On a couple of occasions I was secured to the side of the peak near the actors so as to be closer to what we were shooting. The second time I landed on the summit, I remember stepping out of the helicopter with actor Vittorio Mezzogiorno. I turned around and he was on the ground lying as flat as he could go with his nails dug as deep into the ice as he could get them. He looked up at me and I asked him what was wrong. Very meekly he replied, 'Well, I want to get up but my body will not co-operate. Give me a little more time.' He was so afraid, and it really made me somehow solidify my friendship with Vittorio.

He was probably petrified because he had overheard my conversation with Hans Kammerlander – the climber who appears in *Dark Glow of the Mountains* and who plays a small part in *Scream of Stone* – where we talked about the cave in the ice that had been built on the peak and stocked with provisions for eight days, just in case we needed to take refuge. The rope that secured this whole thing was somehow loose, so Hans and I tried to pin it back down. When he saw me about to grab hold of this rope flying about he grabbed me and said, 'Do not lean towards the slope, walk straight, otherwise you will start to slide. If you start to slide there is nothing that can hold you any more. You will just accelerate and then you will be airborne for two kilometres.' And he looked me right in the eye and said, 'If that happens, promise me one thing: enjoy the vista.'

You said you made Dark Glow of the Mountains *to see if a feature film like* Scream of Stone *was possible. You seemed to conclude that it wasn't. So what problems did you have during filming?*

At one point our helicopter took the actor and world champion free-climber Stefan Glowacz, one of the cinematographers – who was also a climber – and me up on to a ridge not far from the peak of Cerro Torre to prepare a sequence. Normally a team of climbers would make extensive preparations, like building an emergency shelter, taking provisions and equipment up, and then the actors and technical crew would follow. But a storm had been raging for ten days, and suddenly we had a calm, crystal clear night followed by a beautiful morning without wind. It looked so good that we made the mistake of flying up there without sending a vanguard. Once dropped at the ridge the three of us walked towards our location, when all of a sudden, out of the corner of my eye, I saw something that I am sure I will never see again in my life. Something absolutely outrageous. As far as the eye could reach, I saw clouds below us exploding like gigantic atomic bombs. I immediately called the helicopter, which was still in sight. I saw it make a loop towards us, it came as close as fifty metres and then, all of a sudden, the storm hit us like a bullet. The clouds were over us, there was a 200 kilometre per hour storm and the temperature fell thirty degrees below. After twenty seconds my moustache was a lump of ice. The helicopter was literally tossed away from us and we found ourselves alone with no sleeping bags, no tents, no food, no ropes. Nothing whatsoever, except two ice-picks. We had to dig ourselves into the snow immediately, otherwise we would have frozen to death in a few hours.

We spent a bit more than two days and two nights in this snow hole. You can get by with nothing to eat for fifty hours, but water is another thing. You have to drink at least a gallon of water a day otherwise your toes and fingers will freeze away. Ninety-five per cent of all losses of fingers and toes is the result of dehydration. After twenty hours the cameraman, a very tough man, was in bad shape. He was running a temperature and having cramps, and he radioed down that he would not survive another night. We had a walkie-talkie which we only used every two hours for a few seconds in order to save batteries, and this stark message alarmed our team in the valley. Two teams of four climbers were sent out to reach us. The strongest of them became delirious, threw his gloves into the storm and snapped his fingers. He insisted on calling the waiter to pay for his cappuccino. They had to guide him down back to the glacier, but an avalanche swept them down some 200 feet. They now had no choice but to dig a snow cave themselves, since one of them had lost his sunglasses and showed signs of snow blindness. After fifty hours the clouds burst open for ten minutes, and with this lull in the storm the helicopter was able to pick us up. The pilot was in a panic and could not wait until the last person – me – had scrambled inside, so I crouched in a metal basket outside the helicopter holding on to an aluminium bar. When we finally touched down my hand was solidly frozen to the bar and we could not get it off. Finally one of the Argentinian climbers urinated on to it, thawing my hand out and thus releasing it from the bar.

Your eight half-hour films entitled Film Lesson *were shot in Vienna during your time as head of the Vienna Film Festival in the early 1990s. The guests you invited to lecture certainly seem to demonstrate that film truly is the art of illiterates, and that cinema's roots are most definitely in the 'country fair and the circus'.*

Film Lesson showed the general public my approach to how I would run a film school. Every day at a fixed hour in the circus tent at the festival I invited a guest, for example, the New York magician Jeff Sheridan. Like my magician son Rudolph, whose mentor Jeff was, I am absolutely fascinated by the way this man presents his magic to audiences with his silent performances. Sometimes I wish I could be a magician instead of a filmmaker because I would be in direct physical contact with people in the street, playing out all these little dramas with my bare hands just as Jeff Sheridan does. The trick to magic is directing our attention wherever the magician wants to, and this is surely also one of the secrets of cinema. As a director, you must be capable of pushing and pulling the audience's attention in whatever direction the story demands. After all, the great pioneer of early cinema, George Méliès,[12] was actually a magician before he became a filmmaker. As Jeff said during his demonstration, the whole point of the magician is to destroy the logical and the rational. Film seems like reality but it is not reality at all, merely a complex illusion.

Another guest was the tightrope walker Philippe Petit,[13] who is also an expert at picking locks, a basic skill that every filmmaker should have. Imagine you need to get a shot of a street and there is a truck blocking your view: it must be removed. When this happened to me and the owners refused to move it, I temporarily stole it, moved it a hundred yards away and brought it back a few hours later. One discussion was with Kamal Saiful Islam, a cosmologist from Bangladesh who had worked at the Max Planck Institute in Munich. The title of this segment of the film was 'Fantastic Landscapes and the Algebraization of Unthinkable Spaces'. I projected small details of fantastic landscapes in paintings by Altdorfer, Hercules Segers, Grünewald and Leonardo da Vinci and spoke about landscapes of the mind in cinema, while Kamal Saiful Islam proved that there are spaces unthinkable for our minds yet which can be conclusively proven algebraically; for example, a bottle which has only an inside, but definitely no outside. He spoke of the future directions that cinema might move in, proving the existence of objects and images that are impossible for us to imagine today. It reminded me of what people thought during the time of Columbus. They were scared to travel to the other side of the earth because they thought they would hurtle down into empty space. Today, every schoolchild can tell you why this is not so, why the force of gravity keeps us on the ground regardless of where we travel. Similarly, a cinema may be created in the future that is just as inconceivable to us today as basic gravitational physics was to the contemporaries of Columbus.

That absolutely no one in the tent understood this kind of imaginative and exotic mathematics did not matter at all. We would rave and rant about questions which have bothered me for a long time, such as immovable positions within the universe. It is easy to relate this to three-dimensional spaces: if you hang yourself by the neck in your attic, and somebody finds your body dangling, what would this person need to do to fix you in a completely immobile position? Answer: one more rope from your ankles down to the floor to prevent you from swinging and one more from your belt to a wall in order to prevent you from spinning around your axis. But how many ropes would be necessary to fix yourself in a totally immovable position within the universe?

I believe our audience understood that it is not the curriculum of a traditional film school that makes you a filmmaker, but wild fantasies and an agitation of mind over seemingly odd questions. As I said, the question about moving big boulders of stones in prehistoric times was more the starting point for *Fitzcarraldo* than anything else.

But surely you do think analytically when it comes to film, at least a little. What about your talk earlier of Zorro *and* Dr Fu Manchu *and your realization of how film is put together?*

Analytical is probably not the right word because I am not a very analytical person. As a child I just increasingly started to look at films in a different way, asking myself questions like: why is it that in a Zorro film there are never any chickens on the ranches? Why does a Western hero never eat noodles? Why is Zorro dressed in black, which is normally the costume of the Bad Guy? In the final shoot-out is the Good Guy shooting left to right or right to left? Things like that. Hardly analytical in the traditional meaning of the word.

Very early on I could see there was a certain grammar of film-making that most filmmakers adhered to. Just imagine the hero of a Western lying in bed, tucked under a thick eiderdown blanket. An impossibility! If the hero is tired he has to sleep outside next to the camp fire with his saddle as his cushion and a crude blanket to keep himself warm. The only exception to this rule would be when he walks up the saloon staircase to the pretty singer's room where there will be a perfectly made bed waiting for him on which he will lie down. But he will lie down on the cover – never under it – and will cross his legs and prop his spurred boots on the brass bedrail. Again, covering himself with the blanket is totally out of the question! And when the Good Guy appears, he always appears from nowhere, riding on horseback, and when he leaves, he disappears into the landscape, riding towards the horizon. There is inevitably a real vagueness about where the hero comes from and about where he is headed. I suspect there are also very strict laws that govern the way a showdown is filmed, laws that are just as rigid as other iron rules of the genre. All these kinds of things point to some deeply rooted inherent laws which have to do with nomadic existence versus sedentary existence.

For the same reason you will almost never see chickens in Westerns. Of course, there were plenty of chicken on real ranches, but chickens belong to a more sedentary form of life which is foreign to the world of Westerns. And one might well ask oneself what is it exactly that the cowboy eats? Of course, he could never eat anything indoors, though he is permitted to have a drink. But it absolutely must be a whisky that comes skidding along the saloon bar. Under no circumstances can it be orange juice! Juice is just as much a no-no as eating spaghetti. The hero eating noodles or potatoes? Forget it. It could only be beans and bacon cooked in a pan on an outdoor fire. Under no circumstances may he fry an egg as this would be a violation of the genre's iron laws. And coffee, always without milk and sugar, always strong and always from tin mugs. So these questions are not really analytical, but neither are they as ridiculous as they may at first sound. Ask questions, try to discover the hidden mechanics. You will surely discover countless other rules that apply to Westerns, or those that govern other genres.

What about your own lecture for Film Lesson *entitled 'Orientation in Film'.*

I am someone who likes to travel on foot and this is one reason why orientation is so important to me and why I find the idea of losing my way very threatening. One thing you will surely have observed is that when you sit down at a table with your brother, your sister, or some other family member, there will automatically be some sort of a seating arrangement. It is the same kind of thing as when I occasionally get confused when I go to the cinema. I only feel comfortable if I can seat myself some way to the left of the centre of the screen, and when I take someone along to the movie it is important that he or she sit on my right. Of course, this type of seating arrangement is not always possible, but it really does make me uncomfortable and cramped if I have to seat myself in a way that goes against my inner orientation.

'Orientation in Film' deals with my need for orientation, but also with the unspoken need of cinema audiences. The classic case would be an invisible optical axis between two actors which the camera must not cross, otherwise both of them would look into the same direction instead of opposing each other on screen. This gets more tricky if you have three people involved. A shot of a barman serving two guests is easy to solve since the bar can serve as the axis, but what if there is no bar? I cannot stand disorientation in movies, and films like *Waterloo* are wonderful examples to learn from: three armies march from three different directions and meet at the battlefield, and you always know who is who, and coming from where. *Aguirre* deals a lot with orientation: the army moves on with a clear purpose and sense of direction, but somewhere in the film they lose their orientation and by the end are going in circles. The problems of orientation and rhythm can never be resolved in the editing room; they are established only during shooting.

My favourite film in this respect is one of Jean-Pierre Melville's. A little gypsy gangster is summoned to meet some rivals and he secretly checks out the small attic where the meeting is going to take place. He tests the possible seating arrangements and notes where he would be pushed if threatened with a gun. The only logical place is a cupboard. He tests how he would stand there, hands raised. He leaves his gun hidden on top of the cupboard, just inches away from where his raised right hand would almost certainly be. But when he leaves the building he is spotted by one of the rival gangsters who checks out what the little gypsy might have been doing up there. He starts to take potential positions himself and finds the gun. All of a sudden space and orientation become the leading characters in the film – as they do in other Melville films – and I love him for that.

Could we go back to Aguirre *in this respect. What about the final shot of the film with the camera circling around the raft?*

In that shot all orientation is lost thanks to the movement of the camera, and only a circling, dizzying movement remains. The camera circles around the raft which is pretty much stationary, an image that mirrors the story of this man who has no way out and no hope of salvation. There were real problems with *Aguirre* because so many of the scenes were set on the moving rafts, which meant that if we filmed dialogue from one angle, the riverbank in the background would move from left to right on the screen, but on the reverse angle from right to left. To avoid confusion I would normally pan from one man to the other. If there is no cut, the spectator stays orientated, but on a raft that keeps turning and spinning the editing possibilities become tricky.

Let me add something else. During the Second World War, Joseph Goebbels[14] gave a rather laconic order to all cameramen at the front: 'The German soldier always attacks from left to right.' That was it, no further explanation. Sure enough, if you take a look at old newsreels, you will discover that the Germans always advance from the left to the right of the screen. There was some logic to this when Germany attacked Russia, as Russia lies east of Germany, but what about the war against France? But again, in the newsreels of the invasion westwards into Europe, the German forces are seen to attack from left to right. Goebbels' trick is still used today. You just have to look at television commercials, a couple of which I screened during my talk. I think that the question we need to ask ourselves is this: why does the direction of their movement make the soldiers look so victorious, so optimistic? Some people have argued that we read and write from left to right, which could be the reason why such a movement will be perceived as harmonic. But how does it work in the Arab world, where people write from right to left? There must be something within us, some hidden law. What it is, I cannot say. I just know that it exists.

While we are on the subject, let me talk about the way directors show vast distances covered by their heroes on film. I might have just imagined the whole thing, but I seem to remember in Buñuel's *Nazarin*[15] there is a scene in which Nazarin crosses Mexico on foot, walking a thousand miles with a cross over his shoulder. Buñuel uses a mere three shots, each one not more than five seconds long, to give the audience a sense of the immense distance that is being covered. How does Buñuel manage to economize in this way? How does he compress weeks of walking in fifteen seconds? The trick in 'Buñuel's Shot' is that the camera starts almost on the ground, pointing up to the sky while the frame remains empty for a fraction of a second. Then the character suddenly steps into the image and the camera twists and pans after him, watching him walk away into the distance. Five seconds of walking will do fine. After that, the whole process is repeated elsewhere and the two shots are cut together. Now we suddenly get the impression that Nazarin must have walked a thousand miles! A very remarkable phenomenon, how vast distances can be compressed by using an odd, twisted camera movement. I have no idea why it works, though it is a technique I actually used in *Heart of Glass* for the scene at the start of the film when Hias the prophet descends from the mountain and walks into the valley below.

What about the forged document you brought to one class? Why is forgery a skill useful to film directors?

The document you are speaking of was a four-page document that I myself had forged in Peru while I was making *Fitzcarraldo*. It was a very extravagant piece of paper with beautiful water marks which gave me all kinds of permission to move about the country in places where I would not otherwise have been able to go, areas that were swarming with the military. The soldiers were constantly stopping us and telling us we were not permitted to proceed. The document was apparently even signed by the President of the Republic and Supreme Commander of the armed forces, Belaunde, though of course it was one of our people who had put their pen to it. We needed to stamp it so it looked more authentic and I found a very impressive one in German that said something like 'To acquire the reproduction rights of this photo contact the author', something I knew nobody out there in the jungle would be able to decipher. That particular document opened so many doors for me, and *Fitzcarraldo* would not have been made without this fabrication. I did no harm to anyone by fabricating such a thing, I just needed to navigate downriver – through the militarily controlled areas – and when I showed the document to the soldiers and they saw the signature of the President on this impressive piece of paper they immediately saluted and let us through.

Take my advice and be prepared, study how to fake a document. Carry a silver coin or medal with you at all times. If you put it under the paper and make a rubbing you will create a kind of 'seal'. Top that with a bold signature and you have got something that looks just right. There are so many obstacles in filmmaking, but the worst of all is the spirit of bureaucracy. You have to find your own way to battle this menace. You have to outsmart it, outnumber it, outfilm it. And, moreover, bureaucracy loves nothing more than paper. You have to keep feeding it, and even a forgery pleases the bureaucrats so long as it is on impressive looking paper.

In recent years, with the growth of DVD, there has been a trend to go back and re-cut films, maybe releasing the so-called 'Director's Cut'. Is this something you've ever thought about doing?

No, I have almost always been the producer of my own films and so have always had final cut on all my work. Every film of mine you have seen has been a director's cut. To speak of out-takes, I have none of them. It is too expensive to store things like this – endless reels of material from all my films – so six months after the release of a film I always throw footage that has not been used in the final film into the garbage. This includes both negatives and and printed out-takes. A carpenter does not sit on his shavings either. When I was in New York during the closing stages of the *Fitzcarraldo* shoot I looked through all the rushes I had and decided what was useful and what was not. I just threw out everything I did not want to transport back to Germany, which meant a considerable saving in freight and customs charges. Just an example: in both *Aguirre* and *Kaspar Hauser* there was at least an hour of beautiful footage which did not make it to my final cut, and all this material is gone.

I do, of course, have the negatives of the cut films. People speak to me with alarm in their voice when they learn that many of them are already in decay with the colours fading away, or that for example the whole final reel of a film has been ruined by damp or something like that. But I never had the money to pay for a safety dupe negative on some of them. Originally my feelings about this had to do with my belief that film has a shorter shelf-life than literature. Decay is a natural phenomenon and to a certain extent I feel that celluloid's inevitable deterioration is a natural part of what cinema is. Most of the films that have been made in the past one hundred years are no longer with us, and much of what is left today is only stills. In the future people will have to read books like Lotte Eisner's *The Haunted Screen* to find out what films we were making at the turn of the millennium: two photos, a description of the story, some notes on the director. That is all there is.

I do appreciate there has been a new attitude developing about film preservation and of late I have maybe shifted in my attitude, perhaps against my better judgement. I can certainly see the other point of view, especially because I am very glad that German films from the 1920s, for example, are still in existence. I am happy that much of the work of Griffith, Méliès and the Lumière brothers is relatively well preserved. My change of heart is due to my fascination with many of the films from the early twentieth century, work I find of such stunning actuality. It was Henri Langlois who said the responsibility existed to preserve even the bad films. After all, attitudes and trends shift so radically over time that what is today a third-rate B-picture might be heralded a masterpiece tomorrow.

What's more, when you think about people 400 years from now trying to understand civilization today, I think they will probably get more out of a Tarzan film than out of the State of the Union address by the President that same year. So I have no clear attitude, but in recent years I have become more aware of the changing feelings about film preservation. My brother Lucki, who is also the producer of my films, is very methodical in at least collecting for our archives all the audio tracks, subtitles and negatives of all the films, something that I thank him for. But I am under no illusions: my existence on this planet is a very fleeting one and so, perhaps, should be the lives of my films.

But your films are the things that people will be able to remember you by. By preserving at least the negatives future generations would then be able to watch them 400 years from now.

I would not dare to predict that. People might watch them, they might not. And I would not know how to deal with posterity anyway.

You wouldn't need to. You'll be dead.

Well then, that's fine.

NOTES
1 See Bruce Chatwin's *The Songlines* and Chapter 9, footnote 4.
2 A book that served as a strong influence on Chatwin, and one that Herzog also read, was J. A. Skertchly's *Dahomey as It Is: Being a Narrative of Eight Months' Residence in that Country* (Chapman and Hall, 1874). Skertchly was investigating beetles and insects on the coast when he was taken captive by the King of Dahomey, who wanted him to explain how to work some new rifles he had just received, and ended up being kept against his will for eight months.

3   See Chatwin's essay 'Werner Herzog in Ghana' in *What Am I Doing Here* (Vintage, 1998).

4   See Brian Titley's *Dark Age, The Political Odyssey of Emperor Bokassa* (McGill-Queen's University Press, 1997).

5   Ryszard Kapuściński (b. 1932, Poland) has written many books about his travels in Africa, Latin America and the Middle East. He has often referred to his work as 'literature by foot', something that will resonate strongly with Herzog (see Chapter 9), and when asked recently where his sense of vocation comes from, he replied: 'I don't know where it came from: my father? My childhood? Or simply from seeing these people who have nothing to expect from life. But mostly I think I understood that to know anything at all about these cultures – in Rwanda, say, or Ethiopia – and to have the gift of describing them – you have to have a bit of the zeal, the humility, the craziness of the missionary. If you are staying in the Hilton or Sheraton you will never know, you will never write these things.' See his recent autobiography, *The Shadow of the Sun* (Penguin, 2001). Kapuściński also appeared as one of Herzog's guests in *Film Lesson*.

6   Brendan Behan (1923–64, Ireland) was a playwright whose works include *The Quare Fellow* (1956) and *The Hostage* (1958).

7   Luis Trenker (1882–1980, Italy) worked as a mountain guide in the Alps before becoming a leading writer and director. He also played opposite Leni Reifenstahl in many of Arnold Fanck's 'mountain films'.

8   Arnold Fanck (1889–1974, Germany) was a writer, producer and director. Inspired by his love of geology and fuelled by his frequent trips to the Swiss Alps as a child, Fanck was perhaps the most important director working within the mountain genre. See Thomas Elsaesser's *Weimar Cinema and After* (Routledge, 2000), pp. 391–4.

9   The *Bergfilm* [mountain film] was a very popular German genre in the 1920s and 1930s. It combined excessive melodrama, patriotism and death-defying mountain-top heroism with (because most were filmed on location) a documentary style of filmmaking. A good example is *Das Blaue Licht* [*The Blue Light*] (1932), directed by Béla Balázs and Leni Riefenstahl, and starring Riefenstahl.

10 The *Heimatfilm* was a wildly successful genre of the immediate post-war era. '*Heimatfilme* depict a world in which traditional values prevail: love triumphs over social and economic barriers, and the story is usually set in an idyllic German countryside, highlighting maypoles and other folkloric traditions.' (Elsaesser and Wedel, p. 133.)

11 Leni Riefenstahl (b. 1902, Germany) was a leading actress in the 1930s before becoming a director and photographer. Controversy has surrounded Riefenstahl's post-war reputation due to her propaganda film made for the Nazi party in 1934, *Triumph des Willens*

[*Triumph of the Will*]. See Ray Müller's 1993 film *The Wonderful, Horrible Life of Leni Riefenstahl*.

12 George Méliès (1861–1938, France) is generally considered one of the great pioneers of cinema. A professional magician by training, he built Europe's first film studio in Paris in 1897 and made his most famous film, *Voyage to the Moon*, in 1902.

13 Philippe Petit (b. 1949, France) is a magician and high-wire walker. On 6 August 1974 he became the first (and subsequently the only) person to tightrope walk between the twin towers of the World Trade Center in New York. See his books *On the High Wire* (Random House, 1985) and *To Reach the Clouds: My High Wire Walk Between the Twin Towers* (North Point Press, 2002).

14 Joseph Goebbels (1897–1945, Germany) was the Propaganda Minister of the Third Reich. He helped orchestrate Hitler's 1933 election victory and soon wielded control over all forms of media in Germany. Especially interested in film, Goebbels created the Reich Chamber of Culture, which in 1935 resulted in the world's first regular television service. See Hake's *German National Cinema*, p. 61.

15 Buñuel himself described the character of Nazarin (1958) as 'a Quixote of the priesthood; instead of following the example found in tales of knighthood, he follows the Gospels'. (*Objects of Desire: Conversations with Luis Buñuel*, edited and translated by Paul Lenti, Marsilio, 1992.)

8

Fact and Truth

In Hollywood there's a strong emphasis on 'story structure' and how each 'act' of the film fits into a structure. Do you have any time for things like that?

Not at all. I am just a storyteller who knows if a good story is working or is not, and who writes so fast he cannot afford to think about the structure of the writing. There is such an urgency of telling the tale that inevitably it creates its own structure. Hollywood films might have 'structure' to them, but they have scripts that press the right buttons at the right time, which is essentially filmmaking by numbers. There is a great production and distribution system in Hollywood, something we in Europe should be envious of, a great star system and special effects facilities too. But you hardly ever find a really good story any more, a deficit that is known to most of the people who work out there. I see the role of the film director as being akin to that of a storyteller at the market in Marrakech who has a crowd standing around him. This is who I am.

What was the starting point of your Minnesota Declaration?

The Minnesota Declaration[1] is somewhat tongue-in-cheek and designed to provoke, but the ideas it deals with are those that my mind has been engaged with over many years, from my earliest 'documentaries' onwards. After wrestling with these issues – certainly since *Land of Silence and Darkness* – the question has become much more intense than ever in the last ten years with films like *Bells from the Deep*, *Death for Five Voices* and *Little Dieter Needs to Fly*. The word 'documentary' should be handled with care because we seem to have a very precise definition of what the word means. Yet this is only due to our need to easily categorize films and the lack of a more appropriate concept for a whole range of cinema. Even though they are usually labelled as such, I would say that it is misleading to call films like *Bells from the Deep* and *Death for Five Voices* 'documentaries'. They merely come under the guise of 'documentaries'.

The background to the 'Minnesota Declaration: Truth and Fact in Documentary Filmmaking' is a very simple one. I had flown from Europe to San Francisco and back again in a very short space of time and had ended up in Italy, where I was directing an opera. Jet-lagged as I was, I could not sleep and turned on the television at midnight to be confronted by a very stupid, uninspiring documentary, something excruciatingly boring about animals somewhere out there in the Serengeti, all very cute and fluffy. At 2 a.m. I turned the television on again and watched something equally bad, the same kind of crap you find on television wherever you go. But then at 4 a.m. I found some hard-core porno, and I sat up and said to myself, 'My God, finally something straightforward, something real, even if it is purely physical.' For me the porno had real naked truth. For some time I had wanted to write some kind of manifesto, my thoughts about fact and truth in filmmaking – and ecstatic truth – a rant against *cinéma vérité*.[2] That same night I wrote the twelve points in a few minutes. They contain, in a very condensed form, everything that has angered and moved me over the years.

Your conclusion about so-called cinéma vérité *documentaries is that they don't penetrate into the deeper truth of the situations that they portray. This form of cinema is, in your words, merely 'the accountant's truth'.*

Cinema, like poetry, is inherently able to present a number of dimensions much deeper than the level of the so-called truth that we find in *cinéma vérité* and even reality itself, and it is these dimensions that are the most fertile areas for filmmakers. I truly hope to be one of those who finally bury *cinéma vérité* for good. Thankfully, there seem to be more and more filmmakers – and audience members – who understand this. Chris Marker[3] and

Errol Morris are two names that spring to mind. *Cinéma vérité* is the accountant's truth; it merely skirts the surface of what constitutes a deeper form of truth in cinema.

When you have an idea for a story, do you immediately know whether it is going to be a feature or a 'documentary'?

I do not sit and ponder whether I should articulate the story in one way or another. The next few films I will make are all features. Why? I do not know, this is just how it is. I do know the media have never picked up on the 'documentaries' as much as the other films, but I could not care less. I just do the things that are urgent to me. So for me, the boundary between fiction and 'documentary' simply does not exist; they are all just films. Both take 'facts', characters, stories and play with them in the same kind of way. I actually consider *Fitzcarraldo* my best 'documentary'. So I fight against *cinéma vérité* because it reaches only the most banal level of understanding of everything around us. I know that by making a clear distinction between 'fact' and 'truth' in my films, I am able to penetrate into a deeper stratum of truth most films do not even notice. The deep inner truth inherent in cinema can be discovered only by not being bureaucratically, politically and mathematically correct. In other words, I start to invent and play with the 'facts' as we know them. Through invention, through imagination, through fabrication, I become more truthful than the little bureaucrats. This is an idea that will become clearer when we discuss some of the later films like *Bells from the Deep* and *Lessons of Darkness*.

Land of Silence and Darkness seems an important film in this respect because it marks the start of your 'investigations' into 'truth' and 'fact' in cinema.

Yes, though I suspect at the time it was probably not so conscious but more a kind of instinctive attitude I had. The line that is quoted at the end of that film – 'If a world war were to break out now, I would not even notice it' – is not something that Fini ever said. This is something I wrote that I felt encapsulated, in only a few words, how someone like her might experience the world. And the lines at the start of the film when Fini speaks about the ecstatic faces of the ski-flyers whom she says she used to watch as a child are also written by me. It is all pure invention. She had actually never even seen a ski-jumper, and I just asked her to say the lines that I wrote. Why? Because I felt that the solitude and ecstasy of the ski-jumpers as they flew through the air was a great image to represent Fini's own inner state of mind and solitude. Of course, when making the film no scenes were shot contrary to Fini's wishes and she did not mind speaking the lines that I had written for her. The wonderful thing about her was that she never argued about it; she immediately understood and squeezed my hand. Sometimes she would say that she understood in a very strange way, almost like an Egyptian priest: 'I . . . have . . . understood . . . you.'

In my 'documentaries' I have constantly explored the intensified truths of the situations that I have found myself in and of the characters I have met, whether it be abused people who lose their speech in *Lessons of Darkness* or the chain-smoking African chimp of *Echoes from a Sombre Empire*. It is permissible to stylize certain parts of a film only if the subject is co-operative, and so with my film about my work with Kinski, *My Best Fiend*, I felt that such an approach would not be healthy. Not being around to defend himself, the facts about Kinski had to be presented as coherently as possible and a very clear concept had to be maintained, even though, the film was undeniably from my own perspective.

And now you seem to be doing this by playing with the facts surrounding a real-life character in your latest feature film.

What I did with *Invincible* is a good example of how I used these ideas and applied them to a feature film. I looked at the facts about the life of the Polish blacksmith Zishe Breitbart in the 1920s and realized – though there was clearly a story there – much of it did not interest me. I knew I had to reinvent Zishe for the film and transplant the character to the early 1930s because everything that is fascinating about the relationship between Germans and Jews was exacerbated in that era and, of course, turned into the most monstrous crime and tragedy afterwards. The 'truth' about Zishe's life is brought much more to life when we are able to see his story through the lens of 1930s Germany.

But this isn't an approach that you use for every single one of your 'documentaries', is it? And even when you do, it is done with extreme subtlety.

Even in a film like *Ballad of the Little Soldier*, perhaps my most political film, you can see signs of these ideas. I could have made a straightforward study of the political situation down there and called it *The Children's War Against the Sandinistas*. But I called it *Ballad of the Little Soldier* for a reason: for a long time I have wanted to make a musical. I have hours of footage of the villagers and the soldiers singing and maybe one day will edit it together to produce a real oratorio. The existing film is my compromise, as I very much wanted to tell the story of the child soldiers who were dying in Nicaragua every day.

But the stylizations of truth in the 'documentary' films are generally very subtle indeed. You probably would not know about most of them unless you were paying close attention to the films, and even then you might need to have some background to the subject matter. A good example is the last scene of *Echoes from a Sombre Empire*. In the decrepit zoo we found one of the saddest things I have ever seen: a monkey addicted to cigarettes thanks to the drunken soldiers who had taught it to smoke. Michael Goldsmith looks at the ape and says something like, 'I can't take this any longer' and tells me I should turn the camera off. I answer back from behind the camera, 'Michael, I think this is one of the shots I should hold.' He replies, 'Only if you promise this will be the last shot in the film.' While this dialogue and my use of the animal was a completely scripted invention, the nicotine-addicted monkey itself was not. There was something momentous and mysterious about the creature, and filming it in the way I did brought the film to a deeper level of truth, even if I did not stick entirely to the facts. To call *Echoes from a Sombre Empire* a 'documentary' is like saying that Warhol's painting of Campbell's soup cans is a document about tomato soup.

I would like to point out also the opening quote from Blaise Pascal at the start of *Lessons of Darkness*. 'The collapse of the stellar universe will occur – like creation – in grandiose splendour.' Well, it may sound like Pascal, but actually it is all invented. I enjoy doing things like this because I am a storyteller, plain and simple, not a traditional 'documentary' filmmaker. In *Little Dieter Needs to Fly* I open the film with a quote from Revelation – 'And in those days shall men seek death, and shall not find it, and death shall flee from them' – and then show a regular guy walking into a downtown tattoo parlour. With this quote you are immediately prepared for something almost otherworldly when the film starts. You just do not expect to see a kind of seedy tattoo parlour after the Bible has just been quoted to you.

What the Pascalian pseudo-quote does is lift you from the first minute of the film to a level that prepares you for something quite momentous. We are immediately in the realm of poetry – whether or not the audience knows the quote is a fake – which inevitably strikes a more profound chord than mere reportage. With Pascal you are immersed in the cosmic even before the first picture appears on the screen, and *Lessons of Darkness* never lets you down until its last frame. It holds you up there without shame, something I do with real pride and with the confidence that I am not manipulating the audience in any way. Pascal himself could not have written it better! After the quote the film continues with the voice-over talking of 'Wide mountain ranges, the valleys enshrouded in mist.' What I actually filmed were little heaps of dust and soil created by the tires of trucks. These 'mountain ranges' were no more than a foot high.

I keep telling young people who always ask with hesitation in their voice about history and concoction and invention that *this* is what cinema is about.

Lessons of Darkness was made very soon after the Gulf War. How did audiences react to seeing in cinemas the images of the oil fires that they'd been watching on television for months?

Lessons of Darkness was very well received in America. It was interesting to see the reaction to the film there because the whole country – and the whole world in fact – had repeatedly watched the same kind of images of the burning oil wells in Kuwait on CNN during and after the war. But these images saturated the public's consciousness only via news broadcasts and made very little impact because of their tabloid style. We have all watched so many horrific things on the news that we have become totally –

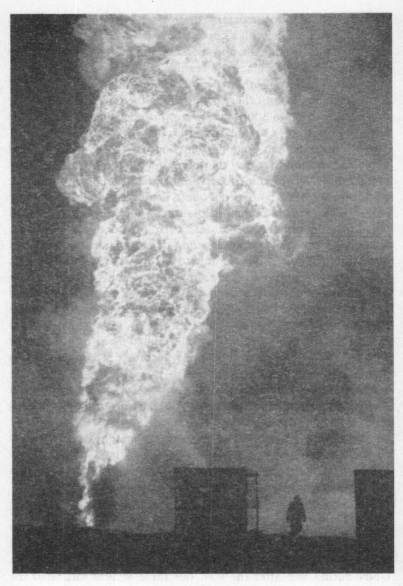

Lessons of Darkness

and dangerously – inured to them. When it came to these spectacular fields of burning oil, everyone seemed to forget them the very next day. Yet to look at the surface of pitch-black oil is to see what looks like a vast serene lake reflecting the blue sky and the clouds. It is very strange, and I knew I was watching something momentous that had to be recorded for the memory of mankind.

The stylization of the horror in *Lessons of Darkness* means that the images penetrate deeper than the CNN footage ever could, something that bothered audiences in Germany a great deal. When *Lessons of Darkness* was shown at the Berlin Film Festival, with one voice nearly 2,000 people rose up in an angry roar against me. They accused me of 'aestheticizing' the horror and hated the film so much that when I walked down the aisle of the cinema I was spat at. They said the film was dangerously authoritarian, so I decided to be authoritarian at my very best. I stood before them and said, 'Mr Dante did the same in his inferno and Mr Goya did it in his paintings, and Brueghel and Bosch too.' You should have heard the uproar. The German critics took the film as if it were a dangerous attack on everyone's decency. Everyone else liked the film very much and it received tremendous reviews around the world. Sitting here now ten years later I would dare an assumption: if I showed the film today to an audience at the Berlin Film Festival they would probably like it.

Was it a particular conceptual decision you made to use the scenes of the burning oil wells with the abused Kuwaitis?

I made contact with various organizations who were documenting torture victims and through them got in touch with the people I filmed. They had lost their ability to speak because of the atrocities they had witnessed. I feel that there is actually a slight imbalance to the film because there were some other people I wanted to film, but the Kuwaiti government basically expelled me. The authorities were constantly scrutinizing what I was doing there. From the start they hoped I would make a film that would show the positive, optimistic reconstruction of everything with the cleaning up of the oil wells and an apparently heroic fresh new start. They had objections against me going into the deepest wounds that the war had created for some of the people. One afternoon I was handed a letter by the Ministry of Information which quite simply stated I was wished a pleasant flight out of the country tomorrow morning at 7 a.m. It was clear this was an expulsion order. If I had insisted on continuing filming they would have confiscated my footage, so I was prudent enough to wrap up my things and go instantly. It seemed the world the Kuwaitis wanted to portray on film consisted only of the fires and the heroic firemen, not the scarred victims. I wish I had been able to put more human beings in *Lessons of Darkness*, yet it still has something very humane about it. Not only where you see human beings; you see it everywhere. Every single shot somehow.

Did the bureaucrats criticize you for not identifying Kuwait?

They did indeed, but of course I did that on purpose. There was just no need to name Saddam Hussein and the country he attacked. And you know, even if people are watching *Lessons of Darkness* in 300 years' time, it still would not be important for them to know the historical facts behind this film. *Lessons of Darkness* transcends the topical and the particular. This could be *any* war and *any* country. The criticisms of the film in Germany come down to this: if you do not make a black-and-white political statement you are on the side of the devils, a point of view that is clearly overly simplistic and stupid. But at the end of the day all this good and bad dissipates into thin air, and thankfully only the films remain. Films have their own lives and their own ways to travel straight to the hearts of audiences. Anyway, everyone knew that it was Kuwait because, as you said, the war was still in people's minds.

I should stress that *Lessons of Darkness* is as much a film by Paul Berriff as it is mine. It was a very fortunate collaboration. There was the danger of two cooks preparing one meal, but in this case Paul was a man of such calibre that our collaboration worked very well. The result is something very special, and ultimately I owe this film to him. I knew after watching CNN that I wanted to go out to Kuwait and luckily I found Paul Berriff by searching for someone – anyone – with a shooting permit for Kuwait. The oil fires were being extinguished unexpectedly fast so I had to hurry.

Berriff is English and has made a lot of very physically daring films, like sea rescues by helicopter with him dangling from a cable and things like that. A courageous man, very physical in his methods of seeing and creating images. He has a really physical curiosity. Paul already had an expert helicopter pilot he wanted to work with, and for a project like this a good pilot is as important as a cinematographer. He had to understand the terrain and air flows around the burning oil wells and establish a pattern of flight to facilitate a sequence of travelling shots. I was never actually in the helicopter; the footage was shot two days before I arrived in the country. The cameraman, an expert in aerial photography, knew what I wanted: as many unbroken travelling shots of the landscape as possible. But I would not have been able to plan every single one of the shots even if I had been up there. The pilot would not have been able to just follow my directions all the time because if he had flown into an area where the heat might be suddenly blown towards it, the helicopter would immediately explode. Up there the temperatures reached over a 1,000 °C. So in flying into a burning oil field the pilot has to make his own choices for safety reasons. He did an outstanding job and allowed the cameramen to hold the shots for as long as he possibly could.

Who are the firefighters on the ground? Is that Red Adair and his crew?

No, Red Adair had already quit at that point. Initially, I was advised to make a film about him and his efforts to put out the fires, but his working methods involved the heaviest imaginable machinery with every precaution in the book. He predicted it would take four or five years to put out these fires, which it certainly would have done if Adair had gone his own way. As I said, it was actually done within about six months, though the crews who did extinguish the fires were running much higher risks of course. The men in the film are, I think, an American or Canadian team. There were also Iranians, Hungarians, teams from all over the world. The Iranians were the most impressive because they did not have much equipment and they fought the fires almost with bare hands. Everyone who worked with these men spoke of them with great respect.

What kind of cameras did you use?

We used regular cameras, and the crew had only nomex suits for protection, the kind of suits Formula One race drivers wear. What was not well protected were hands and shoes, and our soles would melt away quite quickly if we were not careful. One time Paul Berriff jumped from behind our barricade to get a shot and immediately I could see that the half of his face not protected by the camera was reddening and getting burnt. I held my two hands with thick leather gloves on to try to protect his face, and within ten seconds my gloves were burning. We were recording all the sound live and one of the boom microphones just melted away. In fact, to really appreciate the film you have to see it in the cinema with Dolby stereo because for me the sound was actually the most impressive thing. These geysers of fire shooting 300 feet up into the sky with such pressure sounds like four jumbo jets taking off simultaneously. It really was quite something.

One of the reasons my collaboration with Paul worked so well was because of this understanding of hearts we had, something that became obvious when we both decided we did not want to use long zoom lenses when filming on the ground. This meant that if something interested us we decided to go as far in as possible and were right there with the firefighters themselves. Paul did the camerawork, though there was a second cameraman sometimes, and we shot it all on film, nothing was on video. Sometimes this was a problem because raw stock has to be acclimatized to wherever you are shooting, and it was exceptionally hot in Kuwait that summer. So we could not just take the film out of the refrigerator and then expose it in the camera, and when it came to the shots of the oil wells we had to protect the film with aluminium foil and take it out of the camera as soon as we had finished the roll to get it away from the heat. Thankfully we never lost any of the footage.

You've said that Lessons of Darkness, *like* Fata Morgana, *is a science-fiction film. What do you mean by this?*

Calling *Lessons of Darkness* a science-fiction film is a way of explaining that the film has not a single frame that can be recognized as our planet, and yet we know it must have been shot here. I spoke earlier of our 'embarrassed landscapes'. Well, the landscape you see in *Lessons of Darkness* is not just embarrassed, it is completely mutilated. The film plays out as if the entire planet is burning away, and because there is music throughout the film, I call it 'a requiem for an uninhabitable planet'. Unlike *La Soufrière*, which tries to document a natural catastrophe, *Lessons of Darkness* is a requiem for a planet that we ourselves have destroyed. The film progresses as if aliens have landed on an unnamed planet where the landscape has lost every single trace of its dignity, and – just like in *Fata Morgana* with the debris-strewn desert landscapes – these aliens see human beings for the first time. There is a line I speak in the voice-over when one of the firemen signals something: 'The first creature we encountered tried to communicate something to us.'

You become quite explicit about this idea when showing the shot of the firefighter lighting up a plume of gushing oil.

The voice-over says something like, 'Seized by madness, they reignite the flames because they cannot imagine a life without fire, and now there is something to extinguish they are happy again.' There was actually a practical reason for igniting the flame because in this case the gush of oil had created a lake which was approaching other burning fires, and had the oil been ignited by other fires there would have been an even bigger problem. I asked them to let me know when they were going to reignite the flame so I could be there with a camera. I am a storyteller, and I used the voice-over to place the film – and the audience – in a darkened planet somewhere in our solar system.

The ideas of 'fact and truth' you started exploring in Land of Silence and Darkness *have of late been taken to the* reductio ad absurdum *with films like* Death for Five Voices *and* Bells from the Deep: Faith and Superstition in Russia. *How did you hear about this array of bizarre characters out there in Siberia?*

Oh, I find them. I engaged some Russian collaborators and told them to scour Siberia for the best Jesus Christ they could find and eventually they came up with Vissarion. He is an ex-policeman who all of a sudden realized that he was, in fact, Jesus. There were about a 110 competing Jesus figures roaming Siberia at that time,

Bells from the Deep

and Vissarion actually had an agent in Moscow. But this did not turn me away from him because I had the feeling that he truly was someone very special with great depth, and he lived a very ascetic life in a tiny apartment in Krasnojarsk in Siberia. The faith healer in the film, Alan Chumack, used to be a very well-known media figure on Russian television where he would re-enact alien abductions and things like that. One day, after discovering he was so popular with mass audiences, he decided he had psychic powers himself, something which has made him ten times more money than his television work.

What about Yuri Yurevitch Yurieff, the orphaned bell ringer who used to be a cinema projectionist?

An incredible man, yes. When he was found as a child and was asked what his name was – first name, middle name and family name – all he would say was 'Yuri'. For me the man is a true musician; the way he has strung up all the ropes in the bell tower is incredible. The sound he gets from tolling the bells has such depth to it. I actually planned to start the film at a monastery with one single monk playing one single bell and wanted to show bigger and bigger bell-ringing orgies throughout, and Yuri would have been somewhere in the middle. I also spent some time looking for a hermit. Of course, it is not very productive advertising for hermits but I did eventually find one. Actually, he was not a textbook hermit, rather someone condemned to life in prison for murder in a huge prison colony near St Petersburg. Within the huge compound next to the soccer field, he had built himself a small monastery and lived a monastic life. I looked so hard for a genuine hermit and had so many knowledgeable people engaged in this search that I do not believe there are any left. Very few anyway, and very well hidden at that.

So what part of the film is made up? Are some of the characters actors?

When it comes to 'fact and truth', I admit that the best of the film is 'fabricated'. The film begins in the Tuvinian Autonomous Republic, just north-west of Mongolia. An old man is throat singing about the beauty of a mountain. Later in the film there are two young kids – one is twelve, the other is fourteen – and they sing a love song. What does that have to do with a film about faith, you might ask? And yet it does belong; just by dint of declaration this becomes a religious hymn. Later on we see what seems to be people deep in prayer. We were *en route* to one of the locations when I stopped the bus because I saw a frozen lake in the distance with hundreds of people on it who had drilled holes in the ice and were fishing. As it was so cold they were all crouching down with their backs against the wind, all facing the same direction as if they were all in deep meditation. So the film somehow declares them all pilgrims in prayer.

When you look at a film like *Bells from the Deep* you are not watching a film that in any way strives to report facts about Russia, like an explicitly ethnographic documentary might do. This sounds like someone who reads a poem by Hölderlin where he describes a storm in the alps claiming, 'Ah, here we have a weather report back in 1802.'

Is the legend of the Lost City of Kitezh real or a figment of your imagination?

I heard of the myth while I was out there. It is a very real belief these people have. The legend goes that the city was systematically ransacked and demolished by hundreds of years of Tartar and Hun invasions. The inhabitants called on God to redeem them and He sent an archangel, who tossed the city into a bottomless lake where the people live in bliss, chanting their hymns and tolling the bells. During the summer you find pilgrims on their knees crawling around the lake saying their prayers, though I was there in winter when there was a very thin layer of ice covering the lake. I wanted to get shots of pilgrims crawling around on the ice trying to catch a glimpse of the lost city, but as there were no pilgrims around I hired two drunks from the next town and put them on the ice. One of them has his face right on the ice and looks like he is in very deep meditation. The accountant's truth: he was completely drunk and fell asleep, and we had to wake him at the end of the take.

What do you say to those who feel this kind of filmmaking is cheating?

It might seem like cheating, but it is not. *Bells from the Deep* is one of the most pronounced examples of what I mean when I say that only through invention and fabrication and staging can you reach a more intense level of truth that cannot otherwise be found. I took a 'fact' – that for many people this lake was the final resting place of this lost city – and played with the 'truth' of the situation to reach a more poetic understanding. We react with much stronger fervour and passion to poetry than mere television reportage, and that is the reason why *Lessons of Darkness* struck such a chord. We have known for a long time the poet is able to articulate a deep, inherent, mysterious truth better than anyone else. But for some reason filmmakers – particularly those who deal in the accountant's truth – are unaware of this as they continue trading their out-of-date wares.

Is what we see in Bells from the Deep *in any way representative of the general attitudes and feelings in Russia today?*

There is something very profound about Russians. I am married to a Russian from Siberia and many of these people have truly ecstatic depths to them when it comes to beliefs and superstitions. I feel the borderline between faith and superstition is very blurred for them. The question is: how do you depict the soul of an entire nation in an hour-long film? In a way, the scene of the drunken city-seekers is the deepest truth you can have about Russia because the soul of the entire country is somehow secretly in search of the lost city of Kitezh. I think the scene explains the fate and soul of Russia more than anything else, and those who know about Russia best, Russians themselves, think this sequence is the best one in the whole film. Even when I tell them it was not real pilgrims out there on the ice, it was people whom I hired, they still love it, and understand the scene has captured some kind of ecstatic truth.

Let's talk about your career as an opera director. Around this time you made your film at the Bayreuth Wagner Festival, The Transformation of the World into Music. *You'd been directing opera around the world for some time before you made the film. Was it an attempt to summarize on film your ideas about this side-profession you've found for yourself?*

In 1987 I directed *Lohengrin* at Bayreuth,[4] which ran for seven consecutive years until 1994, when I made *The Transformation of the World into Music*. You have to see the film in the right context as it is a piece that serves a very clear purpose. Over the previous few years operas staged in Bayreuth were being recorded for transmission on the French/German station Arte. They wanted an introductory piece and asked me to make a film about the festival. Initially they suggested a very dubious approach, something like 'The Myth of Bayreuth'. I said no, but they accepted my proposal to focus on the workshop aspect of the festival. I explained that the best time to shoot would be right now because it was the last year I was working there restaging *Lohengrin*. Working there meant it would be relatively easy to talk with colleagues and musicians and singers whom I would see every day anyway.

Why this desire to start directing opera in the 1980s?

I never had any aspirations to stage opera. I was literally dragged into it. After much hesitation I was persuaded to visit the opera house in Bologna, and all of a sudden I found myself surrounded by about forty stagehands, electricians and other personnel who formed a solid circle of bodies. They just physically held on to me and declared they would not let me leave unless I would sign a contract. I love the Italians for their gift of physical enthusiasm. So I had no choice and staged *Doctor Faustus* by Ferruccio Busoni in 1986. I immediately felt very confident and safe in what I was doing. What was so important was that I was appreciated with an immediacy and enthusiasm by others, something I have never experienced with my films. Opera has brought me joy and inner balance, even though I am also the first to admit that when I started I really did not know what opera was supposed to look like, how it truly 'functions' up there on the stage.

I never do any research. Before I started work on *Lohengrin*, an assistant handed me a huge pile of literature and opera theory, none of which I read. Apart from my own productions I have watched maybe four or five operas in my entire life, though I have listened to recordings of many productions. I know nothing about the different stylistic approaches to opera, I just seize upon what I see when I listen to the music. Today hardly anyone believes me when I tell them that the first production I ever saw was at La Scala in Milan two years after the filming of *Fitzcarraldo*, a film that of course is in part about opera.

But the key to my opera work is my love of the music. When I heard Wagner's *Parsifal* for the first time in Bayreuth during a rehearsal, the auditorium was almost empty. There is a moment when for twenty minutes Kundry is lying on the ground, somewhat hidden. She looks like a piece of the rock formation, and then suddenly she rises up and screams. It was such a shock for me, with my knees propped up against the seats in front of me, that I was jolted violently and ripped this entire row of seats from its anchoring. Along with Wolfgang Wagner, the grandson of Richard Wagner, I tumbled backwards. Wagner got to his feet and rushed over to me. Bowing, he took my hand and shook and said something like, 'Finally, an audience who knows how to really respond to the music!' It was like being struck by lightning. Beautiful.

You said that music is the most important influence for you when it comes to your films. Does this include opera?

Music has always been very important to me. Audiences surely do not need me to explain this; they are able to understand just by listening to my films. When you watch *Fata Morgana* and *Pilgrimage*, my use of music is very obvious. And even though it has lots of dialogue I feel that *The Great Ecstasy of Woodcarver Steiner* is also one of these. I have always felt that there are very few film directors who truly understand what is possible with music in cinema. Two names that spring to mind when I think of masters of film music are Satyajit Ray, the wonderful Indian director, particularly *The Music Room*, and the Taviani brothers from Italy. I doff my hat to them. They are so incredibly lucid in their use of music they make me ashamed, particularly their film *Padre Padrone*, where the music suddenly starts up and builds until it makes an entire landscape appear as if it were in mourning.

It seems that it was with Fata Morgana *that you really started to work intensively with music. Throughout the film the music seems to fit so well to the images, even though there is such a wide selection of different composers, from Leonard Cohen to Mozart.*

An image does not change *per se* when you place music behind it, but with *Fata Morgana* I found that there were certain qualities and atmospheres in the images that could be seen more clearly when there was certain music playing. The music changes the perspective of the audience; they see things and experience emotions that were not there before. Of course this can also work the other way around: if you choose the right images, a piece of music we think we understand can be utterly transformed and resonate with completely new meaning. With *Fata Morgana*, in particular, there does sometimes seem to be a contradiction between what you see and what you hear, but for me this actually creates a kind of tension that makes many things transparent that otherwise would not be so.

What about your working relationship with Florian Fricke, the man behind the cult German band Popul Vuh.

It is a very bitter loss for me that Florian Fricke has recently died. Kinski was 'my best fiend', but Florian was 'my best friend' when it came to my films. He appears as the pianist in *Signs of Life* and *Kaspar Hauser*, and did the music for many of my films including *The Great Ecstasy*, *Fitzcarraldo*, *Nosferatu* and *Heart of Glass*. Florian was always able to create music I feel helps audiences visualize something hidden in the images on screen, and in our own souls too. In *Aguirre* I wanted a choir that would sound out of this world, like when I would walk at night as a child, thinking that the stars were singing, so Florian used a very strange instrument called a 'choir-organ'. It would sound just like a human choir but yet, at the same time, had a very artificial and eerie quality to it. Florian was always full of ideas like this.

And what about the sound design in your films, something that again seems very important.

One thing that I realized very early on, practically in my very first film, was the importance of sound quality if a film was to succeed. I have often seen young filmmakers who when they finally manage to make their first film – when they finally overcome the problems of finance and organization and all the rest – frequently fail with their use of sound. It is because of this that I have spent some time concentrating on how sound functions in cinema. Almost all my films have been shot in direct sound, which means it takes more time and energy to prepare. Often it takes more time preparing the sound than setting up the shot and determining where the camera will move. But it is sound that will decide the outcome of many battles on a film set. Good sound adds dimensions to a film that you never ever knew existed. Someone like Bresson was very aware of this, and in each of his films he gives us so many silences, yet every one different and full of noise. Compare his subtlety with a film like *Apocalypse Now*, where the sound is not handled well conceptually and where the sledgehammer effects are constantly hitting you over the head. It is like watching very early colour films which have absurdly bright primary colours screaming out at you.

Would you ever make a narrative feature without any dialogue?

Isn't that what I did with *Fata Morgana*? For me storytelling has to do with human speech, and relationships between humans are established primarily through speech, so I would certainly hesitate before making a wholly silent film without dialogue and even music. I do not see *Pilgrimage* as a silent film because the music is inextricably bound up in the images. The only form I immediately see would work without any dialogue and music would be a porno where you would only need the gasps and the shrieks and panting.

Can you read music?

I must be one of the few opera directors who cannot read music scores. This is due to one of those little childhood school tragedies when I was thirteen. The music teacher asked every-body in alphabetical order to stand up and sing a song. The whole thing had an ideology behind it: at that time there were these ideas floating around that everyone is an artist and has innate musical talent, whether he sings well or not. When it came to the letter H, I was asked to stand up. 'I am not going to sing,' I told him. The thing immediately turned nasty, and bold as I was at that age I said, 'Sir, you may do a somersault forward and backward, you may run up the walls and on to the ceiling. I . . . am . . . not . . . going . . . to . . . sing.' This pissed him off so much that he brought in the headmaster, and in front of the whole class, while I was standing there, they discussed whether I should be thrown out of the school altogether. It was that serious, but I remained stubborn. Then what they did was really bad: they took the whole class hostage. 'Nobody is going to leave until Herzog sings.' All my friends started to push me, saying, 'Don't worry, we will not listen to you, we just want to go outside during the break.' And the headmaster interrupted and said, 'There is no break for you if Herzog does not sing.' But I stood my ground, knowing that they just wanted to break my back. After forty minutes, for the sake of my classmates, I sang. And while I sang I knew I would never, ever sing in my life again. And I have not until this very day, nor have I sat down and learned how to read musical scores. Truly, it pains me to think back about this incident, and at the time I told myself, 'No man, ever, will break me again. It will not happen, no matter what.' So I continued in school, but during music classes I became completely autistic. I would not listen; I was on a different planet. Between the ages of thirteen and eighteen no music existed for me.

When I left school I sensed this huge void and voraciously dug into music without any guidance at all. I started with Heinrich Schütz, some kind of point of reference to me, and from there into earlier music. Only very much later did I start listening to Wagner and more contemporary composers. Then, of course, there was Gesualdo's *Sixth Book of Madrigals*. That was a moment of complete enlightenment for me. I was so excited I called up Florian Fricke at three in the morning and did not stop raving about it. Finally, after half an hour, he said, 'Werner, everyone who is into music knows about Gesualdo and the *Sixth Book*. You sound as if you have discovered a new planet.' But for me it *was* as if I had discovered something tremendous within our solar system, and out of that sprung a film about Gesualdo which I carried within me for many years.

I became fascinated by Wagner relatively late. Wolfgang Wagner sent me a telegram asking me to direct *Lohengrin*. I immediately replied, answering his request with a single word: 'No.' Wagner kept on insisting, and I kept on saying no. Finally, after weeks, he became suspicious and finally asked whether I had even heard the opera. I said, 'No.' So he asked, 'Would you please listen to my favourite recording that I am going to send you? Then, if your answer is still no, I will never bother you again.' This I did, and when I heard the *Vorspiel* – the overture – I was totally stunned. Hearing it for the first time was a moment of complete illumination for me; it was a deep and beautiful shock and I knew this was something very big. And I had the feeling, 'I should have the courage to tackle this one,' so I immediately accepted his offer to direct at Bayreuth. And I said to Wagner, 'Let's just do the overture – musically it contains the entire opera – and keep the curtain closed. And when people start to make noise and demand the opera, we will play it again and again until we chase them out of the theatre.' Wagner, I think, started to like me.

What do you mean when you talk of 'transforming a whole world into music'?

I consider opera a universe all its own. On stage an opera represents a complete world, a cosmos transformed into music. I love the gross stylizations of the performances and the grandeur of human emotions, whether they be love or hate or jealousy or guilt. I often ask myself do we humans *really* recognize these archetypes of emotional exaltation and purity that are being enacted on the opera stage? Of course we do, this is what makes opera so beautiful even though the stories being told are often so implausible. Emotions in opera are almost like mathematical axioms: extremely reduced and concentrated. It matters little that most of the libretti are bad, or like in the case of *Giovanna d'Arco*, a true catastrophe. In fact, so many of the opera plots are not even within the calculus of probability; it would be like winning the lottery jackpot five consecutive times over. And yet, when the music is playing, the stories do make sense. Their strong inner truths shine through and they seem utterly plausible.

When I was first asked to direct opera it seemed a strange request, but after thinking about it I realized that it was something not foreign to me. 'Why should I not try at least once in my life to transform everything into music, every action, every word?' As I have explained throughout our conversations, since my very earliest days as a filmmaker I have to a certain degree worked in a similar way by transforming things that are physically there into more intensified, elevated and stylized images.

Do opera and cinema work well together?

Film is about transforming a world into images, and is very different from opera where the veracity of facts does not seem to matter any longer and where suddenly everything is possible. Film and opera are like cats and dogs; they will never marry, and this is the reason why some very able directors have failed when trying to film operas in original settings.

Are you as fast at directing opera as you are at writing and directing your own film scripts? And unlike with your films, do you rehearse a great deal?

I am relatively quick at the job, yes. In less than a week I move through the entire opera, every scene, and try to locate the big questions quickly. And just as I do not like to over-rehearse scenes before I shoot them, I dislike rehearsing opera too much, otherwise it gets very stale. As an opera director at Bayreuth and other places, it is important for me to forget I am principally a filmmaker. I wipe it from my mind. Opera is such a different process; the director needs to be aware of what the stage looks like from every possible angle in the auditorium. If a singer takes a step to the right the whole right side of the house cannot see her any more. I am aware there are a hundred different angles for the spectators, but with a camera there is only one position at a time. Emotions flow very differently in opera, and so does the flow of time.

Am I right in thinking that with Death for Five Voices *many of the scenes are again subtly stylized?*

Subtly stylized? No, in this case they are complete fabrications. Most of the stories in the film are completely invented and staged, yet they contain the most profound possible truths about Gesualdo. I think of all my 'documentaries', *Death for Five Voices* is the one that really runs amok, and it is one of the films closest to my heart.

It tells the story of Carlo Gesualdo, the sixteenth-century musical visionary and Prince of Venosa.[5] Gesualdo is the composer who keeps stunning me more than anyone else, and I wanted to make a film about him because his life is almost as interesting as his music.

For a start he murdered his wife, and as he was the Prince of Venosa he was never financially dependent on anyone and was able to finance his own voyages into the musical unknown. The other books are more within the context of his time, but with his *Sixth Book of Madrigals* all of a sudden Gesualdo seems to step 400 years ahead of his time, composing music that we hear only from Stravinsky onwards. There are segments in *Death for Five Voices* when we hear each of the five voices of a madrigal individually. Each individual voice sounds perfectly normal, but in combination the music sounds so ahead of its time, even of our own time.

So for Death for Five Voices *you took the most basic facts about Gesualdo and illustrated them with stylized scenes that would reinforce the major elements of the story?*

Yes. Take, for example, the scene shot in the castle of Venosa where there is a museum. In one of the glass showcases there was one piece – a clay disc with enigmatic script-like symbols on it – that really engaged my mind with puzzlement and gave me sleepless nights. I very much wanted to use the object in the film, so I wrote for the director of the museum – in actuality the dean of Milano Law School – a monologue about the disc that he should speak whilst standing next to the showcase. He presents a letter from Gesualdo to his alchemist, enlisting his aid in deciphering the mysterious signs on the disc. 'The prince had spent sleepless nights trying to unravel the secret of these strange symbols,' the professor explains. 'In the course of this activity, he became lost in a labyrinth of conjectures and hypotheses. He almost lost his reason in the process.' What I wanted here was to play on the fact that in the final years of his life Gesualdo was basically mad; he really did lose his mind. He single-handedly chopped down the entire forest around his castle and hired young men who had the task of flogging him daily, something that gave him festering wounds and apparently killed him. There is also a scene when we meet a woman running around the Prince's decrepit castle singing his music who says she is the spirit of Gesualdo's dead wife. She is there to stress the profound effect Gesualdo's music has had on people over the centuries, though we hired Milva, a famous Italian actress and singer to play the part.

Death for Five Voices

And what about the story of Gesualdo killing his own son?

I invented the story of Gesualdo placing his two-and-a-half-year-old son – whom he doubted was actually his child – on a swing and having his servants swing him for two days and two nights until the child was dead. There is an allusion in some of the existing documents to him killing his infant son, but no absolute proof. That he would have a choir on either side of the boy on the swing singing about the beauty of death is also invented, though in one of Gesualdo's compositions there is such a text. It is absolutely certain, however, he caught his wife *in flagrante* and stabbed her and her lover to death. The court documents attest to this being historical fact.

The last scene of the film was shot at a local mediaeval tournament, something the Italians love. I wanted to have the musical director speak about boldness and adventure in music, and as I was talking to him I noticed the face of a young man who was playing a footman to one of the knights. The whole scene with this footman picking up his mobile phone and speaking to his mother was, of course, staged. The person who actually called up was my own brother who knew exactly when to call as he was standing ten feet away. I told the young man to act as if it was his mother calling him and she wanted him to come back for lunch. I knew it was going to be the last scene in the film, and he says, 'Mom, don't worry, I'll be home very soon, because the film about Gesualdo is almost over.' I asked him to look straight into the camera after saying this line and look very serious. I was right next to the camera, playing around and making all sorts of jokes and things. There is a strange expression on his face because he didn't know whether to laugh or be serious, so he just stares for a long time into the camera, and the film ends.

Little Dieter Needs to Fly is one of my favourites, a very moving story told so incredibly by Dieter Dengler himself. How did you first meet him?

Dieter Dengler was the greatest rapper I ever met. He died recently of Lou Gehrig's disease, and the way the illness attacked him was to take his power of speech first. How scandalous that in his final days he was bereft of words. Being with Dieter was a constant joy. The man had such an intense enjoyment of life, something I think you really can feel throughout the film. Even when he could not talk any more we still managed to have long conversations together. Of course I had to do most of the talking, but he was still capable of getting stories across with his face and hands and feet. He could even tell jokes without being able to speak. I truly feel a great void now he is not around.

Dieter's story is an amazing one. Born in Germany, his earliest memories are of Allied bombers diving down from the clouds and bombing his small village in the Black Forest into dust. One bomber came so close to the house where Dieter lived, firing as it flew, that it whipped past the window where he was standing. For a split second Dieter's eyes locked with the pilot's. Rather than being afraid, Dieter was mesmerized: he had seen some strange and almighty being fly down from the clouds, and from that

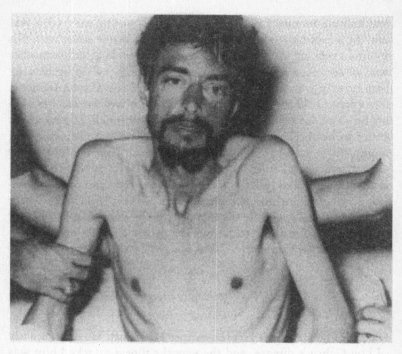

Little Dieter Needs to Fly

moment on Little Dieter Needed to Fly. After his apprenticeship as a blacksmith and church clock maker, he emigrated to America and after years of struggle became a pilot. During the very early stages of the Vietnam War he was shot down over Laos, where he was held prisoner for six months. There was a real innocence about the man. He had such a healthy and impressive and jubilant attitude to life, something that comes through in the film. One time after Dieter spoke in detail about the tortures he had experienced during captivity, my wife asked him, 'How do you sleep at nights?' 'You see, darling, that was the fun part of my life.' I like this attitude; he never made a fuss about it.

Sure, he had to develop certain safeguards once back home, but he never had to struggle for his sanity and certainly was not possessed by those things that you see so often among Vietnam veterans who returned home destroyed inside. I do not feel that Dieter was as changed by his experiences as much as most other

264

people would have been. Clearly it was the event that shaped the rest of his life, for better or for worse, but Dieter had such a difficult and hard childhood in the devastation of post-war Germany that he was actually extremely well prepared for an ordeal of that nature. He had all the qualities that make America so wonderful: self-reliance and courage, a kind of frontier spirit. He had grown up in a remote area of the country without his father, who had been killed in the war. As a child, Dieter saw things that made no earthly sense at all. Germany had been transformed into a dreamscape of the surreal, and this is exactly what we see in the film, shots of the bombed-out cityscapes. Like me, Dieter had to take charge of his life from a very early age, and because as children we both knew what real hunger was, we had an immediate rapport.

When did you first meet Dieter?

I was invited by a German television station to contribute to their series called *Voyages to Hell*. Immediately I thought, 'Ah yes, that sounds very good. My kind of thing.' The television executive actually wanted me to make a film about myself, all the stuff about landing in prison in Africa and the problems on *Fitzcarraldo*. 'This was difficult work,' I told him, 'but they were not voyages into hell.' I vaguely remembered reading about Dieter in the 1960s, though by now he was very much forgotten.

In what way was the film stylized?

This time the stylizations were more subtle. Actually, the film was shot twice, in both English and German. We were very careful about editing and stylizing Dieter's reality. He had to become an actor playing himself. Everything in the film is authentic Dieter, but to intensify him it is all re-orchestrated, scripted and rehearsed. It was my job as the director to translate and edit his thoughts into something profound and cinematic. Sometimes I had to push him to condense a story that rambled on for almost an hour into only a couple of minutes. There is hardly a scene in the film that was not shot at least five times until we got it exactly right. If Dieter did start to move away from the crucial details of the story, I would stop him and ask that he stick to the absolutely essential points.

The film starts with Dieter visiting a tattoo parlour in San Francisco and looking at a design of death whipping a team of horses down from Hell through fire and brimstone. He tells the tattoo artist that he could never put this image on his body because for him it was different. 'It wasn't death,' he says, 'it was the angels who steered the horses. Death really didn't want me.' Though it is true that he had hallucinations when he was near death by starvation in the jungle, of course Dieter never had any intention of really getting a tattoo. The whole thing was my idea.

Then we cut to him driving in the hills of northern California and see him getting out of his car, opening and closing the car door and then going into his house. Dieter repeatedly opens and closes his front door, a scene I created from what he had casually mentioned to me, that after his experiences in the jungle he truly appreciated the feeling of being able to open a door whenever he wanted to. It is a scene also sparked by the images of open doors we see inside his house, all of which were really his, something he also talks about in his autobiography.[6]

All the big substantial elements in *Little Dieter* are real. All the food under the floorboards of his kitchen really was there, and the story of being followed by a bear in the jungle is also true. But one of the best examples of stylization in any of my films comes at the end of the film, a scene shot at Davis-Monthan Air Force Base near Tucson, Arizona, a kind of aeroplane graveyard where there are tens of thousands of mothballed aircraft just sitting there on the ground, as far as the eye can see. Previously Dieter has spoken about his nightmares right after his rescue and explains how his friends would pack him into a cockpit to sleep at night. That was where he truly felt safe. It was my idea to have him look around at all the planes and exclaim what a haven for pilots this is.

Wasn't it a bit much to march Dieter back through the jungle with his hands bound behind his back?

Dieter had been back to Asia and the jungle many times since the war. He loves Asia and the people very much. We actually filmed in Thailand in some jungle areas at the Loatian border and on the Mekong river itself because the Loatians did not allow us to cross the border and film there. Reconnaissance planes had photographed the remains of his plane just before we made the film so we knew exactly where it was, and Dieter said he was willing to swim across the Mekong river and film there, but in the end this idea was abandoned. The German television network wanted me to film re-enactments of the events Dieter was talking about, the kind of stupid thing you can see on television worldwide. I hate this kind of stuff so much and thought it better that Dieter do it all himself. He exuded so much sanity it was not a problem for him to walk through the jungle with his hands tied behind his back being led by a couple of guys with guns whom we hired from the nearest village. 'This is a little too close to home,' he says, but it was just a relatively safe way of getting something extraordinary from him.

How was Little Dieter *received in the United States?*

The film was generally very well received by American audiences. Inevitably I was asked why I did not denounce American aggression in the Vietnam war and why the film made no political statement about the war. Though I feel that the war is always very much in the margins of the film, you have to remember that for Dieter it lasted only forty minutes. It was never his aim to go to war; he just wanted to fly, and the only chance as a German to do this was to emigrate to the United States. It is only a chain of coincidences that he ended up in a war three weeks after he got his wings. One has to remember this was 1965. At that point America was still only giving small-scale military assistance to the South Vietnamese generals who were tying to push back the infiltration from the north. Dieter was delighted to go over there because all his buddies had told him about the go-go girls in Saigon. He really never had any intention to go to war, and like so many people thought the whole thing would be over in a few weeks. In 1965 no American could have possibly known they were getting involved in a war that was to last so many years. Once he was down on the ground, of course, the entire country was not an abstract grid on a map any more. All of a sudden it was filled with voices and human beings, people who were starving and under pressure of air attacks. And almost immediately he started to change his attitude, to understand that there were real people down there, real suffering and death.

So the humanity of the film is somewhere else; it was not in political sloganeering. After spending time with Dieter, I realized that his story had the quality and structure of an ancient Greek tragedy. Dieter's story is that of a man and his dreams, his punishment and redemption.

Wings of Hope seems almost like a sequel to Little Dieter, *another tale of horror in the jungle.*

The film was one of those things dormant in me for many years. The film is the story of Juliane Köpcke, a seventeen-year-old German girl, the sole survivor of a plane crash in the Peruvian jungle on Christmas Eve in 1971. Juliane's mother was killed along with ninety-four others. What is so astonishing is that after ten days the intensive search was called off, and on the twelfth day Juliane emerged from the jungle. It is such a miraculous story, and what I like very much about Juliane is that she did everything right in order to survive her ordeal.

The other reason for my fascination with the story is that in 1971 I was in Peru filming *Aguirre* and, along with my wife, some actors and technicians, was booked on the very same flight. I had to bribe an airline employee to get the boarding passes, but at the last minute the planned stop at Cuzco, where we needed to get off, was cancelled and the plane ended up flying directly to Pucallpa. Only later did I discover that we were filming *Aguirre* just a few rivers away from Juliane as she was fighting for her life. As I had flown in the very same plane several times already back and forth into the jungle I knew many of the crew who later died on the flight. The airline was notorious for its crashes, and only months before, the pilots – who happened not to have valid pilots' licences – missed the runway in Cuzco and crashed into a mountain nearby. One hundred and six bodies were retrieved from the wreckage, even though the maximum capacity of the plane was only 96. The airline employees had sold an additional ten standing places in the aisle and pocketed the cash. I always knew that I would make the film one day, but it took quite a while to locate Juliane. She had disappeared and covered her tracks because she had been harassed by the press so intensely after her rescue, becoming very low-key, getting married and changing her name. I managed to find her father, who immediately ranted against me saying he would never give the name and address of his daughter to anyone. There was no way of convincing him that I might be different from the press. I had a suspicion that she would be in Peru because that was where she had grown up. I knew she loved the jungle and thought that she might be working as a biologist in one of the ecology stations down there.

In the end I found her through some old newspaper clippings about her mother's burial in a small Bavarian town. I finally located the retired Catholic priest who buried Juliane's mother, and he told me that one aunt was still alive and lived in the next village. I went straight over there, but she would not tell me anything. I asked her to pass my phone number on to Juliane, which she did. Juliane called me, and it turned out she lived in Munich and not Peru. I explained to her that it would be enough for me to talk with her for thirty minutes, not a minute longer, and that of course I would not record the conversation. I also explained that exactly five minutes into our meeting I would offer to withdraw if she wanted me to. So when we met I put my wristwatch on the table and exactly 300 seconds into the meeting I stood up, took my wristwatch, bowed to her and said, 'This is the deal. I am withdrawing unless you would like to continue for the next twenty-five minutes.' And she took my arm and said, 'Sit down and stay. We haven't finished yet.'

Did Juliane have any idea who you were before you met?

She had seen a couple of my films, which was quite helpful because she liked them. The thing was she was still somewhat traumatized by the media's treatment of her back then. I touch on this in *Wings of Hope* when talking about the trashy film made about her experiences. Our first meeting was over two hours, but it took one full year for her to decide that she would co-operate with me on a film. Once she had said yes she really went for it, knowing there would be no mercy, and so it was not surprising for her that I asked her to sit in window seat F, row 19 on the aeroplane when we went back to the jungle. This was the same seat she had when her plane disintegrated over the Amazon. Her ill-fated plane back then had come apart in a thunderstorm at an altitude of 15,000 feet, and Juliane had sailed to earth strapped to her row of seats. The fact that she landed in the jungle without being killed is a miracle, but her escape from the jungle was not. It was sheer professionalism. She knew the jungle very well from her time spent at the ecological station her parents had built, and she never panicked when crocodiles splashed from the sandbanks left and right into the river in which she was wading. She knew that crocodiles always flee from human beings and they hide in the water, never in the jungle. Everyone else, including me, would have fled into the jungle and inevitably perished there.

What is stylized in Wings of Hope? *Is it the dream sequences?*

When it comes to Juliane's dreams and Dieter Dengler's dreams or Fini Straubinger's in *Land of Silence and Darkness*, it is all pure invention. The invention serves these real people and our own insight into who these characters are. There is a scene in *Little Dieter* where Dieter is standing in front of a water tank full of jellyfish explaining what death looks like. In our conversations he described his dream to me in such a way that immediately an image of a jellyfish floated into my mind. It was almost dancing in a kind of slow-motion transparent movement, exactly the image that was needed to enable his dream to be articulated on screen. Dieter could not express it, so I did it for him and had him stand next to the water tank. I just took his words and enriched them with images, much like a scientist enriches uranium. He then has a bomb.

In *Wings of Hope* all the dream sequences are invented. The film opens with a dream sequence with Juliane walking down a street and seeing broken dummies in shop windows. The voice-over talks about how in her dreams the faces she encounters are broken. 'The heads are smashed, but she is not afraid.' There were some very personal things that Juliane did not want to talk about, and she knew I would always respect her wishes on things like that. My decision not to introduce too many stylized elements into the film was probably something to do with her character. Juliane is a scientist, very straight-talking and clear-headed, and the only reason she survived her ordeal was because of her ability to act methodically through those absolutely dire circumstances. I wanted these qualities to shine through in the film. Look, for example, at how much the mosquitoes bothered her husband, while Juliane does

not think twice about them as she is so used to dealing with creatures like this. Of course, there is real grief in the film but it is done
with tenderness and discretion. Not dwelling on the pain that
Juliane went through back then means the story is much more
haunting for audiences. Again the television executives wanted re-
enactments of her experiences. They certainly never expected me
to take Juliane herself back to the jungle. But by doing this, and by
tying Dieter Dengler up and walking him through the trails where
he almost perished thirty years before, we ended up ploughing a
deeper reality.

*A friend insisted I ask you this question. I know that for you film
is not art, but what is the purpose of art in general?*

I have never asked myself such a question. I only know that the
work of great poets and artists does not change the course of my
life. But it makes it better.

In what way?

Just write that it makes my life BETTER. And make sure you spell
it with capital letters.

NOTES
  1 See page 303.
  2 *Cinéma vérité* [cinema truth] is the name given to the work of film-
    makers (Frederick Wiseman, Richard Leacock, D. A. Pennebaker,
    Robert Drew, Jean Rouch, etc.) who emerged primarily in the
    United States and France in the late 1950s. Drawing on the early
    work of Flaherty (*Nanook of the North*) and Vertov (*The Man with
    the Movie Camera*), the practitioners of *cinéma vérité* were very
    aware of the effect their cameras had on the events they were trying
    to capture, and as such acted more as 'participant observers'. Their
    approach, born in part out of methods of television journalism,
    resulted in films that seemed to be more objective in their presenta-
    tion of real life. One major reason why the movement emerged
    when it did was due to the new portable cameras and sound equip-
    ment (including synchronous sound 16 mm and faster film stock).
    Some filmmakers, for example the Maysles brothers (*Salesman* and
    Gimmie Shelter), preferred to use the term 'direct cinema'. See films
    such as Drew's *Primary* (1960), Rouch and Mourin's *Chronicle of a*

Summer (1961) and Pennebaker's *Don't Look Back* (1967), and Peter Wintonick's historical documentary *Cinéma Vérité: Defining the Moment* (1999).

3 Chris Marker (b. 1921, France) is best known for his short feature *La Jeteé* (1962), which was the inspiration for Terry Gilliam's *Twelve Monkeys* (1995). Since the 1960s Marker has produced a series of challenging and somewhat experimental 'documentaries', including *Le Jolie Mai* (1963), *Sans Soleil* (1982) and *The Last Bolshevik* (1992).

4 See Frederic Spotts's *Bayreuth, A History of the Wagner Festival* (Yale University Press, 1994).

5 See Denis Arnold's *Gesualdo* (BBC, 1984).

6 *Escape from Laos* (Presido Press, 1979). 'Above me the golden door opened again. Racing chariots dashed out, and I threw up my arms to protect myself from the sharp, trampling hooves.' (p. 199)

9

The Song of Life

One person we haven't talked about is Beate Mainka-Jellinghaus who edited many of your films, including Signs of Life, Aguirre *and* Land of Silence and Darkness, *and with whom you worked until* Fitzcarraldo. *How did you work with her, and what is your general approach to editing?*

The way I worked with Beate was simple: very fast, with great urgency. It is not that I have a slovenly attitude to the editing process, it is just that I take quick decisions and Beate was always very good at instantly sensing what was the best footage sitting in front of her. She would unfailingly identify which sequences worked and which did not. I have learned so much from Beate over the years and without her input I would be only a shadow of myself. On our first collaboration, *Signs of Life*, the first reel we checked at the flat-bed was a 600-metre roll. It had been coiled the wrong way from the end, so she put it on the machine and spun it backwards through the reels, about five times as fast as it would normally be viewed. At the end of this, she grabbed the whole reel and threw it into the garbage, saying, 'This is so bad I am just not going to touch it again.' And of course I was aghast, but after a couple of weeks I looked at this reel again in the context of the rest of the film and she was right. Just as quickly she would always be able to spot the good footage.

Have you continued to work in this way with other editors?

I have always been able to work through the footage and put together a first assembly of what I feel the final film should be in less than a fortnight. And I never look at things I have edited the day before. Every morning I get into the editing room and start from the point where we finished the previous night, and only at the end do I look at what we have put together. This approach does require a certain amount of recklessness, I admit, but it is the only way to keep the material absolutely fresh and ensure that only the footage of the highest calibre remains. All in all, editing of a feature film takes two or three months.

Everything that is not useful is immediately junked, which means when it comes to fine-tuning we never have endless takes to view. Being able to establish a film's rhythm on location is for me what real filmmaking is, as big mistakes can rarely be rectified in the editing room, and this is the reason why I am so careful about ensuring I make the right choices on location. I never shoot endless amounts of footage. On *Aguirre*, for example, I shot only about 50,000 feet of film in total. There are very few exceptions to this, the most obvious one being *Fata Morgana*, which was structured entirely in the editing room, though in a strange way I still say that the rhythm of the film was established during shooting, even though I had no idea what I was going to do with the footage when I was shooting it.

Have you ever got into the editing room and found that all the footage you have to work with is an unusable mess?

Never, though sometimes it is clear that a certain scene will not work properly, so I cut it. But the film as a whole has always been what I planned. With *Invincible* I realized very quickly that the film would be too long and sat for some time on a version that was almost three hours. The footage was all good and coherent, but I put it aside for six weeks and tried to forget about it. I knew somehow that I needed to condense the film and tighten it. When I went back to it, within a day I had cut forty minutes from the film and was left with the version that you can see today. For *Kaspar Hauser* I had a seven-minute-long sequence between Kaspar and an impoverished farmer in the countryside. The farmer in his despair had killed his last surviving cow. It was a very intense and beautiful scene, but somehow disrupted the flow of the story. It meant the audience would have to take some time to get back into the story once the scene was over, so I threw it out even though it was one of the two or three best sequences I had shot. I am not speaking here of the mechanics of the story. It fit in the story and it made a lot of sense when placed in the context of this story of Kaspar being pushing into this world around him. But there was something about it that disrupted the flow of the film in terms of how I felt audiences would receive it; they were detoured too far, and the return journey would have been too arduous. In such a case, as I work for audiences and for no one else, I had no problems throwing the scene out. During the editing of every film you have to undergo the cruelty of tearing scenes out and throwing them into the garbage. This is one of the most painful lessons to learn as a filmmaker: in each film there is some sort of unique inner timing that must be discovered and respected so the story will properly function on the screen.

One thing that Beate taught me is that when you look at the material you have in the editing room, forget about yourself, forget any ideas you might have had before you stepped into that room, forget about the story and the screenplay. When confronted by your footage you must become smaller than a midget, less than the black under my nail. Very often I see filmmakers ruin their films by squeezing the footage into a preconceived notion that has been brought into the editing room from the original script.

But you must let the material escape the clutches of the script, let it enlarge or shrink itself as it needs to. Your film is like your children. You might want a child with certain qualities, but you are never going to get the exact specifications right. The film has a privilege to live its own life and develop its own character. To suppress this is dangerous. It is an approach which works the other way too: sometimes the footage has amazing qualities that you did not expect. I always approach footage as a surprise that was dumped in my editing room. It is a real joy to dig away and discover the gems.

Why did you ask Beate to join you on the set of Stroszek?

From the first film we made together, *Signs of Life,* Beate was always complaining how bad my films were. She thought they were so embarrassingly terrible that she never went to the opening night of any of my films, with the exception of *Even Dwarfs Started Small*, which she did like. For *Nosferatu*, as usual she grumbled about the terrible footage that I had dumped on her doorstep. But I think that this kind of response was somehow a challenge. It was meant to push me to do the very best that I possibly could.

It was wonderful seeing her working with these reels which she truly felt had such little value. By the end she was fighting for the footage. As she saw it, she was working hard to salvage what little good she could from it, protecting it from incompetents like me. I truly liked this attitude. For years I said to her that much of what she complained about was due to the physical circumstances of shooting and that there were always so many obstacles to struggle with on location. Every single shot always involved some sort of a compromise, and it is vital to be lively and intelligent enough to take these difficult situations and make something remarkable out of them. 'If you do not believe me,' I finally said to her, 'why not come to the set of the next film and be with me during the shooting?' So she came to do continuity and watch the filming of *Stroszek* in Germany and America. Of course, she hated every single day of shooting much more than the time she later spent editing the film.

I was always very aware of Beate's skills as an editor – she originally edited for Alexander Kluge – and I worked with her because of that. No matter that she disliked much of what I brought to her, or that she truly found the whole experience on the set of *Stroszek* and the story itself absolutely disgusting. She hated everything we shot so much that sometimes she would signal to the cinematographer to cut and shut it down and stop the whole damned thing. One time she did this when I was watching Bruno and Eva Mattes who were acting in some of the best footage I have ever shot in my life. I could have killed her like a coward, with a snow shovel from behind. But of course that is life; you have to accept strong collaborators. I do not need 'yes' men and women around, a docile crew that tells me everything I do is great. What I need is people like Beate, creative people with a strong independent spirit and attitude.

Having said that, after filming I am always loaded with subjective feelings and certain irrational preferences, and after *Stroszek* I realized that there is a certain value to keeping the editor as far away from the location as possible. It is very important the editor is able to look as clearly and objectively as possible at the footage sitting in the cans, and if she is witness to all the trouble and effort that goes into shooting a scene – maybe one that I particularly like – she might decide that though it does not work in the context of the film, we should keep it in because of all the trouble it caused us. 'What a waste to lose it!' So, generally, I think it is good to keep editors away from the filming in order to preserve the purity of their opinions.

If the technology had been available at the time, would you ever have made a film like Aguirre *on digital video? And would you ever make a Dogme 95[1] film, for example?*

Under no circumstances. Video is a different approach to film primarily because there is this unhealthy pseudo-security a director has about instantly knowing what the image he has just captured is. But this is very misleading. When I know in my guts we have got the best we possibly can out of a scene, then I stop. It does not matter whether I see dailies or not. I know this is going to be the best take that I have done and everything else becomes meaningless. I have never liked watching dailies, and I have always found them dangerously misleading. To check certain technical things they are useful, but when you take an individual shot out of context not only from the scene where it sits but also from the rest of the film – much of which we might not have even shot yet – there is no way of knowing just how competent and useful it really is.

But you can see how appealing the new technology is for young filmmakers?

Absolutely. It means they can become much more self-reliant. But again, I suggest caution should be exercised, or at the very least these filmmakers need to understand the differences between what they are shooting with and what kinds of images can be obtained with celluloid. I am not one to tell others what they should do and what they should use, but I myself am a man of celluloid; it has its own depths and force which you do not easily achieve when you work with digital technology. Of course, video will improve over the years and I have shot two films on video, *Pilgrimage* and *Lord and the Laden*, both of which were filmed in places where we were not allowed to put up lights, so film would not have worked. So clearly there are some real advantages to video technology. It is just that for a feature like *Aguirre* or *Fitzcarraldo* it would not be acceptable to shoot on anything but film.

Anyway, I would never be accepted into the Dogme 95 movement because I use lights, tripods, costumes, etc. And I would not like to make a film without music either. I do everything in the book that is contrary to the basic Dogme recipes. Even though they themselves do not take it that seriously, I know it is not for me. The physical immediacy of making a film like *Aguirre* – even though it is a period film – the Dogme people really love and this was the reason Harmony Korine wanted me to play the father in his Dogme film *julien donkey-boy*. Originally, he was going to act as my son, but in the end he did not feel comfortable enough to be behind and in front of the camera at the same time. So he did not just cast me in the role only because I was the right age and looked right; it was much more significant for him than that. He wanted his 'cinematic father' to be in the film even if the character I play is completely dysfunctional and hostile.

One morning in 1984 you left Sachrang, the village where you spent your childhood, and proceeded to walk around the entire border of West and East Germany. What little I've read about your walk suggests that it was something like a political act.

Not explicitly, no. Some years ago, before the revolutions that swept through eastern Europe in 1989, it seemed that for many Germans reunification was a lost cause as the nation was in fragments with no real centre. The country had no centre or middle, it was without a real metropolis, and there was no heart beating at its core. It was almost as if the country had become homeless within its own territory, and while the real capital city was a divided enclave deep in a separate country, we had to make do with a small provincial town. I was upset by politicians like Willy Brandt,[2] who in a public statement as Chancellor declared the book on German reunification closed. But I had a very clear 'knowledge' about the inevitability of reunification. In fact, back then I insisted that it was a historic necessity, even though prominent figures like Günter Grass insisted that Germany should never be reunified.[3]

Ireland will be reunified one day. It might take another few hundred years, but it will eventually become one nation. Korea too, no matter when. I truly believe there is a geographical fate to nations, not only a cultural or political fate. The unification of Germany was very dear to my heart. I still remember the deep feeling of joy and jubilation when the Berlin Wall came down. My great hope was that in an explosion of freedom, everyone in East Germany would crawl out of their holes and display to the world their creative energies. However, I found it appalling that after the first week of sheer jubilation and ecstasy in Germany almost everyone lapsed into a climate of complaint, something that is still all-pervading. I find it very sad and it is one of the reasons why I do not want to physically live in Germany. In the early 1990s everything seemed to be overshadowed by committee meetings and bureaucratic wranglings. There was also the incessant talk and debate that went on for months about moving the government to Berlin. How could parliament, we were told, move to Berlin and start sessions in the new Reichstag without having all the offices ready for the parliamentarians? Such worry about this. Godammit, a parliament can hold its session in an open field if it needs to!

Back in 1984 I had the increasingly strong feeling that Germany was an extremely godforsaken country. What, I asked myself, was actually holding it together? What was capable of binding the country together again until it was reunited in the distant future? I felt that the only things we Germans were held together by were our culture and language, and for this reason I truly felt that it was only the poets who could hold Germany together and so set out from Sachrang and started walking westwards around the border. I was careful to walk clockwise so I would always have Germany on my right side. What happened was that after about 2,000 kilometres I became ill and had to return, so I jumped on a train home, where I was hospitalized for a week. To this day the journey remains some kind of unfinished task for me.

It should be clear that I never had a nationalistic attitude to my task. There was no doubt that Germany would, after its unification, disappear into the abyss of history, just as historically – and for other reasons – former world powers like Holland and Portugal have. But at the same time Germany is returning to the bosom of the civilized world. It is not completely there yet, but has undergone profound changes and made real progress. We should not overlook this.

Has travelling on foot always been very important to you?

Humans are not made to sit at computer terminals or travel by aeroplane; destiny intended something different for us. For too long now we have been estranged from the essential, which is the nomadic life: travelling on foot. A distinction must be made between hiking and travelling on foot. In today's society – though it would be ridiculous to advocate travelling on foot for everyone to every possible destination – I personally would rather do the existentially essential things in my life on foot. If you live in England and your girlfriend is in Sicily, and it is clear that you want to marry her, then you should walk to Sicily to propose. For these things travel by car or aeroplane is not the right thing. The volume and depth and intensity of the world is something that only those on foot will ever experience. I have never been a tourist, for a tourist destroys cultures. I have a dictum that connected me instantly with Bruce Chatwin, one that I put in the Minnesota Declaration: 'Tourism is sin and travel by foot is virtue.' Cultures around the world visited by tourists are having their basic dignity and identity stripped away.

My voyages on foot have always been essential experiences for me. For many hours during my walk around Germany, sometimes even a day or two at a time, there was no well or creek to drink from. I would knock on the door of a farmhouse and ask for something to drink. 'Where are you from?' the farmer would ask. I would say Sachrang. 'How far away is this?' 'About 1,500 kilometres,' I would reply. 'How did you get here?' And the moment I would explain that I walked, there is no more small talk. It is the same when you cross the Sahara, not necessarily on foot but in a car. Those people who have crossed the Sahara somehow recognize each other. And when people take note of how far you have walked, they start telling you stories they have bottled up for forty years. One evening in a mountain hut I spoke with a retired teacher who told me a story about the Second World War. It was the final day of the war in Europe and he was in Holland, with Canadian forces only a little over a hundred metres away advancing on him with their tanks. He had been given orders to take a group of soldiers prisoner at a farm beyond the advancing line of enemy tanks. He explained that only by turning his gun against his own superior officer did he manage to prevent the execution of the prisoners. Then, together with the Dutch captives and the superior officer he had taken prisoner, he was intercepted by the Canadian tanks which he had overtaken and outrun on an open field heading back to his own lines, and was taken prisoner himself.

When you come on foot, you come with a different intensity. Travelling on foot has nothing to do with exercise. I spoke earlier about daydreaming and that I do not dream at nights. Yet when I am walking I fall deep into dreams, I float through fantasies and find myself inside unbelievable stories. I literally walk through whole novels and films and football matches. I do not even look at where I am stepping, but I never lose my direction. When I come out of a big story I find myself twenty-five or thirty kilometres further on. How I got there I do not know.

Your friendship with Lotte Eisner was so strong that when she fell ill you refused to let her die. You said German film just wasn't ready for her death, that it still needed her. Was this the reason why you walked to Paris to see her, a voyage you wrote about in your book Of Walking in Ice?

In 1974 we German filmmakers were still fragile, and when a friend told me Lotte had suffered a massive stroke and I should get on the next plane to Paris, I made the decision not to fly. It was not the right thing to do, and because I just could not accept that she might die, I walked from Munich to her apartment in Paris. I put on a shirt, grabbed a bundle of clothes, a map and a compass, and set off in a straight line, sleeping under bridges, in farms and abandoned houses. I made only one detour to the town of Troyes because I wanted to walk into the cathedral there. I walked against her death, knowing that if I walked on foot she would be alive when I got there. And that is just what happened. Lotte lived until the age of ninety or thereabouts, and years after the walk, when she was nearly blind, could not walk or read or go out to see films, she said to me, 'Werner, there is still this spell cast over me that I am not allowed to die. I am tired of life. It would be a good time for me now.' Jokingly I said, 'OK, Lotte, I hereby take the spell away.' Three weeks later she died.

When you travel on foot with this intensity, it is not a matter of covering actual ground, rather it is a question of moving through your own inner landscapes. I wrote a diary of the walk which I pulled out during the shooting of *Nosferatu* and decided to publish as *Of Walking in Ice*. I actually like the book more than my films; it is closer to my heart than all my films together, I think, because of the many compromises that filmmaking always entails.

Have you thought since about writing similar books of 'prose poetry'?

Sometimes I feel that I should have done more writing, that I might be a better writer than I am a filmmaker. The writer is the one inside me who remains to be properly discovered. There is a lot of written material I have not even dared to read myself since I wrote it, for example, notebooks from the time I worked on *Fitzcarraldo*. The texts are all in subminiaturized handwriting; it could not get any smaller because no pens exist that give a finer stroke. Why I wrote it like this I do not know, as my longhand is of normal size. I know it was not to stop people from reading it, though you do need a magnifying glass to make it out. I have not read it since I wrote it. I think I am scared to dive back in there.

You were good friends with the writer Bruce Chatwin. What do you think it was that drew you so closely together?

The fact that we both travel on foot made us instant friends. And I always felt Chatwin[4] was the most important writer of his generation in the English language, somehow in the same league as Conrad.

Where did you first meet him?

In Melbourne in 1984. I was in Australia working on *Where the Green Ants Dream* and read in the paper that he was also in the country, so immediately contacted his publishing company and tried to locate him. They told me he was somewhere in the desert in central Australia and two days later called me back and said, 'If you call this number in Adelaide within the next twenty minutes you will reach him before he goes to the airport.' I called him and asked what his plans were. He was flying to Sydney, but after a very short conversation he changed his plans and flew to Melbourne instead. How would I recognize him? 'Look for a man with a leather rucksack,' he told me. Apparently Bruce knew some of my films and had read *Of Walking in Ice*, which he liked very much, and we spent forty-eight hours together talking and talking. For every story I told him, he would tell me three. It never ended; when he was interested in something nothing could stop him.

Years later when he was very ill he asked me to come and show him my film about the Wodaabe, but he had the strength to watch only ten minutes at a time. Before I arrived I was not aware that he was dying. But he insisted on seeing the film, bit by bit. He was lucid, but eventually became delirious and would exclaim, 'I've got to be on the road again, I've got to be on the road again.' And I would say, 'Yes, that is where you belong.' He wanted me to come with him, and I told him we would walk together if he got stronger. 'My rucksack is so heavy,' he said. 'Bruce, I will carry it,' I said. His bones were aching and he would ask me to move him in his bed. He called his legs 'the boys'. One time he asked me, 'Will you move the left boy to the other side.' And he looked down and saw that his legs were so weak they were almost spindles, and he looked at me and with great lucidity said, 'I will never walk again.' I still carry the leather rucksack he used all his life. He gave it to me saying, 'You are the one who has to carry it on now.' I still carry it, and I had it with me in the snow storm in Patagonia, sitting on it for fifty hours dug into the snow. It is much more than just a tool to carry things. If my house were on fire I would first grab my children and throw them from the window. But of all my belongings it would be the rucksack that I would save.

We've saved the wildest stuff for the end: Klaus Kinski. Why did you make My Best Fiend, *the film about your relationship with the man you directed in five feature films, and the man who had caused you so much grief?*

Sure, sometimes he caused me trouble when we were making those films. Every grey hair on my head I call Kinski. But who really cares about that now. What is important is the five films got made and they are out there for people to enjoy. And he gave truly amazing – and in subtle ways very different – performances in each of them. Undoubtedly, he was the ultimate pestilence to work with. He was such an intense man, something that naturally frightens most people. But often he was a joy, and you know, he was one of the few people I ever learned anything from.

Like what?

There was the 'Kinski Spiral' for example, something I talk about with photographer Beat Presser in *My Best Fiend*. When you enter the frame from the side, showing your profile and then face the camera, there is no tension, so whenever there was a reason for it, Kinski would make his appearance from directly behind the camera. Say Kinski wanted to spin into frame from the left. He would position himself next to the camera, with the left foot next to the tripod. Then he would step over the tripod with the right leg, twisting the foot inward. The whole body would organically unwind before the camera allowing him to smoothly spin into frame. It really did create a mysterious and disturbing tension. By the way, there is also a move called 'Kinski's Double Spiral' where the initial movement is followed by a counter-spin, but I could never explain it to you in words. It is complex stuff. I adapted the single spiral for a shot in *Kaspar Hauser* when Kaspar is at the party with Lord Stanhope.

Our creative relationship was so pronounced and intense that I felt I had to make a film about our struggles and friendship and distrust. It sounds like a contradiction, but it is not. People think we had a love–hate relationship. Well, I did not love him, nor did I hate him. We had mutual respect for each other, even as we both planned each other's murder. Klaus was one of the greatest film actors of the century, but he was also a monster and a great pestilence. The fact that he constantly threw tantrums, created scandals and broke contracts scared other directors, and every single day I had to domesticate the beast. But he also really knew so much about the cinema, about film lighting, stage craft, the choreography

My Best Fiend

of the body on screen. He created a climate of unconditional professionalism on every set he worked on that he would not allow me to step back from.

Was there a particular reason you made My Best Fiend *when you did?*

It was a question of the right timing. When I first heard Kinski had died, the fact really did not enter my heart until months later when I stood with his ashes in my hands and threw them into the Pacific Ocean. Even to this day I still catch myself sometimes talking in the present tense about him. I needed to let time pass and I knew time would have the mysterious power to change perspective, and only because of that has the film humour and warmth. I had always felt something was missing from the five films we made together. I needed something to bind them together and fill that missing link. And had I made the film right after Kinski's death, I am sure it would have been a much darker work. Now I can laugh much more about what happened, see the bizarre side of everything and look back with a certain serenity. The film was easy to make, almost effortless.

It's not a biography of the actor nor anything like a nostalgia film. How do you see the film?

My Best Fiend is neither a work about Kinski, nor about me. Rather it is about an extraordinary working relationship. My choice of interviewees – I am speaking here primarily of Eva Mattes and Claudia Cardinale – was very carefully planned. I could have found untold numbers of people who had only terrible things to say about Kinski, that he was the ultimate scum. But I wanted to show his other side, one that shines through not one bit in his autobiography: someone full of humour and warmth and love and generosity. For example I am glad I included the sequence of Kinski and me embracing at the Telluride Film Festival. In fact I am glad this footage even exists otherwise no one would believe that we were so good with each other. He always complained about the money he was offered to be in certain films. He refused offers from Kurosawa, Fellini and Pasolini, always talking about them as vermin who did not pay enough. Yet I always had relatively small budgets and paid him less than what he would have earned working with these other directors. I truly believe that with me he had a rapport which meant money just was not that important. In public Kinski claimed to hate my films, but when you spoke to him privately it was obvious he was proud of them.

Whenever I watch the film with audiences there is always so much laughter, maybe more than with any other film of yours.

I get that too. It is something that really pleases me about the film. The scenes when he is screaming at our production manager Walter Saxer on the set of *Fitzcarraldo*, the shots at the beginning of the film during his infamous 'Jesus Tour' and when we visit the apartment in Munich are all very funny.

How did you come to live with him in Munich for a time when you were a young boy?

It was a complete chain of coincidences. My mother, struggling to raise three sons on her own, found a room in a boarding house for the four of us. The owner of the boarding house, Klara Rieth, an elderly lady of sixty-five with wildly dyed orange hair, had a soft spot for starving artists as she herself had come from a family of artists. Kinski had been living nearby in an attic, without furniture, just bare beams, and everything covered knee-high with dead leaves. He posed as a starving artist and walked around stark naked. When the postman rang Kinski rustled through his leaves, stark naked, and signed. But from the very first moment he arrived, he terrorized everyone. He locked himself into the bathroom for two days and two nights and for forty-eight hours in his maniacal fury he smashed everything to smithereens. The bathtub, the toilet bowl, everything. You could sift it through a tennis racket. I never thought it possible that someone could rave for so long.

He had a tiny room with a small window. One day he took a huge running start down the corridor while we were eating. I heard a strange noise and then, like in an explosion, the door came off its hinges crashing into the room. He must have jumped against it at full speed, and now he stood there flailing wildly, completely hysterical, foaming at the mouth. Something came floating down like leaves – it was his shirts – and three octaves too high he screamed, 'Klara! You pig!' His screams were incredibly shrill, and he could actually break wine glasses with his voice. What happened was this poor woman who let him live there for free, feeding and cleaning for him, had not ironed his shirt collars neatly enough.

One day a theatre critic had been invited for dinner. He hinted that having watched a play in which Kinski had a small role, he would mention him as outstanding and extraordinary. At once, Kinski threw two hot potatoes and the cutlery in his face. He jumped up and screamed, 'I was not excellent! I was not extraordinary! I was monumental! I was epochal!' I think I was the only one around the table who was not afraid, merely astonished. I looked at him the way you would look if an extraterrestrial had just landed or a tornado had just struck.

Was Kinski a classically trained actor?

No, he was self-taught and at times I could hear him in his tiny room for ten hours non-stop doing his voice and speaking exercises. He pretended to be a genius who had fallen straight from heaven and who had obtained his gift by the grace of God, but in reality it was incredible how much work he did training himself. Having seen him at such close range I suppose I should have known better than to work with him as a director. When I was fifteen I saw Kinski in the anti-war film, *Kinder, Mütter und ein General.*[5] He plays a lieutenant who leads schoolboys to the front. The mothers of the boys and the soldiers go to sleep for a few hours. Kinski is awakened at daybreak, and the way he wakes up will forever stay in my memory. I replay it several times in *My Best Fiend.* I am sure it looks like nothing special to most people, but this one moment impressed me so profoundly that later it was a decisive factor in my professional life. Strange, how memory can magnify something like that. Today, the scene where he orders Maximillian Schell to be shot seems much more impressive to me.

It seems that he really needed you as much as you needed him. Without films like Aguirre *and* Fitzcarraldo *he would have been totally unknown outside of Europe.*

Kinski and I completed each other in a strange way. It is certainly true that I owe him a lot, but also that he owed me a great deal too, only he could never admit it. It was very fortunate for both of us, fortunate for me that he did a film like *Aguirre* and fortunate for him that I took him seriously as an actor. You look at his filmography, something like 200 films, and you know exactly what I am talking about. He was totally reckless with his own possibilities. He respected and truly liked me, but he would never admit that in public. On the contrary, he would heap the wildest expletives over me, which has a very funny side to it.

In his autobiography, Kinski Uncut,[6] *he describes his feelings towards you.*

It is a highly fictitious book, not only when he describes me and our relationship. Page after page he keeps on coming back to me, almost like an obsessive compulsion. In some passages of this book I kind of had a hand in helping him to invent particularly vile expletives. Sometimes we sat on a wooden bench, looking over the landscape, and he said, 'Werner, nobody will read this book if I do not write bad stuff about you. If I wrote that we get along well together, nobody would buy it. The scum only want to hear about the dirt.' I came with a dictionary and we tried to find even fouler expressions. He needed money at the time and knew – quite rightly – that by writing a semi-pornographic rant against everyone and everything it would get some attention. He describes his childhood as one of such poverty that he had to fight with the rats over the last piece of bread. In reality he grew up in a relatively well-to-do middle-class pharmacist's household.

Did you ever feel that he was some kind of alter ego for you?

Though we worked together five times, I never saw him as some kind of *doppelgänger*. We were similar in many ways, and I think the reason he returned again and again to work with me was because we shared a real passion for our work. I suppose you might argue he was my screen alter ego, but only because all the characters in my films are so close to my heart. Maybe he was as much a *doppelgänger* for me as I was for him. It is hard to explain, but Kinski had always wished he could direct, and he really envied me for certain qualities that I had. He wanted to articulate certain things that were brooding inside of him but was not able to.

Kinski sometimes believed I was completely mad. This is not true, of course. I am quite sane, clinically sane, so to speak. Together we were like two critical masses which created a danger-ous mixture whenever they came into contact with each other. One day I seriously planned to firebomb him in his house, a wonderful 'infallible' plan sabotaged only by the vigilance of his Alsatian shepherd dog. Later he told me that around the same time he planned to murder me as well. But although we often kept our dis-tance, we would seek out one another again at the right time and equally often could understand one another without words, almost like animals. I could see through him like no one else could. I knew what was in there and what could be mobilized and articu-lated. Whenever he really got going, I would get the shooting underway as quickly as possible, and often we managed to capture on film something unique. Sometimes I would even provoke him so he ended up shouting and screaming for a couple of hours, after which he would be so exhausted and in the right mood, very silent, quiet and dangerous. I did this for the speech in *Aguirre* when he calls himself 'the Wrath of God'. He wanted to play the scene screaming with real anger while I wanted him almost whispering, so I provoked him and after a particularly vicious tantrum he was literally foaming at the mouth and utterly exhausted. Then I insisted we start shooting, and he did the speech in one single take. So sometimes I had to trick him into a performance, though he always believed he was doing it all himself. I knew how to nudge him, even trick and cheat him, just to get the best possible performance out of him.

The way I communicated with Kinski was rather strange. A lot of the time we did not even use words, almost like a set of identical twins. During the making of *Fitzcarraldo* we did takes where everything was just perfect, the camera and sound were flawless, the actors did not make a single mistake and Kinski was great. But I would say to him, 'Klaus, I think there is more to this. Turn the pig loose.' And somehow he knew what I was talking about, and I would roll it again and he would go straight into something new, something totally exceptional. Whenever I saw him go into one of those wild things, I would double over and had to muffle my laughter with a handkerchief for the sake of the sound recording, even if the scene was not funny at all. But he knew he was good when my face turned purple due to my suppressed laughter. And sometimes, even though the scene was coming to a close, I would not call 'cut', but let the camera continue rolling to see what might happen because I would see that Kinski was up to something. Kinski would kind of look at me out of the corner of his eye, instantly sense I was not going to stop the camera and of course the whole thing would just explode and get even wilder and better than anything that had come before it. This synchronicity was quite incredible sometimes, and there were many times when we would communicate almost through these kinds of currents. I knew his hysterical energy and his so-called insanity, I understood his innermost qualities and how to evoke them, bring them to life before the camera. He felt safe working with me, and the closeness between us became such that we almost changed roles; I felt that if necessary I could have played the role of Fitzcarraldo, though not nearly as well as he did.

Is the story of you threatening to kill him on the set of Aguirre *really true?*

Yes. For Kinski to have left the set meant he would have violated a duty I felt was beyond and more important than each of us. I only told him very quietly that I would shoot him, but I had no rifle in my hand. He had enough instinct to understand this was no joke or hollow threat, and screamed for the police, even though the next outpost was 300 miles away. The press later wrote that I directed Kinski from behind the camera with a loaded gun, a beautiful image. I love the press for its ability to be so lyrical.

The fact is Kinski was well known for breaking contracts and walking off films in the middle of shoots, and this was clearly unacceptable to me. In the middle of the opening night of a play he broke off in the middle of a speech, threw a lit candelabra into the audience and then wrapped himself in the carpet that was lying on the stage. He remained coiled in the carpet until the audience was cleared from the theatre. It was probably because he had forgotten his lines. Once, for insurance reasons, he had to have a check-up before we shot *Aguirre*. The doctor asked routine questions about allergies, hereditary diseases, and then: 'Mr Kinski, have you ever suffered from fits of any kind?' 'YES, EVERY DAY!' screamed Kinski at the highest pitch possible before he proceeded to lay waste to the doctor's office.

In Aguirre *and* Fitzcarraldo *you worked closely with the native Indians of Peru. How did they react to Kinski's antics?*

On *Fitzcarraldo* his raving fits strained things with the Indian extras. He was quite frightening to them and became a real problem as the native Indians would solve their conflicts in a totally different manner. They would huddle together and whisper, keeping very quiet while listening to Kinski's tantrums. Towards the end of shooting one of the chiefs came to me and said, 'You probably realized that we were afraid, but not for one moment were we scared of that screaming madman, shouting his head off.' They were actually afraid of me because I was so quiet.

Kinski's fits can be explained partly by his egocentric character. Egocentric is perhaps not the right word; he was an outright egomaniac. Whenever there was a serious accident it became a big problem because, all of a sudden, he was no longer the centre of attention. On *Fitzcarraldo* a lumberman was bitten by a snake while cutting a tree. This happened maybe once every three years even with hundreds of woodcutters in the jungle always working barefoot with their chain saws. The snakes naturally flee from the smell of gasoline and the noise. Suddenly a deadly poisonous snake struck the man twice. It only takes a few minutes before cardiac arrest occurs, so he thought about it for five seconds, grabbed the saw and cut off his foot. It saved his life because the camp and serum was twenty minutes away. When that happened, I knew Kinski would start raving with some trifling excuse, because now he was just a marginal figure. And he did not fail to throw a tantrum.

In another incident, a plane which was bringing six people to the jungle location crashed. Luckily they all survived, but some people were seriously injured. There were confusing and garbled reports on the radio and Kinski saw that he was no longer in demand, so he threw a fit claiming his coffee was only lukewarm that morning. For hours he screamed at me, three inches away from my face. I did not know how to calm him down because we needed to listen to the radio in case we needed to send a search party into the jungle. Then I had an inspiration. I went to my hut where for months I had hidden a piece of Swiss chocolate. We all would almost have killed one another for something like that. I went right into his face and ate the chocolate in front of him. All of a sudden he was quiet. It was just utterly beyond him. Towards the end of shooting, the Indians offered to kill Kinski for me. I declined at the time, saying, 'No, for God's sake! I still need him for shooting. Leave him to me.' But they were dead serious and if I had only given a nod they would have done it.

Kinski was a peculiar mixture of physical cowardice and courage. A wasp could cause him to scream for his mosquito net and for a doctor with a syringe. And yet on *Fitzcarraldo*, I think it may have even been Kinski's idea to get on the boat as it went through the rapids. He said to me, 'If you go on board then I'm coming with you. If you sink, I shall sink too.' But he never liked the jungle or nature, even though he styled himself as the 'Natural Man'. I believe that everything he said about the jungle was just posing. He declared everything in the jungle erotic, but on *Fitzcarraldo* he stayed in the camp for months and never set foot in the jungle. Once he penetrated it for about a hundred feet to where a fallen tree lay, and the photographer had to go with him to take hundreds of photos of him tenderly embracing and copulating with this tree. Poses and paraphernalia were what mattered to him. His alpine gear was more important than the mountains themselves. His camouflage combat fatigues, tailored by Yves Saint Laurent, were much more important than any jungle. In this regard, Kinski was endowed with a fair share of natural stupidity.

Do you miss him?

Maybe very rarely, I have to admit, but my relationship with him had ended some years before he died. There were moments in *Cobra Verde* that I will never forget. The final scene where he tries to push the boat out into the ocean is full of such despair, and Kinski is magnificent as he collapses into the water. But I knew at the time we could go no further after the film, and I told him so. There was nothing I would like to have discovered with him beyond that which I had already discovered in these five films. He had certain qualities I sensed and that we explored together, but anything beyond *Cobra Verde* would have been repetition.

The final scene of *Cobra Verde* was the last day of shooting that we ever did together. He had put so much intensity into this final scene that he just fell apart afterwards. Even at the time we both sensed it, and he even said to me, 'We can go no further. I am no more.' He died in 1991 at his home north of San Francisco. He had just burnt himself out like a comet. Like me, Kinski was a very physical person, but in a different way. We complemented each other well because he drew everyone together. He attracted the herd magnetically and I held it together. Kinski was made for me, for my cinema. Sometimes I want to put my arm around him again, but I guess I only dream about this because I have seen this in old footage of the two of us. I do not regret a moment, not one. Maybe I do miss him. Yes, now and then I do miss him.

After My Best Fiend *come two shorts,* The Lord and the Laden *and* Pilgrimage. *Both are very much concerned with the question of faith and religious worship.*

Well, I am good with religious subjects and feel I understand them. Both films were made for television. For *The Lord and the Laden*, the network asked me to contribute to a series about 2,000 years of Christianity. I told them I wanted to do something about the church in Latin America, but that they should not expect anything encyclopaedic because I knew I wanted to go to a very specific place. The main sequences are shot at the Basilica of the Virgin of Guadalupe in Tepeyac on the outskirts of Mexico City, and the main sequences are shot at a shrine to the Mayan god Maximón in San Andres Itzapá in Guatemala, where the mixture of paganism and Catholicism is very evident. There is nothing organized about the religious ceremonies you see in the film. It is in a private yard, regular people run the place, and worshippers do not have to pay anything to go there.

The figure they are all worshipping is a mannequin in a glass case dressed like a ranchero. It is actually Maximón, an ancient Mayan god who is dressed up like a rich Spanish ranchero to show his power. Part of the veneration of this pagan god involves fumigating him with cigar smoke and putting cigarettes in his mouth, so lots of people are smoking. Worshippers also spit and spray alcohol over him and each other, part of a ritual of cleaning and purification in the presence of God. The Catholic church, not knowing what to do with this phenomenon, have kind of adopted Maximón. They want just a foot in the door to places like this and so they have squeezed a Catholic saint in there that everyone ignores. You would never see a Catholic priest there, and the whole place is completely chaotic and unorganized with no hierarchy or dogma.

Were the books you show in the film actually real or did you make them yourself?

During the making of the film I held in my hands, within two consecutive days, two of the greatest treasures of humankind: the *Codex Florentino* and the *Codex Telleriano-Remensis*. They are most definitely real; you could never invent anything like these texts. For me the *Codex Florentino* is one of the greatest honourable deeds of humankind. Even as the Aztec culture was being destroyed by the Spanish invaders, within all this destruction there was one man, Bernardino De Sahagún, who, with a couple of other monks, started to collect accounts from Aztecs who still had the knowledge of their culture, their history, and all aspects of life. The work is a monumental achievement. Amidst all the destruction this far-sighted monk tried to preserve the culture of the Aztecs for our memory, and even purposely mistranslated some of the original accounts in Nahuatl about their religion and human sacrifices, otherwise the Spanish Inquisition would have burnt the text.

Pilgrimage *is a beautiful little film you made for the BBC last year, part of the 'Sound and Film' series. How did you and composer John Tavener approach the project?*

When I first talked to the BBC I heard 'music and film', not 'sound and film', which is the concept that the four other filmmakers seemed to work with. So maybe *Pilgrimage* is slightly different from the other films in the series. Of course *Pilgrimage* was also an opportunity to work with John Tavener,[7] for me one of the greatest living composers. Initially I was very uncertain whether this would work because Tavener had always refused to write music for films. But in this case it was not writing music for a film, nor was I making a film to his music. It was to be music and images finding some common ground. So I contacted him to see if he was willing, and surprisingly – to me anyway – he had heard of some of my films and immediately said he wanted to work with me.

The context that Tavener and I worked within was religion. He is Greek Orthodox, while I experienced a short and dramatic religious phase in my adolescence. This meant we approached the film from very much the same point of view, one that seemed quite obvious for both of us. I proposed that our collaboration should be about the fervour and woe of pilgrims and prayers and hopes. I wanted music that had a depth to it that seemed proper for prayer and religion, so it seemed very easy to make the right connection with him. When we first met we had such an instant concordance hearts that we did not even discuss the music or the film. He immediately knew what I wanted, and after he had played maybe twenty seconds on the piano, singing along, I just stopped him and said, 'John, stop this. Just compose it. I know what you are doing here.'

It is a short film, only eighteen minutes long, but for me it is an important work. The quote at the beginning of the film is from Thomas à Kempis, the mediaeval mystic: 'It is only the pilgrims who in the travails of their earthly voyage do not lose their way, whether our planet be frozen or scorched: they are guided by the same prayers, and suffering, and fervour, and woe.' If readers have had their eyes on the previous chapters of this book they would have smelt something the moment the text appeared: the quote is my invention. I had some other text in mind but John Tavener wrote a very fine letter full of passion and I immediately knew he was the *melior pars* and had the right to overrule me.

Where did you shoot the film?

In Mexico at the Basilica of the Virgin in Guadalupe. Pilgrims were arriving from all over the country. I know for a fact some came 280 kilometres on their knees. In most cases I did not speak to them. They were arriving exhausted, tormented and at the very end of their physical strength. You just do not start conversations with these people. The camera was never at much of a distance from them and if there was something that interested us we just moved in. We did not have much room for manoeuvre because there were six million pilgrims arriving in the space of two and a half days. It was important never to show exactly who or what the thousands upon thousands of pilgrims are actually venerating, or even where they are. For example, there is a man who holds a photo of his dead wife and talks to the image of the Virgin. We know nothing about him, yet through the images and the music in the context of the rest of the film we seem to know his entire story. Originally, I had some realistic sounds on the soundtrack that I had recorded in the basilica, but the moment I heard John's music I knew I had to leave it all out because the film and the pilgrimage would have been brought down to some pseudo-realistic almost day-to-day event.

Recently you've returned to making feature films with Invincible.
How much of the film is based on fact?

The film is vaguely based on a true story, one that can be told in three sentences. A young Jewish blacksmith, Sigmund 'Zishe' Breitbart, becomes a well-known figure in the world of variety in Vienna, Berlin and even Broadway in the early 1920s. He was apparently proud of his Jewish heritage and once even called himself the 'New Samson'. He died from an absurd little accident when a nail scratched his knee. Breitbart was basically a show-business personality, not much more than that.

One of Zishe's descendants, Gary Bart, had a large collection of photos, letters, newspaper reports and other documents about Zishe from the 1920s. There was also a screenplay in existence that I did not like. But a day after reading it I called Gary and said that I thought there was something big in Zishe's story, something everyone had overlooked. I asked him if he had the nerve to throw away his investment and told him that I would write a screenplay myself, which I did in nine days. I knew I had to reinvent Zishe for the film and transplant the character to the early 1930s because everything that is fascinating about the relationship between Germans and Jews was exacerbated in that era and, of course, turned into the most monstrous crime and tragedy afterwards. Gary had the wisdom to let me do this.

What was the budget?

Slightly over six million dollars, though what we managed to put on the screen makes it look like we had a Hollywood budget of sixty million, which is what a Hollywood studio would have spent on a film like this. Finding money is always difficult, that is a natural concomitant of film production. But the money was found and the film was shot.

What about Hanussen, the character played by Tim Roth?

The character of Hanussen is based much more on reality than Zishe. More is known about him because he published his own magazine and books, including one in the 1920s about how to cheat as a clairvoyant. Later, when he was forging a career as an entertainer and psychic, he tried to suppress the book. Hanussen stepped into the role of a clairvoyant because it paid much more and the climate of the early 1930s demanded a seer, someone who could give real perspective amongst all the political chaos and turmoil of the times with bank collapses, unemployment and attempted coups. He made himself into a Danish aristocrat with his stage name Erik Jan Hanussen, though he was actually a Czech Jew whose real name was Herschel Steinschneider. Hanussen claimed to have predicted Hitler's victory in the November 1932 election and in the film talks about 'the figure of light that has come among us'. But in reality he did something all seers do. He bet on all the horses, predicting the victories of Schleicher, Brüning and von Papen as well. After the election he pointed only to the paragraph he had written about Hitler's victory.

Invincible is also probably the only film about Germany and the Nazis that does not inevitably end with the Holocaust. It ends on 28 January 1933, two days before Hitler takes power. Of course it was my choice to transplant Zishe's story to the early 1930s when

Invincible

the Nazis were gaining power, but I did this simply because it made the story more obvious. The scenes in court between Zishe and Hanussen become more than just legal battles as Hanussen's real identity as a Jew is revealed. He had compromised too many high-ranking Nazi party members and this seems to be the reason he was abducted, riddled with bullets and half eaten by wild boar.

We're at the end now, so let me ask you if there have been any big disappointments in your career.

Not really. I have learned how to cope with flops and bad press. I can handle it and have never hung around licking my wounds. Failures, yes of course. But disappointments, not really. I know something that young filmmakers need to learn very early on: a perfect film does not exist. Filmmakers will *always*, no matter how much time they tinker away at this scene or this frame, have a sense that there are defects in their films that are amplified a thousand times in front of audiences. As a filmmaker you simply have to learn to live with this, the same way a parent has to live with his children. One might have a stammer, the other has a squint, the third one limps. But you love them even more because they are not perfect. To you there is a certain perfection there anyway, no matter what anyone else thinks.

As a filmmaker though, sometimes I do wonder whether what I do is utterly immaterial. Cinema might give us some insight into our own lives, it might change our perspective of things, but there is much that is absurd about it too. Cinema is only a projection of light; it is immaterial and this life can easily turn you into a clown. The lives of film directors have frequently ended badly, even the most powerful and strongest of them. Just look at what happened to Orson Welles or Buster Keaton. The strongest of the animals have all been brought to their knees eventually. A farmer who grows potatoes is never ridiculous, nor is a cook who prepares dishes. I have seen very dignified ninety-year-old cello players and even photographers, but never filmmakers. My way of dealing with the inevitable is to step out of filmmaking whenever I can. I travel on foot, I direct operas, I raise children, I am learning to cook professionally, I write. Things that give me independence outside the world of cinema.

Before we finish, have you any final advice for your readers?

Well, I recently saw a film celebrating the life of Katharine Hepburn, whom I actually like as an actress. It was some kind of homage to her but unfortunately it turns out that she has these vanilla ice-cream emotions. At the end she is sitting on a rock by the ocean and someone off-camera asks her, 'Ms Hepburn, what would you like to pass on to the young generation?' She swallows, tears are welling, she takes a lot of time as if she were thinking very deeply about it all, then she looks straight into the camera and says, 'Listen to the Song of Life.' And the film ends.

I was cringing it hurt so much. I still smart just thinking about it. And hearing this was such a blow that I even wrote it into the Minnesota Declaration, Article Ten, which I repeat here and now for you, Paul. I look you right in the eye and say, 'Don't you *ever* listen to the Song of Life.'

NOTES

1 Richard Kelly's *The Name of This Book Is Dogme 95* (Faber and Faber, 2000) contains a series of interviews that explain and explore this phenomenon of modern cinema and also includes the 'Vow of Chastity'.

2 Willy Brandt (1913–92, Germany) was elected mayor of West Berlin in 1957 and from 1969 to 1974 was the first post-war Social Democratic Party Chancellor of West Germany. From 1974 to 1987 he was SDP party chairman.

3 See Grass's essay *Twin States – One Nation?: The Case Against German Reunification* (Secker and Warburg, 1990).

4 Bruce Chatwin (1940–89, UK) was a writer and traveller, author of several books including *In Patagonia* (1977), *The Songlines* (1987) and *What Am I Doing Here* (1989). See Chatwin's essay 'The Nomadic Alternative' (1970) in *Anatomy of Restlessness* (Picador, 1996) and Nicholas Shakespeare's biography *Bruce Chatwin* (Vintage, 1999).

5 *Kinder, Mütter und ein General* (1955), directed by László Benedek.

6 *Kinski Uncut* (Bloomsbury, 1997) and *Ich brauche Liebe* (Wilhelm Heyne Verlag, 1991). The German edition of the book was cut substantially when translated into English.

7 John Tavener (b. 1944, UK) is a leading composer of works such as *The Whale* (1968), *The Protecting Veil* (1987) and *Song for Athene*, performed at the funeral of Diana, Princess of Wales, in 1998. See also his book *The Music of Silence* (Faber and Faber, 1999).

The Minnesota Declaration
Truth and fact in documentary cinema

LESSONS OF DARKNESS
by Werner Herzog

1. By dint of declaration the so-called Cinéma Vérité is devoid of vérité. It reaches a merely superficial truth, the truth of accountants.

2. One well-known representative of Cinéma Vérité declared publicly that truth can be easily found by taking a camera and trying to be honest. He resembles the night watchman at the Supreme Court who resents the amount of written law and legal procedures. 'For me,' he says, 'there should be only one single law: the bad guys should go to jail.' Unfortunately, he is part right, for most of the many, much of the time.

3. Cinéma Vérité confounds fact and truth, and thus plows only stones. And yet, facts sometimes have a strange and bizarre power that makes their inherent truth seem unbelievable.

4. Fact creates norms, and truth illumination.

5. There are deeper strata of truth in cinema, and there is such a thing as poetic, ecstatic truth. It is mysterious and elusive, and can be reached only through fabrication and imagination and stylization.

6. Filmmakers of Cinéma Vérité resemble tourists who take pictures amid ancient ruins of facts.

7. Tourism is sin, and travel on foot virtue.

8. Each year at springtime scores of people on snowmobiles crash through the melting ice on the lakes of Minnesota and drown. Pressure is mounting on the new governor to pass a protective law. He, the former wrestler and bodyguard, has the only sage answer to this: 'You can't legislate stupidity.'

9. The gauntlet is hereby thrown down.

10. The moon is dull. Mother Nature doesn't call, doesn't speak to you, although a glacier eventually farts. And don't you listen to the Song of Life.

11. We ought to be grateful that the Universe out there knows no smile.
12. Life in the oceans must be sheer hell. A vast, merciless hell of permanent and immediate danger. So much of a hell that during evolution some species – including man – crawled, fled onto some small continents of solid land, where the Lessons of Darkness continue.

Walker Art Center, Minneapolis, Minnesota
April 30, 1999

Filmography

1962
Herakles
Short feature, 12 minutes, 35 mm, b/w
Director/screenplay: Werner Herzog
Producer: Werner Herzog
Director of Photography: Jaime Pacheco
Editor: Werner Herzog
Sound Engineer: Werner Herzog
Assistant Set: Uwe Brandner
Music: Uwe Brandner
Production Company: Werner Herzog Filmproduktion
Cast: Mr Germany 1962

1964
Spiel im Sand (Game in the Sand)
'Documentary', 14 minutes, 35 mm, b/w
Director/screenplay: Werner Herzog
Producer: Werner Herzog
Director of Photography: Jaime Pacheco
Editor: Werner Herzog
Music: Uwe Brandner
Production Company: Werner Herzog Filmproduktion
[Unreleased]

1966
Die beispiellose Verteidigung der Festung Deutschkreutz
(The Unprecedented Defence of the Fortress Deutschkreuz)
Short feature, 15 minutes, 35 mm, b/w
Director/screenplay: Werner Herzog
Producer: Werner Herzog

Director of Photography: Jaime Pacheco
Editor: Werner Herzog
Sound Engineer: Uwe Brandner
Production Company: Werner Herzog Filmproduktion
Location: Deutschkreuz (Austria)
Premièred: Oberhausen Film Festival 1967
Cast: Peter Brumm, Georg Eska, Karl-Heinz Steffel, Wolfgang von Ungern-Sternberg

1968
Lebenszeichen (Signs of Life)
Feature, 87 minutes, 35 mm, b/w
Director/screenplay: Werner Herzog
Producer: Werner Herzog
Director of Photography: Thomas Mauch
Editor: Beate Mainka-Jellinghaus
Sound Engineer: Herbert Prasch
Music: Stavros Xarchaskos
Assistant Director: Martje Grohmann
Assistant Camera: Dieter Lohmann
Assistant Editor: Maximiliane Mainka
Production Manager: Nicos Triandafyllidis
*Assistant Production Managers:*Thasos Karabelas, Mike Piller, Florian Fricke, Thomas Hartwig, Friederike Pezold
Continuity: Ina Fritsche
Still Photography: Bettina von Waldthausen
Production Company: Werner Herzog Filmproduktion
Location: Crete and Kos (Greece)
Premièred: Munich, 5 July 1968
Cast: Peter Brogle (Stroszek), Wolfgang Reichmann (Meinhard), Athina Zacharopoulou (Nora), Wolfgang von Ungern-Sternberg (Becker), Wolfgang Stumpf (Captain), Henry van Lyck (Lieutenant), Florian Fricke (Pianist), Dr Heinz Usener (Doctor), Achmed Hafiz (Greek resident), Julio Pinheiro (Gypsy)

1968
Letzte Worte (Last Words)
Short feature, 13 minutes, 35 mm, b/w
Director/screenplay: Werner Herzog
Producer: Werner Herzog
Director of Photography: Thomas Mauch
Editor: Beate Mainka-Jellinghaus
Sound Engineer: Herbert Prasch
Music: Folkmusic of Crete

Production Company: Werner Herzog Filmproduktion
Location: Crete
Premièred: Oberhausen Film Festival 1968

1969
Massnahmen Gegen Fanatiker (Precautions against Fanatics)
Short feature, 12 minutes, 35 mm, colour
Director/screenplay: Werner Herzog
Producer: Werner Herzog
Director of Photography: Dieter Lohmann
Assistant Camera: Jörg Schmidt-Reitwein
Editor: Beate Mainka-Jellinghaus
Production Company: Werner Herzog Filmproduktion
Location: Munich
Premièred: Oberhausen Film Festival 1969
Cast: Petar Radenkovic, Mario Adorf, Hans Tiedemann, Herbert Hisel,
Peter Schamoni

1969
Die fliegenden Ärzte von Ostafrika (The Flying Doctors of East Africa)
'Documentary', 45 minutes, 35 mm, colour
Director: Werner Herzog
Producer: Werner Herzog
Executive Producer: Eleonore Semler
Director of Photography: Thomas Mauch
Editor: Beate Mainka-Jellinghaus
Narrator: Wilfried Klaus
Production Company: Werner Herzog Filmproduktion
Co-Producers: Gesellschaft für Medizin und Forschung in Afrika e.V.
Location: Kenya, Uganda, Tanzania
Premièred: 3 March 1970 (television)
Participants: Dr Michael Wood, Dr Ann Spoery, Betty Miller, James Kabale

1970
Auch Zwerge haben klein angefangen (Even Dwarfs Started Small)
Feature, 96 minutes, 35 mm, b/w
Director/screenplay: Werner Herzog
Producer: Werner Herzog
Production Manager: Francisco Ariza
Director of Photography: Thomas Mauch
Editor: Beate Mainka-Jellinghaus
Sound Engineer: Herbert Prasch
Music: Florian Fricke (Popol Vuh) and folksongs of the Ivory Coast,
West Africa, Canary Islands

Assistant Camera: Jörg Schmidt-Reitwein
Assistant Editor: Maximiliane Mainka
Assistant Set: James William Gledhill, Martje Grohmann, Felisa Arrocha Martin, Walter Saxer, Wolfgang von Ungern-Sternberg
Continuity: Ina Fritsche
Still Photography: Bettina von Waldthausen
Production Company: Werner Herzog Filmproduktion
Location: Lanzarote, Canary Islands
Premièred: Cannes Film Festival 1970
Cast: Helmut Döring (Hombre), Gerd Gickel (Pepe), Paul Glauer (Erzieher), Erna Gschwendtner (Azúcar), Gisela Hertwig (Pobrecita), Gerhard März (Territory), Hertel Minkner (Chicklets), Alfredo Piccini (Anselmo), Gertraut Piccini (Piccini), Brigitte Saar (Cochina), Marianne Saar (Theresa), Erna Smolarz (Schweppes), Lajos Zsarnoczay (Chaparro)

1970
Fata Morgana
'Documentary', 79 minutes, 35 mm, colour
Director/screenplay: Werner Herzog
Producer: Werner Herzog
Director of Photography: Jörg Schmidt-Reitwein
Editor: Beate Mainka-Jellinghaus
Narrator: Lotte Eisner
Music: Leonard Cohen, Blind Faith, Couperin, Mozart, Handel
Production Company: Werner Herzog Filmproduktion
Location: Southern Sahara, Cameroon, Canary Islands
Premièred: Cannes Film Festival 1971
Cast: Wolfgang von Ungern-Sternberg, James William Gledhill, Eugen des Montagnes

1971
Behinderte Zukunft (Handicapped Future)
'Documentary', 43 minutes, 16 mm, colour
Director: Werner Herzog
Producer: Werner Herzog
Director of Photography: Jörg Schmidt-Reitwein
Editor: Beate Mainka-Jellinghaus
Narrator: Rolf Illig
Production Company: Werner Herzog Filmproduktion
Location: Munich and California

1971
Land des Schweigens und der Dunkelheit (Land of Silence and Darkness)
'Documentary', 85 minutes, 16 mm, colour

Director: Werner Herzog
Producer: Werner Herzog
Director of Photography: Jörg Schmidt-Reitwein
Editor: Beate Mainka-Jellinghaus
Music: J. S. Bach, Vivaldi
Narrator: Rolf Illig
Production Company: Werner Herzog Filmproduktion
Location: Munich, Niederbayern, Hannover
Premièred: Mannheim Film Festival 1971
Participants: Fini Straubinger, Else Fährer, Ursula Riedmeier, Joseph
Riedmeier, Vlamimir Kokol, Heinrich Fleischmann, Resi Mittermeier

1972
Aguirre, der Zorn Gottes (Aguirre, the Wrath of God)
Feature, 93 minutes, 35 mm, colour
Director/screenplay: Werner Herzog
Producer: Werner Herzog
Director of Photography: Thomas Mauch
Editor: Beate Mainka-Jellinghaus
Production Managers: Walter Saxer, Lucki Stipetić
Re-recording Mixer: Bob Oliver
2nd Camera: Francisco Joán
Sound Engineer: Herbert Prasch
Special Effects: Juvenal Herrera, Miguel Vazquez
Assistant Camera: Orlando Macchiavello
Assistant Production: Martje Grohmann, Dr Georg Hagmüller, Ina
Fritsche, René Lechleitner, Ovidio Ore, Gustavo Cerff Arublú
Music: Florian Fricke (Popol Vuh)
Production Company: Werner Herzog Filmproduktion
Co-Producers: Hessischer Rundfunk
Location: Peru (Urubamba Valley, River Huallaga, River Nanay, Cuzco)
Cast: Klaus Kinski (Lope de Aguirre), Helena Rojo (Inez de Atienza), Del
Negro (Carvajal), Ruy Guerra (Ursúa), Peter Berling (Guzman), Cecilia
Rivera (Flores), Daniel Ades (Perucho), Armando Polanah (Armando),
Edward Roland (Okello) and Daniel Farfán, Julio Martinez, Alejandro
Repullés, the Indians of the Lauramarca Co-operative, Peru

1973
**Die Grosse Ekstase des Bildschnitzers Steiner (The Great Ecstasy of
Woodcarver Steiner)**
'Documentary', 47 minutes, 16 mm, colour
Director: Werner Herzog
Producer: Werner Herzog
Director of Photography: Jörg Schmidt-Reitwein

Editor: Beate Mainka-Jellinghaus
Production Manager: Walter Saxer
2nd Camera: Francisco Joán, Frederik Hettich, Alfred Chrosziel, Gideon Meron
Sound Engineer: Benedikt Kuby
Assistant Set: Feli Sommer
Music: Florian Fricke (Popol Vuh)
Production Company: Werner Herzog Filmproduktion
Co-Producers: Süddeutscher Rundfunk, Stuttgart
Location: Oberstdorf and Garmisch-Partenkirchen (Germany), Planica (Yugoslavia, now Slovenia)
Premièred: Munich, 14 November 1974
Participant: Walter Steiner

1974
Jeder für sich und Gott gegen alle (The Enigma of Kaspar Hauser)
Feature, 109 minutes, 35 mm, colour
Director/screenplay: Werner Herzog
Producer: Werner Herzog
Director of Photography: Jörg Schmidt-Reitwein
Editor: Beate Mainka-Jellinghaus
Production Manager: Walter Saxer
Set Design: Henning von Gierke
Costume Design: Gisela Storch
Sound Engineer: Haymo Henry Heyder
Light Design: Dietmar Zander
Assistant Director: Benedikt Kuby
Make-up and Hair: Susanne Schröder
2nd Camera: Klaus Wyborny
Assistant Camera: Michael Gast
Assistant Editor: Martha Lederer
Assistant Sound: Peter van Anft
Unit Manager: Christian Weisenborn
Assistant Costumes: Ann Poppel
Assistant Production: Joschi N. Arpa
Production Secretary: Anja Schmidt-Zäringer
Continuity: Feli Sommer
Still Photography: Gunther Freyse
Music: Florian Fricke (Popol Vuh), Mozart, Pachelbel, di Lasso, Albinoni
Production Company: Werner Herzog Filmproduktion
Co-Producers: Zweites Deutsches Fernsehen (ZDF)
Location: Dinkelsbühl
Premièred: Dinkelsbühl, 1 November 1974
Cast: Bruno S. (Kaspar), Walter Ladengast (Daumer), Brigitte Mira

(Käthe), Hans Musäus (Unknown), Willy Semmelrogge (Circus Direc-
tor), Michael Kroecher (Stanhope), Henry van Lyck (Cavalry Captain),
Enno Patalas (Vicar Fuhrmann), Elis Pilgrim (Second Vicar), Volker
Prechtel (Hiltel), Gloria Doer (Mrs. Hiltel), Helmut Döring (The Little
King), Kidlat Tahimik (Hombrecito), Andi Gottwald (Young Mozart),
Herbert Achternbusch (1st Country Lad), Wolfgang Bauer (2nd Country
Lad), Walter Steiner (3rd Country Lad), Florian Fricke (Mr Florian),
Clemens Scheitz (Scribe), Johannes Buzalski (Police Officer), Dr Willy
Meyer-Fürst (Doctor), Alfred Edel (Professor of Logic), Franz Brumbach
(Showman with Bear), Herbert Fritsch (Mayor), Wilhelm Bayer (House-
hold Cavalry Captain), Peter Gebhart (Cobbler who finds Kaspar), Otto
Heinzle (Old Priest), Dorothea Kraft (Little Girl)

1976
Herz Aus Glas (Heart of Glass)
Feature, 97 minutes, 35 mm, colour
Director: Werner Herzog
Screenplay adaptation: Herbert Achternbusch
Producer: Werner Herzog
Director of Photography: Jörg Schmidt-Reitwein
Editor: Beate Mainka-Jellinghaus
Production Manager: Walter Saxer
Set Design: Henning von Gierke
Costume Design: Gisela Storch
Sound Engineer: Haymo Henry Heyder
Light Design: Alfred Huck
Assistant Camera: Michael Gast
Assistant Editor: Angelika Dreis
Assistant Set: Cornelius Siegel
Assistant Costumes: Ann Poppel
Assistant Sound: Peter van Anft
Continuity: Regine Krejci
Assistant Production Manager: Joschi Arpa
Production Secretary: Anja Schmidt-Zähringer
Still Photography: Gunther Freyse
Collaborators: Dr Claude Chiarini, Ina Fritsche, Alan Greenberg, Patrick
Ieray
Music: Florian Fricke (Popol Vuh), Studio der Frühen Musik
Production Company: Werner Herzog Filmproduktion
Co-Producers: Zweites Deutsches Fernsehen (ZDF)
Location: Bavaria, Alaska, Ireland
Premièred: Paris Film Festival 1976
Cast: Josef Bierbichler (Hias), Stefan Güttler (Factory Owner), Clemens
Scheitz (Adalbert), Volker Prechtel (Wudy), Sonja Skiba (Ludmilla),

Brunhilde Klöckner (Paulin), Wolf Albrecht (Sam), Thomas Binkley (Lute Player), Janos Fischer (Ägide), Wilhelm Friedrich (Factory Owner's Father), Edith Gratz (Innkeeper's Wife), Alois Hruschka (Gigl), Egmont Hugel (Harp-Toni), Sterling Jones and Richard Levitt (Musicians), Wolfram Kunkel (Hurdy Gurdy Man), Werner Lederle (Innkeeper), Sepp Müller (Ascherl), Agnes Nuissl (Anamirl), Andrea von Ramm (Singer), Helmut Kossik, Amad Ibn Ghassem Nadij, Bernhard Schabel, Friedrich Steinhauer (Farmers), Joschi Arpa (The Liar), Claude Chiarini (The Thief), Martje Herzog (Peasant Woman), Werner Herzog, Herbert Achternbusch (Glass Carriers), Helmut Krüger (Workman)

1976
Mit mir will keiner spielen (No One Will Play with Me)
'Documentary', 14 minutes, 16 mm, colour
Director: Werner Herzog
Producer: Werner Herzog
Director of Photography: Jörg Schmidt-Reitwein
Editor: Beate Mainka-Jellinghaus
Sound Engineer: Haymo Henry Heyder
Production Company: Werner Herzog Filmproduktion
Location: Munich

1976
How Much Wood Would a Woodchuck Chuck
'Documentary', 45 minutes, 16 mm, colour
Director: Werner Herzog
Producer: Werner Herzog
Director of Photography: Thomas Mauch
Editor: Beate Mainka-Jellinghaus
Production Manager: Walter Saxer
2nd Camera Unit: Ed Lachman, Francisco Joán
Sound Engineer: Walter Saxer
Production Company: Werner Herzog Filmproduktion
Co-Producers: Süddeutscher Rundfunk, Stuttgart
Location: New Holland, Pennsylvania
Premièred: 14 February 1977 (television)
Participants: Steve Liptay, Ralph Wade, Alan Ball, Abe Diffenbach and competitors at the World Championship of Livestock Auctioneers

1976
Stroszek
Feature, 108 minutes, 35 mm, colour
Director/screenplay: Werner Herzog

Producer: Werner Herzog
Director of Photography: Thomas Mauch
Editor: Beate Mainka-Jellinghaus
Production Manager: Walter Saxer
Set Design: Henning von Gierke
Assistant Set Design: Cornelius Siegel
2nd Camera Unit: Ed Lachman
Sound Engineer: Haymo Henry Heyder
Light Design: Dieter Bähr
Assistant Director: Ed Lachman
Assistant Camera: Wolfgang Knigge (Berlin), Stefano Guidi (USA)
Assistant Set: Anja Schmidt-Zäringer
Assistant Sound: Peter van Anft
Continuity: Anja Schmidt-Zäringer
Still Photography: Gunther Freyse
Music: Chet Atkins, Sonny Terry, Tom Paxton, Beethoven
Production Company: Werner Herzog Filmproduktion
Co-Producers: Zweites Deutsches Fernsehen (ZDF)
Location: Berlin, New York, Wisconsin, North Carolina
Premièred: Munich, 20 May 1977
Cast: Bruno S. (Stroszek), Eva Mattes (Eva), Clemens Scheitz (Scheitz),
Wilhelm von Homburg, Burkhard Driest, Pitt Bedewitz (Pimps), Clayton
Szlapinski (Mechanic), Ely Rodriguez (Indian), Alfred Edel (Prison
Warden), Scott McKain (Bank Employee), Ralph Wade (Auctioneer),
Dr Vaclav Vojta (Doctor), Michael Gahr (Prisoner Hoss), Yücsel
Topeugürler (Turkish Prisoner), Der Brave Beo (Talking Bird)

1977
La Soufrière
'Documentary', 44 minutes, 16 mm, colour
Director: Werner Herzog
Producer: Werner Herzog
Directors of Photography: Jörg Schmidt-Reitwein, Ed Lachman
Editor: Beate Mainka-Jellinghaus
Production Manager: Walter Saxer
Narrator: Werner Herzog
Sound Engineer: Werner Herzog
Music: Rachmaninov, Mendelssohn, Brahms, Wagner
Production Company: Werner Herzog Filmproduktion
Co-Producers: Süddeutscher Rundfunk, Stuttgart
Location: Guadeloupe
Premièred: Bonn, March 1977

1979
Nosferatu – Phantom der Nacht (Nosferatu the Vampyre)
Feature, 103 minutes, 35 mm, colour
Director: Werner Herzog
Screenplay: Werner Herzog
Producer: Werner Herzog
Director of Photography: Jörg Schmidt-Reitwein
Editor: Beate Mainka-Jellinghaus
Production Managers: Walter Saxer, Rudolf Wolf
Set Design: Henning von Gierke, Ulrich Bergfelder
Costume Design: Gisela Storch
2nd Camera Unit: Michael Gast
Sound Engineer: Harald Maury
Make-up and Hair: Reiko Kruk, Dominique Colladant, Ludovic Paris
Props: Hans Oosterhuis
Special Effects: Cornelius Siegel
Light Design: Martin Gerbl, Anton Urban, Erich Labermair
Assistant Director: Remmelt Remmelts
Assistant Set: Josef Arpa, Mirko Tichacek
Assistant Costume: Annegret Poppel, Claire Fraisse (Adjani), Anne Jud, Elisabeth Irmer (Holland)
Assistant Sound: Jean Fontaine
Assistant Make-up and Hair: Dominique Colladon
Continuity: Anja Schmidt-Zäringer
Still Photography: Dr Claude Chiarini
Dialogue Coach: Beverly Walker
Production Manager (France): Jean-Paul Gibon
Production Manager (Netherlands): Jaap van Rij
Production Manager (Czech Republic): Rudolf Wolf
Production Assistant: Hetty Los
Music: Florian Fricke (Popol Vuh), Wagner, Gounod
Production Company: Werner Herzog Filmproduktion
Co-Producers: Gaumont, Zweites Deutsches Fernsehen (ZDF)
Location: Czech Republic, Netherlands, Mexico
Premièred: Paris, 10 January 1979
Cast: Klaus Kinski (Count Dracula), Isabelle Adjani (Lucy Harker), Bruno Ganz (Jonathan Harker), Jaques Dufilho (Captain), Roland Topor (Renfield), Walter Ladengast (Dr van Helsing), Dan van Husen (Warden), Roger Berry Losch (First Mate), Jan Groth (Harbourmaster), Carsten Bodinus (Schrader), Martje Grohmann (Mina), Ryk de Gooyer (Official), Clemens Scheitz (Town Employee), Lo van Hensbergen (Inspector), John Leddy (Coachman), Margiet van Hartingsveld (Maid), Tim Beekman (Coffinbearer), Beverly Walker (Mother Superior), Johan te Slaa (Bellman), Claude Chiarini (Customsman)

1979
Woyzeck
Feature, 81 minutes, 35 mm, colour
Director: Werner Herzog
Screenplay: Werner Herzog (from the drama-fragment by Georg Büchner)
Producer: Werner Herzog
Director of Photography: Jörg Schmidt-Reitwein
Editor: Beate Mainka-Jellinghaus
Production Managers: Walter Saxer
Set Design: Henning von Gierke
Costume Design: Gisela Storch
2nd Camera Unit: Michael Gast
Sound Engineer: Harald Maury
Props: Ulrich Bergfelder
Light Design: Martin Gerbl
Assistant Lighting: Anton Urban
Assistant Director: Mirko Tichacek
Assistant Costume: Ann Poppel
Assistant Sound: Jean Fontaine
Continuity: Anja Schmidt-Zäringer
Still Photography: Dr Claude Chiarini
Music: Fiedelquartett Telč, Rudolf Obruca, Benedetto Marcello, Vivaldi
Production Company: Werner Herzog Filmproduktion
Co-Producers: Zweites Deutsches Fernsehen (ZDF)
Location: Czech Republic
Premièred: Cannes Film Festival 1979
Cast: Klaus Kinski (Woyzeck), Eva Mattes (Marie), Wolfgang Reich-
mann (Hauptmann), Willy Semmelrogge (Doctor), Josef Bierbichler
(Drum-Major), Paul Burian (Andres), Volker Prechtel (Journeyman),
Dieter Augustin (Market Crier), Irm Hermann (Margret), Wolfgang
Bächler (Jude), Rosy- Rosy Heinikel (Käthe), Herbert Fux (Subaltern),
Thomas Mettke (Innkeeper), Maria Mettke (Innkeeper's Wife)

1980
God's Angry Man (Glaube und Währung)
'Documentary', 44 minutes, 16 mm, colour
Director: Werner Herzog
Producer: Werner Herzog
Director of Photography: Thomas Mauch
Editor: Beate Mainka-Jellinghaus
Production Manager: Walter Saxer
Production Assistant: Richard Cybulski
Sound Engineer: Walter Saxer
Production Company: Werner Herzog Filmproduktion

Co-Producers: Süddeutscher Rundfunk, Stuttgart
Location: Glendale, California
Premièred: 17 May 1981 (television)
Participant: Dr Gene Scott

1980
Huie's Sermon (Huie's Predigt)
'Documentary', 43 minutes, 16 mm, colour
Director: Werner Herzog
Producer: Werner Herzog
Director of Photography: Thomas Mauch
Editor: Beate Mainka-Jellinghaus
Production Assistant: Richard Cybulski
2nd Camera Unit: Ed Lachman
Sound Engineer: Walter Saxer
Production Company: Werner Herzog Film Produktion
Co-Producers: Süddeutscher Rundfunk, Stuttgart
Location: Brooklyn, New York
Premièred: 14 June 1981 (television)
Participant: Bishop Huie L. Rogers

1982
Fitzcarraldo
Feature, 137 minutes, 35 mm, colour
Director/screenplay: Werner Herzog
Producers: Lucki Stipetić, Werner Herzog
Director of Photography: Thomas Mauch
Editor: Beate Mainka-Jellinghaus
Production Manager: Walter Saxer
Sound Editor: Petra Mantoudis
Set Design: Henning von Gierke
Costume Design: Gisela Storch
2nd Camera Unit: Rainer Klausmann
Sound Engineer: Dagoberto Juarez
Make-up and Hair: Stefano Fava, Gloria Fava
Special Effects: Miguel Vazquez
Light Design: Raimund Wirner, Hans-Peter Vogt
Assistant Director: Jorge Vignati
Assistant Camera: Beat Presser
Assistant Editor: Carola Mai, Linda Kuusisto
Assistant Set: Ulrich Bergfelder
Assistant Costume: Franz Blumauer
Assistant Sound: Zézé D'Alice
Assistant Make-up and Hair: Jacques Monteiro, Carlos Prieto

Continuity: Anja Schmidt-Zäringer
Still Photography: Beat Presser
Dialogue Coach: William L. Rose
Music: Florian Fricke (Popol Vuh), Verdi, Bellini
Production Company: Werner Herzog Filmproduktion
Co-Producers: Zweites Deutsches Fernsehen (ZDF), Pro-jekt Film-
produktion im Filmverlag der Autoren
Location: Iquitos, Rio Camisea (Peru), Manaus and Iquitos (Brazil)
Premièred: Munich, 5 March 1982
Cast: Klaus Kinski (Brian Sweeny 'Fitzcarraldo' Fitzgerald), Claudia
Cardinale (Molly), José Lewgoy (Don Aquilino), Paul Hittscher (Cap-
tain), Huerequeque Enrique Bohórquez (Huerequeque), Miguel Angel
Fuentes (Cholo), Rui Polanah (Don Araujo), Dieter Milz (Young Padre),
Salvador Godinez (Old Padre), Grande Othelo (Station Master), Milton
Nascimento (Black Doorman), Bill Rose (Lawyer), Jorge Vignati (1st
Sailor), Leoncio Bueno (Police Lieutenant), Peter Berling (Director of
Manaus Opera House) with Ashininka-Campa Indians of the Gran
Pajonal; Cast of Manaus opera house: Costante Moret (voice Veriano
Luchetti) (Enrico Caruso – Ernani), Dimiter Petkov (Silva), Jean-Claude
Dreyfuss (voice Mietta Sighele) (Sarah Bernardt – Elvira), Lourdes Mag-
alhaes (Orchestra Pit Singer), Isabel Jimenes de Cisneros (Donna Elvira),
Liborio Simonella (Arturo), Jesus Goiri (Giorgio), Christian Mantilla
(Walton), Veneta Philarmonia conducted by Giorgio Croci. Sequence in
Teatro Amazones (Manaus) directed by Werner Schroeter; Opera on the
boat, Bellini's *Puritani*, Orquesta Sinfonica des Repertorio, Lima, con-
ducted by Manuel Cuadros Barr

1984
Ballade vom kleinen Soldaten (Ballad of the Little Soldier)
'Documentary', 45 minutes, 16 mm, colour
Director: Werner Herzog
Producer: Lucki Stipetić
Director of Photography: Jorge Vignati
Editor: Maximiliane Mainka
Assistant Editor: Draha Cizek
Sound Engineer: Christine Ebenberger
Assistant Director: Denis Reichle
2nd Camera Unit: Michael Edols
Music: Folksongs: 'Mochila Azul' (Singer Isidoro Reyes), 'Dame la
Mano', 'Evening Song', 'Beautiful Miskito Woman' (singer Paladino
Taylor), 'Flor de mi amor' (singer Isidoro Reyes)
Production Company: Werner Herzog Filmproduktion
Co-Producers: Süddeutscher Rundfunk, Stuttgart
Location: Nicaragua and Honduras

Premièred: 5 November 1984 (television)
Participants: Miskito Indians of Nicaragua

1984
Gasherbrum – Der leuchtende Berg (The Dark Glow of the Mountains)
'Documentary', 45 minutes, 16 mm, colour
Director: Werner Herzog
Producer: Lucki Stipetić
Director of Photography: Rainer Klausmann
Editor: Maximiliane Mainka
2nd Camera Unit: Jorge Vignati
Additional Photography: Reinhold Messner
Sound Engineer: Christine Ebenberger
Music: Florian Fricke (Popol Vuh), Renate Knaup, Daniel Fichelscher
Production Company: Werner Herzog Filmproduktion
Co-Producers: Süddeutscher Rundfunk, Stuttgart
Location: Karakorum (Pakistan)
Premièred: 23 June 1985 (television)
Participants: Reinhold Messner, Hans Kammerlander

1984
Where the Green Ants Dream (Wo die grünen Ameisen träumen)
Feature, 100 minutes, 35 mm, colour
Director/screenplay: Werner Herzog
Producer: Lucki Stipetić
Director of Photography: Jörg Schmidt-Reitwein
Editor: Beate Mainka-Jellinghaus
Production co-ordinator (Australia): Tony Llewellyn-Jones
Set Design: Ulrich Bergfelder
Costume Design: Frances D. Hogan
Sound Engineer: Claus Langer
Special Effects: Brian Pearce
Light Design: Manfred Klein
Assistant Camera: Michael Edols
Assistant Sound: Peter Rappel
Continuity: Christine Ebenberger
Additional Dialogue: Bob Ellis
Advisers Aborigines Affairs: Gary Foley, Jennifer Home
Still Photography: Paul Cox
Music: Fauré, Bloch, Wagner, Klaus-Jochen Wiese, Aboriginal music by
Wandjuk Marika
Production Company: Werner Herzog Filmproduktion
Co-Producers: Zweites Deutsches Fernsehen (ZDF)
Location: Coober Pedy, Melbourne

Premièred: Cannes Film Festival 1984
Cast: Bruce Spence (Hackett), Wandjuk Marika (Miliritbi), Roy Marika (Dayipu), Ray Barrett (Cole), Norman Kaye (Ferguson), Colleen Clifford (Miss Strehlow), Ralph Cotterill (Fletcher), Nicolas Lathouris (Arnold), Basil Clarke (Judge Blackburn), Ray Marshall (Coulthard), Dhungala I. Marika (Malila), Gary Williams (Watson), Tony Llewellyn-Jones (Fitzsimmons), Marraru Wunungmurra (Daisy Barunga), Robert Brissenden (Professor Stanner)

1987
Cobra Verde
Feature, 110 minutes, 35 mm, colour
Director: Werner Herzog
Screenplay: Werner Herzog (from the novel *The Viceroy of Ouidah* by Bruce Chatwin)
Producer: Lucki Stipetić
Director of Photography: Victor Růžička
Editor: Maximiliane Mainka
Production Manager: Walter Saxer
Assistant Production Manager: Salvatore Basile
Sound Editor: Friedrich M. Dosch
Mixer: Milan Bor
Set Design: Ulrich Bergfelder
Costume Design: Gisela Storch
2nd Camera Unit: Jorge Ruiz, William Sefa
Sound Engineer: Haymo Henry Heyder
Assistant Sound Editor: Hans Zeiler
Make-up and Hair: Berthold Sack
Props: Bernd Grotzke
Light Design: Martin Gerbl
Assistant Director: Christine Ebenberger
Assistant Camera: Hermann Fahr
Assistant Editor: Rainer Standke
Assistant Set: Fernando Umaña (Columbia), Ina Lüders, Antonio Jordao Gomes da Costa (Ghana)
Assistant Costumes: Silvia Grabowski
Assistant Sound: Rudolf Hellwig
Continuity: Anja Schmidt-Zäringer
Still Photography: Beat Presser
Music: Florian Fricke (Popol Vuh)
Production Company: Werner Herzog Filmproduktion
Co-Producers: Zweites Deutsches Fernsehen (ZDF)
Location: Elmina and Tamale (Ghana), Cartagena, Cali and Guajira (Colombia)

Premièred: Munich, 3 December 1987
Cast: Klaus Kinski (Francisco Manoel da Silva), King Ampaw (Taparica), José Lewgoy (Don Octavio Coutinho), Salvatore Basile (Captain Fraternidade), Peter Berling (Bernabo), Gillermo Coronel (Euclides), His Royal Highness King Nana Agyefi Kwame II of Nsein (Bossa Ahadee), Yolanda Garcia (Dona Epiphania), Nana Fedu Abodo (Yovogan), Kofi Yerenkyi (Bakoko), Kwesi Fase (Kankpé), Benito Stefanelli (Captain Pedro Vicente), Kofi Bryan (Messenger of Bossa Ahadee), Carlos Mayolo (Governor), Zigi Cultural Troupe HO, Ziavi (Singing Girls)

1988
Les Français Vus Par . . . (Les Gauloises)
'Documentary', 12 minutes, 16 mm, colour
Director: Werner Herzog
Director of Photography: Jörg Schmidt-Reitwein
Editor: Rainer Standke
Sound Engineer: Bernard Aubouy
Production Company: Erato Films, Paris
Participants: Claude Josse, Jean Clemente, the rugby team of Stade Toulousain and the Sport Club of Graulheit

1989
Wodaabe – Die Hirten der Sonne (Wodaabe – Herdsmen of the Sun)
'Documentary', 52 minutes, 16 mm, colour
Director: Werner Herzog
Producer: Patrick Sandrin
Director of Photography: Jörg Schmidt-Reitwein
Editor: Maximiliane Mainka
Production Manager: Walter Saxer
Sound Engineer: Walter Saxer
Assistant Director: Claude Hervaint
Music: Gounod, Mozart, Handel, Verdi
Production Company: Werner Herzog Filmproduktion
Co-Producers: Süddeutscher Rundfunk, Stuttgart and Arion Productions
Location: Southern Sahara (Republic of Niger)
Participants: Wodaabe tribe

1990
Echos aus einem düsteren Reich (Echoes from a Sombre Empire)
'Documentary', 93 minutes, 16 mm, colour
Director: Werner Herzog
Producer: Werner Herzog
Co-producer: Galeshka Moravioff
Director of Photography: Jörg Schmidt-Reitwein

Editor: Rainer Standke
Special Advisor: Michael Goldsmith
Production Manager: Walter Saxer
2nd Camera Unit: Martin Manz
Assistant Editor: Thomas Balkenhol
Sound Engineer: Harald Maury
Music: Bartók, Prokofiev, Lutoslawski, Schubert, Shostakovich, J. S. Bach, Esther Lamandier
Production Company: SERA Filmproduktion and Werner Herzog Filmproduktion
Co-Producers: Films Sans Frontières
Location: Central African Republic
Participants: Michael Goldsmith, François Gilbault, Augustine Assemat, Francis Szpiner, David Dacko, Marie-Reine Hassen

1991

Das excentrische Privattheater des Maharadjah von Udaipur (The Eccentric Private Theatre of the Maharaja of Udaipur)
'Documentary', 85 minutes, 16 mm, colour
Director: Werner Herzog
Producer: Werner Herzog
Staging: André Heller
Photography: Rainer Klausmann, Wolfgang Dickmann, Anton Peschke
Editor: Michou Hutter
Production Manager: Wolfgang Rest
Set Design: Edgar Neogy-Tezak
Costume Design: Heidi Melinc
Sound Engineer: Rainer Wiehr
Assistant Camera: Claudius Kelterborn, Daniel Koppelmann, Bernhard Watzek
Assistant Editor: Ursula Darrer
Assistant Sound: Alois Unger
Unit Manager: Rajesh Shirvaikar
Assistant Production: Ajay Kapoor
Production Company: Neue Studio Film GmbH, Vienna
Co-Producers: ORF (Austria), Zweites Deutsches Fernsehen (ZDF)
Location: Udaipur (India)

1991

Scream of Stone (Schrei aus Stein)
Feature, 105 minutes, 35 mm, colour
Director: Werner Herzog
Original screenplay: Hans-Ulrich Klenner, Walter Saxer, Robert Geoffrion (from an original idea by Reinhold Messner)

319

Producers: Walter Saxer, Henri Lange, Richard Sadler
Executive Producer: Walter Saxer
Director of Photography: Rainer Klausmann
Editor: Suzanne Baron
Production Manager: Erna Erlacher
Sound Editor: Manfred Arbter
Production Design: Juan Santiago
Set Design: Kristine Steinhilber, Cornelius Siegel, Wolfgang Siegel
Costume Design: Ann Poppel
2nd Camera Unit (Climbing): Herbert Raditschnig
Sound Engineer: Christopher Price
Make-up and Hair: Berthold Sack, Ann Brodie, Udo Riemer
Props: Bernd Grotzke
Light Design: Manfred Raab
Assistant Director: Salvatore Basile
Assistant Camera: Claudius Kelterborn
Assistant Editor: Anne Wagner
Assistant Production: Dominique Sidoit, Ruth Charest
Continuity: Andre Gaumond
Still Photography: Stephane Compoint, Frederique de Lafosse
Music: Heinrich Schütz, Wagner, Ingram Marshal, Sarah Hopkins, Alan Lamb
Production Company: Sera Filmproduktions GmbH
Co-Producers: Molecule, Les Stock Films International, Zweites Deutsches Fernsehen (ZDF), Canal+
Location: Patagonia (Argentina), Munich
Premièred: Venice Film Festival 1991
Cast: Vittorio Mezzogiorno (Roccia), Stefan Glowacz (Martin), Mathilda May (Katharina), Donald Sutherland (Ivan), Brad Dourif (Fingerless), Al Waxman (Stephan), Chavela Vargas (Indian Woman), Hans Kammerlander (Mountain Climber), Volker Prechtl (Himalayan Climber)

1992
Film Lesson
'Documentary' (eight parts), Betacam, colour, 240 minutes (total)
Director: Werner Herzog
Producer: Gerda Weissenberger
Directors of Photography: Karl Kofler, Michael Ferk
Editor: Albert Skalak
Sound: Gerhard Sandler
Co-Producers: ORF (Austria)
Location: Vienna
Premièred: December 1991/ January 1992 (television)

Participants: Michael Kreihsl, Jeff Sheridan, Peter Turrini, Volker Schlöndorff, Kamal Saiful Islam, Philippe Petit, Ryszard Kapuściński, Werner Herzog

1992
Lektionen in Finsternis (Lessons of Darkness)
'Documentary', 52 minutes, Super 16, colour
Director/screenplay: Werner Herzog
Producer: Lucki Stipetić
Executive Producer: Paul Berriff
Director of Photography: Paul Berriff
Editor: Rainer Standke
Production Manager: Paul Cotton
Mixer: Manfred Arbter
2nd Camera Unit: Rainer Klausmann
Aerial Camera: Simon Werry
Helicopter Pilot: Jerry Grayson
Sound Engineer: John G. Pearson
Music: Wagner, Grieg, Prokofiev, Pärt, Verdi, Schubert, Mahler
Production Company: Werner Herzog Filmproduktion
Co-Producers: Paul Berriff, Premiere Hamburg
Location: Kuwait
Premièred: 27 February 1992 (television)

1993
Glocken aus der Tiefe (Bells from the Deep)
'Documentary', 60 minutes, Super 16, colour
Director: Werner Herzog
Producers: Lucki Stipetić, Ira Barmak
Supervising Producer: Mark Slater
Director of Photography: Jörg Schmidt-Reitwein
Editor: Rainer Standke
2nd Camera Unit: Martin Manz
Sound Engineer: Vyacheslav Belozerov
Interpreter: Viktor Danilov
Assistant Director: Rudolph Herzog
Still Photography: Christine Ebenberger, Werner Janoud
Mixer: Max Rammler-Rogall
Music: Choir of the Spiritual Academy, St Petersburg, Choir of the Zagorsk Monastery, Choir of the Pühtica Dormition Convent
Production Company: Werner Herzog Filmproduktion
Co-Producers: Momentous Events, Inc., New York
Location: Russia

1994
Die Verwandlung der Welt in Musik (The Transformation of the World into Music)
'Documentary', 90 minutes, Super 16, colour
Director: Werner Herzog
Producer: Lucki Stipetić
Director of Photography: Jörg Schmidt-Reitwein
Editor: Rainer Standke
Costume Design: Henning von Gierke
Sound Engineer: Ekkehart Baumung
Light Design: Lutz Reitemeier
Assistant Camera: Martin Manz
Mixer: Klaus Handstein
Music: Wagner (Choir and Orchestra of the Bayreuth Wagner Festival)
Production Company: Werner Herzog Filmproduktion
Co-Producers: Zweites Deutsches Fernsehen (ZDF)
Location: Bayreuth, Linderhof Castle
Participants: Wolfgang Wagner, Sven Friedrich, Yohji Yamamoto, Placido Domingo, Dieter Dorn, Heiner Müller, Waltraud Maier, Siegfried Jerusalem

1995
Gesualdo – Tod für fünf Stimmen (Death for Five Voices)
'Documentary', 60 minutes, Super 16, colour
Director/screenplay: Werner Herzog
Producer: Lucki Stipetić
Director of Photography: Peter Zeitlinger
Editor: Rainer Standke
Production Manager: Lucki Stipetić
Sound Engineer: Ekkehart Baumung
Light Design: Norbert Erben
Assistant Directors: Pietro Medioli, Rudolph Herzog
Assistant Camera: Thomas Prodinger
Assistant Sound: Klaus Handstein
Continuity: Jenny Erpenbeck
Still Photography: Werner Janoud
Music: Gesualdo, Wagner
Production Company: Werner Herzog Filmproduktion
Co-Producers: Zweites Deutsches Fernsehen (ZDF)
Location: Ferrara, Castel Gesualdo, Arezzo, Venosa, Naples
Participants: Pasquale D'Onofrio, Salvatore Catorano, Angelo Carrabs, Milva, Angelo Michele Torriello, Raffaele Virocolo, Vincenzo Giusto, Giovanni Iudica, Walter Beloch, Principe D'Avalos, Antonio Massa, Alan Curtis, Gennaro Miccio, Silvano Milli, Marisa Milli, Gerald Place, Alberto Lanini, Il Complesso Barocco, Gesualdo Consort of London

1997
Little Dieter Needs to Fly (Flucht aus Laos)
'Documentary', 80 minutes (theatrical), 52 minutes (English/German television), Super 16, colour
Director/screenplay: Werner Herzog
Producer: Lucki Stipetić
Executive Producer: Andre Singer
Director of Photography: Peter Zeitlinger
Editor: Rainer Standke
Sound Editor: Josh Rosen
Additional Photography: Les Blank
Sound Engineer: Ekkehart Baumung
Light Design: Norbert Erben
Narrator: Werner Herzog
Assistant Director: Herbert Golder
Assistant Camera: Erik Söllner
Assistant Editor: Glenn Scantlebury, Joe Bini
Assistant Set: Rudolph Herzog
Continuity: Anja Schmidt-Zäringer
Still Photography: Helen Kim
Music: Bartók, Carlos Gardel, Glenn Miller, Kongar-ol Ondar, Wagner, Dvořák, J. S. Bach, folk music of the people of Sayan Altal and the Ural Mountains
Production Company: Werner Herzog Filmproduktion
Co-Producers: Zweites Deutsches Fernsehen (ZDF)
Location: Thailand, San Francisco, Tuscon, San Diego, Wildberg (Black Forest)
Participant Dieter Dengler

1999
Julianes Sturz in den Dschungel (Wings of Hope)
'Documentary', 70 minutes (theatrical), 42 minutes (German television), 49 minutes (English television), Super 16, colour
Director/screenplay: Werner Herzog
Producer: Lucki Stipetić
Executive Producer: Peter Firstbrook (BBC)
Director of Photography: Peter Zeitlinger
Editor: Joe Bini
Production Manager: Ulrich Bergfelder
Sound Editor: Josh Rosen
Mixer: David Nelson
Sound Engineer: Eric Spitzer
Assistant Director: Herbert Golder
Assistant Camera: Erik Söllner

Assistant Editor: Maya Hawke
Continuity: Anja Schmidt-Zäringer
Still Photography: Sylvia Vas
Music: Wagner, Stravinsky
Production Company: Werner Herzog Filmproduktion
Co-Producers: Zweites Deutsches Fernsehen (ZDF), BBC Bristol
Location: Peru
Premièred: Munich Film Festival 1999
Participants: Juliane Köpcke, Moisés Rengito Chavez, Juan Limber Ribera Soto, Richard Silva Manujama, Ricardo Oroche Rengite, El Moro, Simon Herzog

1999
Mein liebster Feind (My Best Fiend)
'Documentary', 95 minutes, Super 16, colour
Director/screenplay: Werner Herzog
Producer: Lucki Stipetić
Executive Producers: André Singer, Christine Ruppert
Director of Photography: Peter Zeitlinger
Editor: Joe Bini
Production Manager: Ulrich Bergfelder
Sound Editor: Eric Spitzer
Narrator: Werner Herzog
Mixer: Hubertus Rath
2nd Camera Unit: Les Blank
Sound Engineer: Eric Spitzer
Assistant Director: Herbert Golder
Assistant Camera: Erik Söllner
Assistant Editors: Thomas Staunton, Thad Povey, Renate Hähner
Assistant Sound: Chris Simon
Continuity: Anja Schmidt-Zäringer
Still Photography: Werner Janoud, Silvia Vas
Music: Florian Fricke (Popol Vuh)
Production Company: Werner Herzog Filmproduktion
Co-Producers: Café Productions Ltd., Zephir Film GmbH
Location: Peru, Netherlands, Czech Republic, Germany, Paris, USA
Premièred: Cannes Film Festival 1999
Participants: Klaus Kinski, Eva Mattes, Claudia Cardinale, Beat Presser, Guillermo Rios, Andres Vicente, Justo Gonzalez, Benino Moreno Placido, Baron und Baronin von d. Recke, José Koechlin von Stein, Bill Pence

1999
Gott and die Beladenen (The Lord and the Laden)
'Documentary', 43 minutes, digital video, colour

Director/screenplay: Werner Herzog
Producers: Martin Choroba, Joachim Puls
Executive Producer: Lucki Stipetić
Director of Photography: Jorge Vignati
2nd Unit Camera: Ed Lachman
Editor: Joe Bini
Sound Engineer: Francisco Adrianzen
Production Manager (Mexico): Luz-Maria Rojas
Production Manager (Guatemala): Alfonso Rios Montt
Assistant Camera: Gonzalo Tapia
Re-recording Mixer: Josh Rosen
Assistant Editor: Thomas Staunton
Mixer: David Nelson
Assistant Director: Herbert Golder
Still Photography: Lena Pisetskaia
Computer Animation: Dirk Engwicht, Stephan Hempel
Accountant: Monika Kostinek
Music: Gounod, Orlando di Lasso
Production Company: Tellux Film
Location: Antigua, San Andrés Itzapá (Mexico), Guatemala

2001
Pilgrimage
'Documentary', 18 minutes, Super 16, colour
Director/screenplay: Werner Herzog
Producer: Werner Herzog
Executive Producer: Rodney Wilson, Christian Seidel
Associate Producer: Lucki Stipetić
Director of Photography: Jorge Pacheco
Editor: Joe Bini
Production Manager: Luz-Maria Rojas
2nd Unit Camera: Jörg Schmidt-Reitwein, Erik Söllner
Music: John Tavener (*Mahámátra* performed by BBC Symphony
Orchestra, conducted by Leonard Slatkin, sung by Parvin Cox and the
Westminster Cathedral Choir)
Production Company: Werner Herzog Filmproduktion
Co-Producers: BBC, Pipeline Films
Location: Mexico
Premièred: London, 1 March 2001

2001
Invincible
Feature, 130 minutes, 35 mm, colour
Director/screenplay: Werner Herzog

Producers: Gary Bart, Werner Herzog, Christine Ruppert
Executive Producers: Paul Webster, Michael André, Simon Stewens, James Mitchell, Lucki Stipetić
Director of Photography: Peter Zeitlinger
Editor: Joe Bini
Production Designer: Ulrich Bergfelder
Costume Designer: Jany Temime
Editor: Joe Bini
Production Managers: Walter Saxer, Mark Popp
Assistant Directors: Rudoph Herzog, Herb Golder
Music: Hans Zimmer, Klaus Badelt
Production Company: Werner Herzog Filmproduktion
Location: Germany, Latvia, Lithuania, The Netherlands, Christmas Island (Australian Territory)
Premièred: Venice Film Festival, September 2001
Cast: Tim Roth (Hanussen), Jouko Ahola (Zishe Breitbart), Anna Gourari (Marta Farra), Jacob Wein (Benjamin Breitbart), Max Raabe (Master of Ceremonies), Gustav Peter Woehler (Landwehr), Udo Kier (Count Helldorf), Herb Golder (Rabbi Edelmann), Gary Bart (Yitzak Breitbart), Renata Krößner (Mother Breitbart)

Bibliography

Even though since the 1970s there have been many books with Werner Herzog's name on the cover, either as author or subject, there is almost nothing currently available in English. As such, most of what is listed in this selected bibliography will not be easy to find.

The most convenient first stop for readers wanting more information on Herzog's work is his own website (http://www.wernerherzog.com), an excellent source of information on film, opera and stage credits. Well designed and regularly updated by his Munich office, it also contains fairly comprehensive details of Herzog's published works (books, articles and translations) and Herb Golder's vast bibliographies of primary and secondary literature (books, dissertations, articles and interviews).

As Herzog explained in Chapter 7 of this book, his own publishing house Skellig produced two volumes of his screenplays (in German) in 1977. Only one volume (containing *Aguirre, The Enigma of Kaspar Hauser* and *Land of Silence and Darkness*) was published in English (Tanam, 1980). Over the years Carl Hanser Verlag have published several Herzog scripts in German (including *Fitzcarraldo, Stroszek, Nosferatu, Where the Green Ants Dream* and *Cobra Verde*), some of which are still in print. *Fitzcarraldo* was also published in English by Fjord Press in 1982, and several other language editions also exist, including a photobook (Schimer/Mosel, 1982) which also contains a selection of Herzog's diary entries written whilst on location. The journal *L'Avant Scène du Cinéma* published French translations of the scripts of *Aguirre* and *Kaspar Hauser* in the 1970s. A mention should also be made of *Burden of Dreams* (North Atlantic Books, 1984, edited by Les Blank and James Bogan), a collection of journals, reviews and photographs, plus a transcript of Blank's film shot on the set of *Fitzcarraldo*.

Herzog's book *Of Walking in Ice* was first published by Carl Hanser in 1978. The English translation followed in 1980 (Tanam) and was subsequently reprinted by Jonathan Cape in 1991. In 1976, Skellig published *Heart of Glass*, which contains Herzog and Herbert Achternbusch's prose script of the film intercut with Herzog's long-time collaborator Alan Greenberg's interviews and thoughts compiled whilst on the set of the film.

Though Herzog has suffered somewhat at the hands of the press since his earliest films, he has never been shy to talk to the world's media (even if they at times might have been wary of him). As such, there is a huge number of interviews stretching back at least as far as 1968 in many languages, though a scarcity of substantial pieces from the past ten years or so due to a relative lack of interest in 'documentary' filmmaking in many journals and newspapers (and the fact that very few of the recent Herzog 'documentaries' got a release in Britain and the United States, or were even screened on television). Some of the most important interviews are listed in Herb Golder's bibliography on the website, though I might point out that the many ideas and themes that have preoccupied Herzog and that have repeatedly appeared in his print, television and radio interviews over the past thirty years are all elaborated on at length in this book.

Christopher Lambert's essay on Herzog in *World Film Directors Volume II: 1945–1985* (H. W. Wilson Company, 1988) remains a good introduction, while the only critical study of the films in English is Timothy Corrigan's collection of essays *Between Mirage and History: The Films of Werner Herzog*, Methuen, 1986), of which only Amos Vogel's contribution stands out. There are two critical studies of the films in French (Emmanuel Carrère's *Werner Herzog* and Radu Gabrea's *Werner Herzog et la mystique rhénane*), neither of which have been translated into English. Carl Hanser published *Werner Herzog* in 1979, which contains a lengthy interview and commentaries on the films (up to *Woyzeck*), and the relevant chapters in the same publisher's *Herzog/Kluge/Straub* (1976) are similarly structured.

For more in English on twentieth-century German cinema, Sabine Hake's *German National Cinema* (Routledge, 2001) is a good summary, though for specifics on New German Cinema, James Franklin's *New German Cinema* (Columbus Books, 1986) and Thomas Elsaesser's *New German Cinema* (Rutgers University Press, 1989) are more substantial. Elsaesser and Michael Wedel's *The BFI Companion to German Cinema* (BFI, 1999) is also a good alphabetical listing, while Eric Rentschler's *West German Filmmakers on Film, Visions and Voices* (Holmes and Meier, 1988) is a useful collection of writings by West German directors (including Kluge, Straub, Syberberg, Achternbusch, Schlöndorff, Wenders, Fassbinder and Herzog). It also contains the texts of the Oberhausen, Mannheim and Hamberg Manifestos. For those interested in East German cinema, *DEFA: East German Cinema, 1946–1992* (Berghahn, 1999) by Seán Allan and John Sanford is well worth reading.

Klaus Kinski's crazed autobiography, *Kinski Uncut* (Bloomsbury, 1997), is a grotesque and sensational rant, certainly worth twenty minutes of your time. *Kinski* (Parthas, 2000), is a beautiful book of photographs by Herzog's long-time collaborator and friend Beat Presser, and several other books on Kinski have appeared recently, including a volume of his poetry entitled *Fieber, Tagebuch eines Aussätzigen* (Eichborn Verlag, 2001) and another photo book, *Ich, Kinski* (Deutsches Filmmuseum, Frankfurt am Main, 2001). Presser's book on Herzog, *Werner Herzog* (Jovis, 2002), contains photos from the sets of *Fitzcarraldo*, *Cobra Verde* and *Invincible*, plus short texts by Volker Schlöndorff, Herbert Achtern-busch and Claudia Cardinale.

Finally to the films themselves, and an appreciation must go to Anchor Bay Entertainment who are currently doing such a good job of their North American and European DVD and video re-releases of Herzog's films. Many of the DVDs contain commentaries with Herzog talking through the films scene by scene, and the digital transfers have been supervised by the director himself. As such, they look and sound wonderful.

Index

Page references in *italics* are to illustrations; suffix n indicates endnotes

335